Pedagogy of Multiliteracies

Routledge Research in Education

For a full list of titles in this series please visit www.routledge.com

Pedagogy of Multiliteracies
Rewriting *Goldilocks*

Heather Lotherington

Routledge
Taylor & Francis Group
NEW YORK   LONDON

First published 2011
by Routledge
711 Third Avenue, New York, NY 10017

Simultaneously published in the UK
by Routledge
2 Park Square, Milton Park, Abingdon, Oxon OX14 4RN

*Routledge is an imprint of the Taylor & Francis Group,
an informa business*

© 2011 Taylor & Francis

The right of Heather Lotherington to be identified as author of this work
has been asserted in accordance with sections 77 and 78 of the Copyright,
Designs and Patents Act 1988.

Typeset in Sabon by IBT Global.

Library of Congress Cataloging-in-Publication Data
Lotherington, Heather.
  Pedagogy of multiliteracies : rewriting Goldilocks / Heather Lotherington.
    p. cm. — (Routledge research in education ; 63)
  Includes bibliographical references and index.
  1. Language arts (Kindergarten)—Canada—Case studies. 2. Bilingual
education—Canada—Case studies. 3. Multicultural education—
Canada—Case studies. 4. College-school cooperation—Canada—Case
studies. 5. Goldilocks and the three bears. I. Title.
  LB1181.L67 2011
  372.6'044—dc22
  2011008265

ISBN13: 978-0-415-88710-6 (hbk)
ISBN13: 978-0-203-80488-9 (ebk)

To the principal, teachers and children of Joyce Public School

Contents

Figures

Tables

Preface

When I think back on my life as a teacher and a researcher, I started thinking about multiliteracies long before the New London Group (1996) had coined the term. In my makeshift Grade 9 palm leaf-roofed English classroom in Papua New Guinea, where the (very few) girls and boys sat at tables fashioned from all manner of crates, I invited the headmaster's housekeeper to talk to us about his war experiences. The year was 1977. Joseph, a man of indeterminate age born at a time and place where births were not recorded, lived in the nearby village still ruled as a cargo cult. He spoke Mengen and Tok Pisin.

The Japanese, whose war detritus lined the walking routes to the bush school at Palmalmal in Jacquinot Bay, New Britain, providing the school bell in the form of an old gas bottle, had been foiled by the New Guineans, who easily permeated their defenses, considered, as they were, somehow outside the major battles being fought on their land and over their coastal fishing grounds. Joseph had distinguished himself as a messenger for the Allied forces, regularly penetrating the Japanese lines. I learned this one night having dinner at the headmaster's house, when Joseph gave us an impromptu performance of his WWII experiences, demonstrating his prodigious and dramatic storytelling abilities. I realized, young and inexperienced volunteer CUSO[1] teacher that I was, that this was first person history brought to life—a far cry from the usual dry textbook accounts, even if Joseph might have found a little liquid support clearing the table after our meal that night. On my way to school as I passed the local plane wreck, hibiscus growing out of the split rusted red dot, I thought about Joseph's elaborate demonstrations of the Japanese fighter planes, and his stories of how each side of the warring factions had treated the New Guineans, whose lives and homes they had severely damaged and disrupted in their deadly WWII battles. It seemed to me nothing short of inspired to bring him into class to talk about an international historic event from a local standpoint.

So Joseph came to my Grade 9 leaf-house classroom and retold history from a perspective never recounted in history books on WWII about what life was like on the ground during occupation. His delivery was colorfully

xviPreface

multimodal: a one-man play in Tok Pisin, with narration, dramatic action, and sound effects. I loved it.

As a class, though, it was a decided failure. The kids believed that school stuff should be in English and come from textbooks—what would a village man know? Especially in Tok Pisin! They had imported a teacher from the white tribe of dead people who wore glasses, had slippery hair and spoke the language of books: English. Authentic knowledge was imported, found in books written in English. This was the literacy they came to school for, not the stories of an old man.

Decades later, I had earned an MA in Linguistics for English Language Teaching and a PhD in Education, and I was lecturing at the University of the South Pacific in Fiji, responsible for TESL certification for teachers across the islands of the vast South Pacific. By this time, I had a family myself, and my daughter attended a local school, which gave me a vantage point into education on the ground not available to me as a university lecturer making formal visits to schools, where celebratory welcoming rites would be held, and model classes would be shown. The children had developed their own pidginized playground English, which I was amused to hear them use together. English was the medium of education in this city school, though the children learned rhymes and songs in Fijian and Hindi, too (see Shameem, 2002, for a discussion of language proficiencies in primary schools in Fiji). The teachers spoke a variety of languages. Though not the dazzling plethora of languages spoken in Papua New Guinea, I heard Fijian and Fiji Hindi, other Pacific languages, including pidgins related to the one I spoke from my PNG days, Fijian communalects, and international languages: Chinese, at my favorite bakery where the coconut twists were to die for, French spoken in numerous nearby island countries, and, of course, English. I was reassured that maintaining a multilingual microcosm was not only possible but also natural: English meaningfully added to the local repertoire. However, small incidents began to creep into my rosy vista on local polyglot existence. English was not a benign auxiliary language in educational contexts, such as my daughter's primary school. It was seeping into daily lives like an infection—as the major language of the popular press, and the newly acquired television station, whose stories were intruding on local oral culture (Lotherington, 1998; Lotherington-Woloszyn, 1995), and increasingly into daily conversations. Though my work was guiding and supporting teachers of English, a language that was fast becoming a lingua mundi, I began to feel concerned that it was steamrolling local language ecologies. Learning to read was understood as learning to read *in English*.

This growing anxiety hit me in the face one day as I turned into the main stairway of the School of Humanities. I encountered the departmental administrator, soothing her small granddaughter, who had tripped on the stairs, hurting her tooth against a soft drink bottle, and spilling some of her drink. But she was not speaking Fijian to the little preschooler; she was using English. Confused, I asked her later why she would choose to use English as a Fijian grandmother talking to her granddaughter. She looked at me and answered plainly that she wanted to give her granddaughter a head start for school by using English with her—a story that was to become a familiar refrain.

In this global era, cultures and languages are remixed in conversations taking place in local neighborhoods and on multimedia social networking sites that were unimagined only a decade ago. Preschoolers are exposed to a variety of digital technologies alongside more traditional media, such as storybooks in their language and literacy socialization (Dyson, 2003; C. Luke, 2000; Marsh, 2004), and they inevitably meet multiple languages in the urban context—whether in the home, on the street or in the media. In the schools of today, a dynamic, socially responsive and responsible approach to language and literacy education is a must.

This book describes an experiment in emergent multimodal literacy pedagogy that grew from observations about the many gaps facing children entering elementary public school in urban inner-city Toronto in the early 21st century.

Our story is ongoing.

Acknowledgments

Without the warm welcome to undertake research at Joyce Public School extended by the school's remarkable principal, Cheryl Paige, this wonderful exploration would never have happened. This book is dedicated to her, the teachers and the children of Joyce Public School who have worked tirelessly towards a new vision of language and literacy education. I thank her and the teachers from the bottom of my heart for their diligence, faith, imagination and perseverance.

The work we accomplished was funded by the Social Sciences and Humanities Research Council of Canada which I acknowledge with gratitude for awarding the small research grant: *Rewriting Goldilocks: Emergent Transliteracies*, and the standard research grant: *Emergent Multiliteracies in Theory and Practice: Multicultural Literacy Development at Elementary School*. I also acknowledge with appreciation York University Faculty of Education Research and Professional Development for awarding our research team a grant for dissemination of our multiliteracies in practice.

I thank all research assistants and graduate assistants who took part in the research, particularly, Robert Wood, for his beautiful photographs. I extend my thanks to Liza Zawadzka, of the York Catholic District School Board, who so generously volunteered her time and expertise on the Grade 4/5 multimedia project, *Iqbal*; and to Professor Jennifer Jenson— who joined our research collaboration in 2008—and Dr. Nick Taylor for their support in developing a web-based tool with Sandra Chow's Grade 4 class that was used to program *Puppy and Horse Go to the Olympics*. All teachers have been wonderful co-researchers, but I want to specially thank Sandra Chow, whose perseverance in the early days was instrumental in getting us off the ground.

I wish to acknowledge with thanks the valuable expertise of Dr. Leslie McGrath, Head Librarian of the Osborne Collection of Early Children's Books, Toronto Public Library, who facilitated my historical research on *Goldilocks and the Three Bears*. Any omissions or errors in my historical study of Goldilocks' journey are my own.

This book was written in three countries. I collected my thoughts, submitted a book proposal and began writing in the United Kingdom while on sabbatical leave. I am indebted to York University Faculty Association, who generously awarded me a sabbatical fellowship, and to the York University Faculty of Education for a specific research grant. I thank Professor Constant Leung for facilitating my tenure as a visiting research fellow at King's College, University of London, and for including me in scholarly presentations, discussions and meetings, which introduced me to researchers and practitioners whose work has had far-ranging impact on the fields of multimodal literacy, applied linguistics, multilingual education and new literacies. This is a long list; in particular, I want to thank Professors Constant Leung, Brian Street, Ben Rampton, and Roxy Harris at King's College; Professors Gunther Kress and Carey Jewitt at the Institute of Education; and Professor Itesh Sachdev at the School of Oriental and African Studies. I thank Dr. Janet Maybin of the Open University for graciously reading Chapter 6, which I framed around her considered exploration of *voice*.

Most of this book was written in Toronto, Canada, where my first thank-you goes to my daughter, Maya Woloszyn, for supporting me through the long period of intense writing. I am so very grateful for her continuing understanding, and for her good-natured complicity in a rather madcap photographic tour of Toronto. Her photographic skills combined with understanding the linguistic data I sought are evidenced in Figures 2.3 and 2.4. Thank you, Maya! I also wish to acknowledge the continuing support of friend, colleague and former teacher, Professor Jim Cummins at the Ontario Institute for Studies in Education, University of Toronto, who has followed our research at Joyce Public School with continuing interest. Jim's abiding activism for transformational pedagogy in the multilingual classroom first introduced me to educational inequalities in the treatment of languages as a doctoral student over 25 years ago.

The last leg of the writing journey was in Melbourne, Australia, and I thank Dr. Marie-Thérèse Jensen for generously providing me with a quiet and comfortable space to concentrate on writing. My overdue return visit to Melbourne, where I first began to work towards community language maintenance, was too late to catch up with my esteemed mentor and supporter, Professor Michael Clyne, who died at his home in Melbourne suddenly and unexpectedly a few weeks prior to my arrival. His passing is an immense loss to sociolinguistics. Michael's dedicated support for community language maintenance gave shape and direction to my inchoate worries about how English language teaching was snowballing other languages a decade and half ago, and it is my sincere hope that I have done his mentorship justice in our interventionist educational agenda in Toronto.

Permissions

Permission to reproduce two leaves of the manuscript "The Story of the Three Bears, metrically related" written and illustrated by Eleanor Mure, 1831, is acknowledged with grateful thanks to the Osborne Collection of Early Children's Books, Toronto Public Library, Canada. I note with interest and anticipation the new reproduction of this beautiful storybook, sponsored by the Friends of the Osborne and Lillian H. Smith Collections, available from the Osborne Collection with proceeds supporting the Collection.

Figures 3.2, 3.5, 3.6, and Table 3.1 are adapted with permission from material that appeared originally in

Lotherington, H. & Chow, S. (2006). Rewriting *Goldilocks* in the Urban, Multicultural Elementary School. *The Reading Teacher*, 60 (3), 244–252.

Copyright 2006 by the International Reading association: www.reading.org.

Figure 5.2, and picture elements of Figures 3.3, 3.4, and 3.6 appeared in

Lotherington, H. (2008). Digital Epistemologies and Classroom Multiliteracies. In T. Hansson (Ed.), Handbook of Research on Digital Information Technologies: Innovations, Methods, and Ethical Issues (pp. 261–280). Hershey, PA: IGI Global.

Copyright 2010, IGI Global, www.igi-global.com. Posted by permission of the publisher.

Figure 2.5 was retrieved from http://commons.wikimedia.org/wiki/File:Chaucer_knight.jpg. It is an image from the public domain available under the Creative Commons Attribution/Share-Alike License.

1   In Pursuit of a Pedagogy
of Multiliteracies

PREPARATORY THINKING ABOUT MULTILITERACIES

When the New London Group coined the term, *multiliteracies*, to capture the essence of literacy and literacy education "to include negotiating a multiplicity of discourses" (1996, p. 61), I was lecturing in the Department of Linguistics at Monash University in Melbourne, Australia. I had made a bold move from teaching English as a second language pedagogy in a Department of Education and Psychology to Sociolinguistics, focused on bilingual education and minority language maintenance. I had refocused my research from English language and literacy education in a postcolonial context[1] to literacy as lived by bi- and multilingual adolescents in a society whose political and social welcomes to multiculturalism were somewhat at odds.

The context of my research had changed considerably: from the small national capital of Fiji where the dominant language was a nonsettler postcolonial inheritance intended to bridge the diverse languages and cultures of the Island Pacific and orient education to a larger world, to a large cosmopolitan city in an English settler country attracting migrants from around the world through a multiculturalism policy of some 20 years that had pulled the cultural concept of *Australian* from its assumed racial homogeneity (Mishra, 2001). English was part of the magnet. Minority languages in the context of Melbourne were relegated to smaller, less public and very differently valued spaces.

During my tenure at the Language and Society Centre at Monash in the late 1990s, as the world of hypermedia was blossoming, I was dismayed to discover that the multiple literacies of the bilingual, bicultural high school students I was researching were being evaluated through a narrow, deficit lens that translated their multilingual reach as a problem (see Australian Bureau of Statistics, 1997). Political discussions of literacy were framed by the national survey of adult literacy that, in concert with similar surveys in Canada and the United States, tapped prose literacy, document literacy and quantitative literacy (Freebody & Lo Bianco, 1997; Gal, 2002; Watson & Callingham, 2003). As Gal (2002) makes clear, these literacies require the interpretation of complex texts, but it is evident that this interpretation is assessed in terms of cognitive operations. He explains, "Key processes include locating specific information in given texts or displays, cycling through various parts of diverse texts or displays, integrating information from several locations . . . and generating new information" (Gal, 2002, p. 8).

Bilingual and multilingual students' competence in a variety of social literacies, spanning cultures, languages and media, fit poorly into the axiomatic model fixed on cognitive attainment and social fluency in English, so, though technically capable within a broad range of social and academic texts, these students, as nonnative speakers, were labeled a priori at risk of not achieving *adequate* literacy in a skills-based model (Australian Bureau of Statistics, 1997; Lotherington, 2003b). These teens had developed the resources to find their way around a society that made geographic and political but not necessarily social spaces for them. In many cases, they were responsible for managing communications between their families and the broader society, as well. Exactly what risk were they at?

It seemed to me that the New London Group's (1996) concept of *multiliteracies* captured the essence of why reading in more than one language should be a bonus, not a dilemma.

> We want to extend the idea and scope of literacy pedagogy to account for the context of our culturally and linguistically diverse and increasingly globalized societies, for the multifarious cultures that interrelate and the plurality of texts that circulate. Second, we argue that literacy pedagogy now must account for the burgeoning variety of text forms associated with information and multimedia technologies. This includes understanding and competent control of representational forms that are becoming increasingly significant in the overall communications environment, such as visual images and their relationship to the written word—for instance, visual design in desktop publishing or the interface of visual and linguistic meaning in multimedia. Indeed, this second point relates closely back to the first; the proliferation of communications channels and media supports and extends cultural and subcultural diversity. (p. 61)

Freebody and Lo Bianco (1997) collocate the literate subject in Australia over the decades with morality in the 1950s, technical skill in the 1960s, deficit models of the disadvantaged in the 1970s and economics in the 1980s. In the mid-1990s, there was lively critical debate amongst scholars in Australia on literacy and education in a changing world (Freebody & Lo Bianco, 1997; Kress, 1997; Lankshear, 1997; A. Luke, 1993; Muspratt, Luke & Freebody, 1997; New London Group, 1996). A. Luke (2000) locates the trend in Australian literacy education in the 1990s towards enhancement of personal growth and skill development. However, he asserts that, from a sociological point of view, the purpose of literacy education should be to build enabling access to "literate practices and discourse resources" (p. 449). In a rapidly changing world strung together with digital connections of global reach, this is a moving target.

I left Melbourne, Australia, to take up an appointment in the Faculty of Education at York University in Toronto, Canada, in January 1999, informed by my valuable experiences with minority language maintenance in the Language and Society Centre at Monash University, and research associations and mentorship within Language Australia, but stymied by the awkwardly unbridged professional spaces I met in Australia between English as a second language, minority language maintenance, and literacy acquisition and development. I accepted a position in Multilingual Education, aiming to bring language and literacy concerns together for teachers and learners alike, whose needs and concerns are not channeled into neat disciplinary pockets.

FINDING A CONTEXT FOR STUDYING MULTILITERACIES

Shortly after taking up my position at York University, a senior colleague invited me to participate as research associate in an international survey of technologically innovative schools. Delighted to participate, I chose to visit two urban schools in the Toronto area, leaving targeted schools across Canada to research assistants, who, as graduate students, had fewer opportunities to travel.

Both the schools in the greater Toronto area (GTA) visited by our research team provided eye-opening experiences. Children in elementary school at the turn of the millennium were creating websites to illustrate black holes and composing music in a MIDI[2] lab. Teachers and administrators were experimenting with digital technologies in their lessons, professional development programs and school organization in ways that were highly instructive to us at the university level.

One of those schools was Joyce Public School.[3]

I bumped into one of the teachers I had interviewed at Joyce Public School (JPS) some time later and he extended an invitation to attend a celebration scheduled at the school that week. It was a wonderful feeling to walk back into JPS, which literally pulsed with a quest for learning—as messy and beautiful process, not perfect recall and display. In chatting with the principal, Cheryl Paige, I enthusiastically confessed that I would love to do ethnographic research at a school like JPS. This is normally the moment when principals look at the researcher shrewdly and ask what we want, what they get out of it, and then promise to get back on that. Cheryl smiled broadly and said, "What a great idea! When can you start?"

And so it was that in 2003, I spent my sabbatical year at Joyce Public School in Toronto, in a pocket of a city noted for high cultural and linguistic diversity, to understand how literacy in the 21st century was understood, taught and assessed.

JOYCE PUBLIC SCHOOL

Joyce Public School is located in a neighborhood of mixed housing and small industry in the northwest quadrant of the city. The principal explains to me that the surrounding middle-class housing—single-family dwellings with well-kept front and back yards—does not represent the true catchment area of the school. The children of the Italian and Portuguese immigrants who have populated this pocket of the city typically attend the local Catholic school. The children attending JPS live in a nearby densely populated block of four high-rise apartment buildings. The school population, typical of inner-city schools, is characterized by high cultural diversity and low socioeconomic status. These children do not have ready access to the cultural capital (Bourdieu, 1991) that grounds school literacy. Though the percentage of children attending the school who speak a language other than English or French at home and in the community varies from year to year with the new intake, it regularly falls at more than two thirds of the school population. In 2009–2010, it was 68%.[4]

JPS has been federally and provincially designated as a pedagogically innovative school in its uses of information and communications technology.[5] The school developed a focus on technologically enhanced learning at the turn of the century to boost educational opportunities for local children. Many teachers as well as the principal have been honored with prestigious citations and awards for outstanding achievement in education.

What I was introduced to at Joyce Public School was an elementary school that was dynamic and visionary, invested in technological mediation, dedicated to children's learning and supportive of teachers and teaching. Serving a population of children who are culturally and linguistically diverse, and whose families are, on the whole, not well established, socially or economically, the school offered an ideal microcosm of urban Canadian society in which to observe emergent literacy education in practice.

OBSERVING MULTILITERACIES IN
ACTION AT ELEMENTARY SCHOOL

I spent my sabbatical leave in 2003 conducting ethnographic research at JPS. The instigating force behind my participation at JPS as observer, and later, as I became a familiar figure at the school, as class helper, story reader and English as a second language (ESL) assistant, was the late 20th century turn to multiliteracies (Cope & Kalantzis, 2000; New London Group, 1996). The social changes propagating the activist writing of the New

London Group collective (1996) had already changed beyond their vision, websites having morphed from the static Web 1.0 of their times into the interactive web, or, as it is better known, Web 2.0. How well was literacy education keeping up with the onslaught of social change?

Given urban children's realities in learning to communicate in a sophisticated media-saturated society in a language and cultural framework not native to most of them and amid multiple and increasing calls for the revision of traditional literacy curricula in a post–typographic era, I wanted to know:

1. What constitutes success in literacy acquisition for children in the linguistically heterogeneous, urban (elementary) classroom?
2. What obstacles do children face in acquiring school literacies?
3. How does a theory of multiliteracies take shape in practice in the elementary classroom?

BECOMING PART OF THE JPS COMMUNITY

I bemember you! (Kindergartener, 2003)

I loved entering the school, which always hummed with activity. Hallways were filled with bouncing little children trying (and failing) to stay in organized lines, whose gap-toothed smiles and spontaneous comments about little sisters and haircuts counteracted the early morning commute. My regular school visits included a variety of classes and venues around the school from the library to the lunchroom. I studied the gallery of art showcased on the school walls, and attended school meetings and after-school events. I chatted with the principal whenever she had a few moments, discussing social and political issues impacting education amongst the random happenings on the school grounds.

In the principal's bustling office, I was immersed in the nerve center of school administration; she was constantly interrupted by phone calls, secretarial announcements and questions, appointments, children needing help—tears soothed over a lost paper or a serious dressing down for beating up another kid—teachers' queries on issues beyond my prior imagining from what to do about a kindergarten child who had mistimed a trip to the washroom with dire consequences (regulations prohibit a teacher cleaning the child up, which is intimate contact), to 911 calls in response to a child's anaphylactic reaction not responding to his EpiPen (which the school administers via a well-documented file on each child's medical needs). While we wrote grants together in her office, she dealt with bullying parents threatening to sue; a violator entering the school building (and caught promptly by teachers); and the infamous peepee bandit, who mysteriously left a daily afternoon puddle just outside the second floor boys' washroom.

Cheryl always made sure to tell me how happy she was to have me in the school. One day in conversation in her office, talking about kindergarten children, she mentioned in passing that she would love to have volunteers come into the school to read stories to the large number of children who entered school needing exposure to English and narrative structure. I began to think about bringing high school students into the school to read to the little ones as a volunteer task fulfilling their secondary school community service requirements. Unfortunately we never quite worked out how to circumvent time problems, as high school students had to attend their own classes when they were needed in the elementary school, though I did find many teens keen to volunteer. So I read to the children myself.

I began in Sandra Cheng's[6] kindergarten, where there was a small library nook consisting of a bookshelf and a child-sized plastic table and chairs. Sandra, who had previously videotaped children retelling a story to analyze their familiarity with English and with story structure, had concerns about specific children, and referred them to me one at a time in the library corner during their structured play period. In this way, the library (with me in it) was positioned as another *activity station* in the kindergarten classroom. My jump-off-a-cliff orientation to this task was simply to ask children what story they would like me to read to them, and then read what they requested (see Lotherington, 2005). It was enormous fun; shoehorned into my favorite little plastic chair in our library corner, I hammed it up reading the available stories to children who did not know English, or did not recognize books as places where stories were kept, or did not know these stories, or all of the above.

At first the children were generally skeptical. Sandra had to direct them to me as a teacher request. But it did not take long for the children to begin to enjoy the stories, and when I entered the classroom, the children who had been referred would appear spontaneously at the entrance to the library corner. I became known as *the story lady*. This I discovered one day on entering the classroom, when one of the most disadvantaged of the children I read to, brightened up and yelled, "Hey, it's the story lady!" He then proceeded to grab me by the hand and lead me into the principal's office where we unceremoniously interrupted a meeting so he could introduce me to his other *special teacher*, a speech therapist. This was the moment when I realized that I had become a fixture in Ms. Cheng's kindergarten classroom.

In this way, I acquired an identity and space in the school that was productive, reciprocal, revealing and enjoyable, enabling me to develop what Geertz (1973) describes as *thick* description. Though I visited classrooms throughout the school, making observations that were consequential to my thinking from sometimes routine activities or children's unexpected comments, actions or reactions, I spent most of my time in the classrooms of two teachers: Sandra Cheng and My-Linh Hang, both of whom not only included me in their classes (which is not a given) but absorbed me as a helper, thus naturalizing my position in the classroom as teacher assistant.

In Ms. Hang's Grade 4 ESL pullout class, my role included listening to children read, helping them with spelling, prompting their ideas in writing and generally being available as a helper. I sat in her small classroom around a worktable with the shifting members of her pullout ESL class, listening to children and helping as directed by Ms. Hang. In so doing, I learned who was labeled ESL and why, what issues these children faced socially and academically (as I followed them into regular classes and library-lab periods), what languages they spoke and what unrecognized issues were hiding beneath their ESL label, such as special learning needs. My-Linh and I talked regularly; I marveled at her skill as a teacher, and at the behavioral problems she deftly handled, particularly with one child, whose self-absorbed outbursts shocked me, leading me to think deeply about the contemporary remix that is the urban classroom.

My copious field notes from observations, conversations and participation in and around the school were analyzed in keeping with qualitative procedures (Marshall & Rossman, 2006) for emerging themes that were interpreted in line with the initial questions about what counted as literacy, what got in the way of children's literacy acquisition and what multiliteracies were taking shape. I presented my preliminary findings in meetings and workshops at JPS, engaging the teachers and principal in discussion, and adding their feedback, perspectives and thoughts to my evolving understanding of these issues.

WHAT COUNTS AS LITERACY IN ELEMENTARY SCHOOL?

The first research question guiding my research was:

1. What constitutes success in literacy acquisition for children in the linguistically heterogeneous, urban (elementary) classroom?

As A. Luke (2000) instructively states, "If there is an axiom that grounds approaches to critical literacy it is Freire's initial claim that all reading is transitive—that by definition one reads and writes something" (p. 451). Over the sabbatical year, I encountered a number of literacies that children needed to acquire in order to achieve school success, my understanding of which was navigating quotidian classroom and schoolyard needs, both social and academic, and progressing satisfactorily through each year by successfully negotiating the assessments internal and external to the local school context by which they were judged. These I distilled from observations detailed in field notes as *etic* descriptions (Harris, 1976) that were then presented to teachers for discussion, delineation and revision. The upshot of negotiated observations and teacher feedback was that children needed to be able to:

- read and write alphabetic print, as understood in traditional definitions of text (on paper, print-centered, in a majority language);
- demonstrate English language proficiency, in order to communicate in class, read and write assignments, and pass assignments and tests;
- use digital technologies, including a variety of hardware and software required for communicative purposes in school activities;
- produce, interpret and interweave nonlinguistic literacies, including musical notation, photographs and illustrations; this notion includes but is not limited to visual literacies (Petrie, 2003, 2005; Kress & Van Leeuwen, 2006);
- manipulate numerical literacies, understood as numeracy;
- acquire *Canadian* socialization in order to be able to write the standardized tests mandated by the provincial Education Quality and Accountability Office (EQAO),[7] which include cultural knowledge.

HOME-SCHOOL-SOCIETY GAPS IN LITERACY LEARNING

As Heath (1983) identified in her landmark study a generation ago, literacy socialization is viewed through the lens of the *mainstream*. Standards are drawn from the middle class, majority culture and dominant language. They are also romanticized to past models that do not sufficiently take into consideration the media saturation of early childhood (C. Luke, 2000; Marsh, 2004, 2006). The Ministry of Education in Ontario (1994) makes the following recommendation for creating an environment of structured child-centered knowledge building in the home:

In a very real sense, the literacy curriculum of infancy and toddlerhood is the curriculum of the home. It is language- and speech-based, but also involves print. Children who are being readied for future learning (and, therefore, for school) are spoken and listened to; have their questions answered; are offered explanations; and are encouraged to try new words and ideas, to imagine, to guess, to estimate, to draw, and to observe. When they watch television, there is often a parent to mediate, either watching with the child or talking afterwards about what has been viewed. (para. 7)

These recommendations, dated 1994, are posted on the 2011 website. Though useful, they do not question the transitions they assume of Canada's multicultural population, the limited perspective of Canadian culture they describe, the middle-class finances they assume or the media they omit. In the social realities of the children I was observing, being locked in a cramped apartment with a television set as babysitter would have to be added as a prominent literacy socialization activity. Social realities in the JPS community have precipitated a strong demand for extracurricular and summer camp activities at Joyce Public School to afford inner-city children broader social and sociable learning opportunities. These activities, the principal regularly facilitates, organizes and oversees.

My concern was the gaps between language and literacy experiences at home, in the community and at school that vulnerable children with few resources needed to link to become literate. What social, cultural and linguistic interfaces were children facing that were flying beneath the radar of formal literacy education? It was apparent that the gaps to literacy learning confronting many, if not most, children in the kindergarten classroom were, and are, far more complex than those anticipated in curricular documents.

The second question guiding my ethnographic observations specified:

2. What obstacles do children face in acquiring school literacies?

With regard to being able to:

- read and write alphabetic print, as understood in traditional definitions of text (on paper, print-centered, in a majority language); and
- demonstrate English language proficiency, in order to communicate in class, read and write assignments, and pass assignments and tests,

it was clear that the majority of children did not have a satisfactory command of English, which was a prerequisite to being able to read and write in the language/s of schoolwork and tests.

WHO IS AN ENGLISH LANGUAGE LEARNER?

The English language learner is defined very broadly in official documentation:

> For the purposes of this policy, English language learners are students in provincially funded English language schools whose first language is a language other than English, or is a variety of English that is significantly different from the variety used for instruction in Ontario's schools, and who may require focused educational supports to assist them in attaining proficiency in English.
>
> These students may be Canadian born or recently arrived from other countries. They come from diverse backgrounds and school experiences, and have a wide variety of strengths and needs. (Ministry of Education, 2007, p. 8)

Both research-based (Li, 2008; People for Education, 2009) and populist (Duffy, 2004; H.-J. Robertson, 2005) reports on ESL funding outline how it has been cut, stretched and spent in unmonitored ways over the past decade. Duffy (2004) draws an inverse ratio in the proportion of immigrant children in public education and available funding for English language support at the time of this ethnography, quoting survey data from the Ontario-based, parent-led organization, People for Education (PFE):

> In Ontario, a survey published in September, 2003 by the parent advocacy group, People for Education, showed that 76 per cent of urban elementary schools reported having ESL students, but only 26 per cent had ESL teachers. The number of elementary schools with ESL programs has declined by 33 per cent since 1997–98 despite the fact the number of immigrants in Ontario has increased annually by an average of 13.5 per cent during the same period. (p. 2)

The number of immigrant children needing ESL support has continued to rise dramatically and inequitably with urban and suburban areas shouldering much of the increase. PFE (2009) reports, "In places like Markham, Toronto and Mississauga, over 50% of the population are immigrants. Schools in those areas report that as many as 95% of students require English language support" (p. 20).

H.-J. Robertson (2005) remarks, "As other social supports are cut, these immigrants' schools are shouldering much of the burden of delivering on promises they didn't make [re Canadian multiculturalism]" (p. 410). She suggests that official eligibility is not followed through in practice, due partly to the poor lobbying leverage of the population needing ESL services.

Li (2008), examining data available for 2007, describes how funds allocated to those students who are designated eligible for support are reduced over the sequence of 4 years that ESL assistance is granted in Ontario, as specified in the provincial funding formula:

> Ontario provided assistance to ESL students for four years. School boards received $3,349 for each ESL student who was in the Ontario school system for the first time. Boards received 70 percent of $3,349 for each ESL student in the system for the second year. They received 50 percent of $3,349 for each ESL student for the third year, and 25 percent of $3,349 for each ESL student for the fourth year. (pp. 8–9)

However, H.-J. Robertson (2005) states:

> Most jurisdictions now restrict ESL eligibility to students born outside Canada whose mother tongue is not English. Students resident for more than four years or who have had three years of ESL are dropped from the tally. Applying new eligibility criteria may improve the optics, but it obscures the needs of thousands of real students. (p. 410)

People for Education, an Ontario-based, parent-led education watchdog, highlights the fact that though funding for ESL has recently increased, use of ESL funds has been unmonitored, and schools lacking in multiple resources have been reported using ESL funds in unspecified ways.

> There have been increases in funding for English as a Second Language programs over the last several years, and the province introduced [a] new policy in 2007. The policy states students should continue to receive ESL support until they are able to function academically in English. It also states that students should achieve an acceptable standard of English before ESL supports are removed. However, it does not define the "acceptable standard" nor provide for funding based on need rather than numbers of years in Canada. Nor does the new policy make it mandatory to spend all funding for English Language Learners on ESL students. As a result, ESL funds are often used for other programs and services. (PFE, 2009, pp. 20–21)

In 2002–3 JPS had funding for a 0.5 ESL teacher. The 360 children registered in the school that year are on record speaking 25 specified languages, and 4 *others*[8] (which are likely Creoles). In a school where two thirds of children speak a language other than English at home in a community where most parents are recent immigrants, every class is an ESL class, making each and every teacher in the school a teacher of English language and literacy for nonnative speakers as well as native speakers.

Accordingly these children have also had limited opportunity to

- acquire *Canadian* socialization in order to be able to write the standardized tests mandated by the provincial EQAO, which include cultural knowledge.

Access to middle-class mainstream cultural institutions, such as museums, art galleries and historic properties, is low in this population of relative newcomers to Canada who, as new immigrants, are in the process of acquiring the economic, linguistic and cultural capital (Bourdieu, 1991) to successfully navigate Canadian society. This access to Anglo-centric Canadiana, however, affects a student's performance on EQAO gate-keeping tests. Though this background knowledge is most evident in the do-or-die Grade 10 Ontario Secondary School Literacy test (Lotherington, Neville-Verardi & Sinitskaya Ronda, 2009), cultural knowledge is also embedded in elementary reading and writing test questions, such as the following multiple-choice question from the 2007 reading test:

1. The phrase "a real crowd-pleaser" means that celery sticks
   o are a healthy snack
   o are liked by many people
   o come with a cheese spread
   o can be found in most restaurants. (Education Quality and Accountability Office, 2007, p. 2)

The principal tells me that students can confidently

*   manipulate numerical literacies, understood as numeracy,

because the Arabic numerals used in mathematical calculations are cross-cultural. However, she laments that the children have difficulties in showing their strengths in number sense and manipulation when mathematical questions are textually embedded in problems, which then additionally tap their weaker proficiencies in English language and alphabetic reading. Mathematics test questions also embed knowledge of *Canadian culture*. Question 18 in the 2008 mathematics test asks whether an assortment of pictured coins equals:

*   1 toonie, 1 loonie, 3 quarters, 3 pennies
*   1 toonie, 16 dimes, 1 nickel, 3 pennies
*   3 loonies, 1 quarter, 3 dimes, 3 pennies
*   3 loonies, 6 dimes, 2 nickels, 3 pennies. (Education Quality and Accountability Office, 2008, p. 11)

TECHNOLOGICAL IMMERSION

The daily activities of the teachers helped to inform me about how students learn to:

*   use digital technologies, including a variety of hardware and software required for communicative purposes in school activities, and
*   produce, interpret and interweave nonlinguistic literacies, including musical notation, photographs and illustrations.

All children at JPS learn to use a variety of technologies in regular schoolwork. The Joyce Public School website describes its mission to develop innovative technology-enhanced pedagogies:[9]

> Two unique features of Joyce Public School are the technology emphasis and resources, which we are fortunate to have obtained through the support of the Toronto District School Board, the Ontario Ministry of Education and Training, and the Federal Ministry of Industry and Trade. Joyce Public School is a member of the Network of Innovative Schools (NIS). This organization is part of Canada's SchoolNet, funded by the Ministry of Industry and Trade, and supports innovative technology projects in schools across Canada. Joyce is also a Pathfinder School for a technology project called the Innovative Models of Learning. This is part of the Ontario Ministry of Education and Training's Ontario Knowledge Network. (para. 1)

JPS students are immersed in *technology* as a means rather than an end to learning, so it is not singled out for consequential testing, as are *reading* and *writing*. The fact that facility with digital media and nonlinguistic literacies is not part of formal descriptions of school literacy (though *media literacy* is included) led me to the third question:

3. How does a theory of multiliteracies take shape in practice in the elementary classroom?

MULTILITERACIES IN THE ELEMENTARY CLASSROOM

Though children faced many gaps in linking literate expectations and knowledge, they also had many wonderful learning opportunities in a school where digital technologies are given prominence in pedagogical development. The facilitative digital and nonlinguistic literacies I observed in school activities, materials and home communication were woven into everyday learning of print literacies, English conventional usage, subject specific content and Canadian socialization.

In kindergarten I learned that early childhood education inherently combines multiple media for learning, expression, play and communication. To get to my familiar seat in the library corner during structured play period, I stepped past children building wondrous structures from wooden blocks cut from two-by-fours, and others engaged in art work, or racing dinky toys, or playing grown-up in the little kitchen where tiny plastic dishes are used for make-believe food made on a miniature replica stove. Beside the entrance to the library nook, three little girls regularly sat making playdough pizzas and speaking to each other in Cantonese. I would read to students one at a time from the available storybooks. They were called from their activity stations to full class with a song.

It was apparent to me that teachers of early childhood education know how to recognize, create, juxtapose, join and mix multiple making-meaning resources in the classroom. Across a classroom a *clothesline* is strung with children's painted pictures telling a story they had been read. Sitting in classes where children's activities included singing songs, taking turns in telling little stories in a circle, clapping their hands to keep rhythm and playing *Simon says* and other movement games, I participated in musical, oral, spatial, numerical, gestural and aural communication, much of it, ludic: play-oriented. Classrooms were furnished with a rich and eclectic array of communicational resources, including finger puppets, modeling clay monsters, masks, dioramas and critters made from toilet paper rolls, amongst the books, coloring pencils and computers. Utilizing such a diversity of semiotic resources generates creative meaning-making that children can take ownership of. How is it that we lose this immense communicational richness as school becomes more school-like?

My-Linh, the ESL specialist on staff (and also the French as a second language teacher), explains to me that she uses a digital camera to photograph Grade 4 children in everyday learning so she can create collages to show their parents who, often, have less English than their children, and so cannot follow their children's progress in school. On examination, I see that My-Linh has done much more than visually document the children at work. She has made learning inclusive, by putting children inside their own resources. The book I peruse is a homemade book to teach English grammar, focusing on prepositions. "We are under the bridge" captions a photo of four children in full snow gear appropriately standing underneath a bridge in the school playground (see Figure 1.1).

Other locally enacted prepositions are written in children's home languages. The teacher explains that the children write in the languages that are accessible to them at present. The book is multilingual, image-centered and an innately culturally inclusive resource. It is entertaining as well as explanatory, collaboratively involving the children and the teacher to bring to life abstract grammatical usage, anchored in local context. An otherwise banal and confusing aspect of English grammar comes to life in the shape of a handmade picture book. The digital technologies that were used to create this customized resource are simple, everyday and straightforward: a digital camera, a printer and a photocopier. Books that are personalized and tailored to the learning environment insert the learner into the reading experience, a twist on Freire and Macedo's (1987) landmark refrain, *reading the word and the world* that might be restated as *writing yourself into the word and the world*.

Bilingual, image-centered resources are not new. Figure 1.2 presents two pages from Comenius' 17th century Latin grammar.

Figure 1.1 "We are under the bridge."

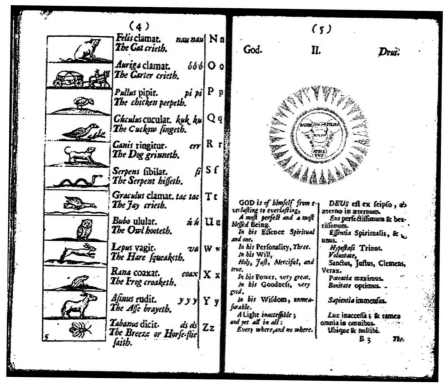

Figure 1.2   Comenius' bilingual *Orbis Sensualium Pictus*, 1689, p. 16.

What is new in the idea of multiliteracies is the complexity building from globalization and digitization. Cope and Kalantzis (2009a) ask:

> What, then, are the core concepts that may be of use in developing a language of the multimodal applicable to literacy learning? Traditionally, literacy teaching has confined itself to the forms of written language. The new media mix modes more powerfully than was culturally the norm and even technically possible in the earlier modernity dominated by the book and the printed page. (p. 362)

USING TRANSMODALITY AS A RESOURCE

In My-Linh's pullout ESL class for those few children who are lucky enough to be designated eligible for scarce specialist support, I meet a child in Grade 4 who has recently arrived from South America. He understands no English. Both My-Linh and I have enough Spanish to grease basic communication, but I wonder at the lassitude of this little fellow, who lays his head on the table in utter exhaustion when he comes to ESL class. Does he not get enough sleep at home? I decide to follow him around to see how he, his classmates and his homeroom teacher manage the language barrier.

In his homeroom, the teacher uses an online translator for daily messages and class procedures, which he projects in English and Spanish from his laptop to a screen. In this class, the children are accustomed to finding daily start-up directions on the screen so they can prepare for class activities when they arrive at their desks in the morning. Though online machine translation is clearly flawed, it is functional in this context, and the messages get through to Carlos, who follows along as best he can. The teacher describes to me that not only has the online translator helped familiarize Carlos with English, connecting meaning to new literate and oral forms, but it has also exposed the other children in the class to written Spanish.

This Grade 4 teacher regularly and very creatively utilizes multiple, juxtaposed media in daily activities that include bilingual directions using the online translator that allow Carlos to hop from the known (Spanish directions) to the unknown (what the rest of the class is doing in English). The teacher splices all students' oral and literate work into a digital universe that facilitates activities such as writing, illustrating and programming poems as timed PowerPoint presentations, which are then recited to the class who simultaneously watch the written and illustrated forms on the screened backdrop. To accomplish this, the children have:

- composed an original poem,
- illustrated their poem,
- programmed their illustrated poem as a timed PowerPoint presentation,
- memorized their poem,
- sequenced their poetry recital with their preprogrammed visual presentation, and
- recited their poetry against a multimedia backdrop to fellow classmates.

This is *multimodal learning*: it encompasses numerous semiotic resources that require different skill sets to master. These means of communication are joined in sequence (i.e., *transmodal* communication), and presented as a collage (i.e., *multimodal* communication). I remind myself that this is Grade 4. And it is 2003.

A few weeks into the ESL class, Carlos perks up. We are discussing soccer, and *fútbol* is clearly his passion. The mental exhaustion on his face caused by the constant effort of trying to understand the world through another language filter is erased, and a lively little boy emerges. As I watch, I find another thread of commonality. In the library-lab he is outgoing and energetic, pointing out to his classmates something on his computer screen. I nudge him playfully to indicate that the teacher is watching. He makes a conspiratorial face and gets back to assigned work. The icons he reads on the screen allow him to move forward, keeping up with his classmates. Manipulating icons is reading he can do, and that helps him to enter the alphabetic world in English that, just a few weeks ago in ESL class, put him to sleep. He is using *transmodality* as a resource.

At JPS, I learn through class moments such as these that children of very different language backgrounds can be introduced to languages and literacies of necessity and importance through digital links and keyholes. This is how I see multiliteracies taking shape in this school—different modes of semiotic communication and representational media being combined to facilitate communication between and among children whose preschool socialization does not fit what is anticipated in curricular documents.

But JPS is unusual in that it strives to find innovative ways of teaching and learning with new technologies. The multiliteracies I see in action are creditable to teachers' creative thinking, rather than to curricular guidance, and they are certainly light years from the brick wall of provincial paper-and-pencil tests the children will face in Grades 3 and 6 in the elementary years.

FINDING A WAY FORWARD

In the year of this study, Kress (2003) sounds the following alert about the rapidly changing face of literacy:

> It is no longer possible to think about literacy in isolation from a vast array of social, technological and economic factors. Two distinct yet related factors deserve to be particularly highlighted. These are, on the one hand, the broad move from the now centuries-long dominance of writing to the new dominance of the image and, on the other hand, the move from the dominance of the book to the dominance of the medium of the screen. These two together are producing a revolution in the uses and effects of literacy and of associated means for representing and communicating at every level and in every domain. Together they raise two questions: what is the likely future of literacy, and what are the likely larger-level social and cultural effects of that change? (p. 2)

My observational study at JPS had at its heart a concern with how formal education was coping with dimensional changes in the fabric of literate communication, given rapid and consequential social change. Being a participant observer had allowed me to create a picture of the emergent literacy requirements and practices that elementary school children had to navigate in order to function at school in 2003. Though such complex needs can be seen in myriad ways, I encapsulated essential literacies in terms of learning to:

- read and write alphabetic print, as understood in traditional definitions of text;
- demonstrate English language proficiency, in order to communicate in class, read and write assignments, and pass assignments and tests;
- use digital technologies, including a variety of hardware and software required for communicative purposes in school activities;
- produce, interpret and interweave nonlinguistic literacies, including musical notation, photographs and illustrations;
- manipulate numerical literacies, understood as numeracy;
- acquire *Canadian* socialization to successfully write the standardized tests mandated by the provincial EQAO.

To achieve sufficient authority over the kinds of knowledge and practices children needed to negotiate, they had to bridge a number of gaps, including

- home, community and school languages,
- social and school literacies, and
- cultural understanding across
  - *Canadian* and home cultures, and
  - school, pop and digital cultures.

The language gap was acknowledged by the state: ESL classes were available to the small percentage of the two thirds of children in the school needing support with spoken and written English who were deemed officially eligible. A 0.5 ESL teacher was calculated in provincial budgetary allocations.

Some gaps were seen as the province of teachers in formal education. Every teacher in the school worked very hard to help children learn to read and write alphabetically in English, and manipulate number systems. Provided with a minimum of technology but a maximum of support to use it, teachers imaginatively developed innovative pedagogies using multiple media for daily classroom activities that were engaging and instructive as working models of multimodal literacies pedagogies; these helped children to interpret the world of school learning and express themselves in multiple ways. The principal facilitated myriad extracurricular opportunities for families that provided access to a slice of cultural life in Toronto, such as art camps, sports clubs and ESL classes for parents.

I had gained an understanding of what constituted literacy acquisition for elementary school children at JPS, obstacles they faced in acquiring school literacies, how a theory of multiliteracies was beginning to take shape in practice in the elementary classroom and how it was being prevented from taking shape. To develop a pedagogy of multiliteracies required two kinds of action, mapped out in Figure 1.3.

This was a huge agenda for change. Where would we start?

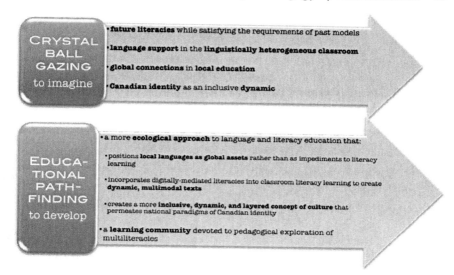

CRYSTAL BALL GAZING
to imagine

- **future literacies** while satisfying the requirements of past models
- **language support** in the **linguistically heterogeneous classroom**
- **global connections** in local education
- **Canadian identity** as an inclusive **dynamic**

EDUCA-TIONAL PATH-FINDING
to develop

- a more **ecological approach** to language and literacy education that:
  - positions **local languages as global assets** rather than as impediments to literacy learning
  - incorporates digitally-mediated literacies into classroom literacy learning to create **dynamic, multimodal texts**
  - creates a more **inclusive, dynamic, and layered concept of culture** that permeates national paradigms of Canadian identity
- a **learning community** devoted to pedagogical exploration of multiliteracies

Figure 1.3   Plan to develop a pedagogy of multiliteracies.

WHO IS GOLDILOCKS?

The upshot of my year at JPS provided plenty to think about, and as in all qualitative studies, some of these observations seemed extraneous to my main focus. For example, my experiences in kindergarten kicked up an issue that fell outside of the guiding questions I was seeking to answer but persisted in my thoughts. In my regular story reading in the kindergarten library nook, a runaway favorite story had emerged: *Goldilocks and the Three Bears*. I wanted to know why.

It had been great fun making the voices of mama, papa and baby bear hidden behind the half-wall of books with the children. But one day I was caught off-guard when one of the three Cantonese-speaking play-dough pizza makers showed up at the entrance to the library nook. The book chosen by the little girl was again *Goldilocks and the Three Bears*. I had never heard her speak English, so I started off with a slow and careful, but lively reading. When we got to the bears, she jumped up with obvious excitement and grabbed three Popsicle stick puppets from a box of junk that I had never bothered to look through. Using no identifiable words, but making a voice appropriate to each character, she belted out a series of monosyllabic grunts moving the appropriate puppet across an imaginary stage to the classic refrain: "Someone has been eating my porridge!" We finished the story with her lively contributions in the appropriate places, and I thought about how much she had contributed to a dynamic reading of a story in a language she did not know.

What was it about *Goldilocks and the Three Bears* that got the attention of children who didn't know much English, or how to read, or stories in the Western canon, or even what a book was? What or who did they see in *Goldilocks*?

As it turned out, answering these questions led us into a long-term collaborative research agenda to develop a theoretical and practical understanding of multiliteracies.

2 Competing Visions of Language and Literacy Education
Theory, Policy and New Directions for Practice

LANGUAGE DEMOGRAPHY, POLICY AND EDUCATION IN CANADA

In 1971, Prime Minister Pierre Elliot Trudeau announced a "policy of multiculturalism within a bilingual framework" (Churchill, 1998, p.15), introducing to the world stage a groundbreaking social perspective on cultural diversity. The policy aimed to nurture a climate of cultural equality, and to preserve cultural pluralism in a nation previously characterized in terms of the two solitudes of English-speaking and French-speaking Canadians. The Multiculturalism Act[1] was passed by Parliament in July 1988, making Canada the first nation in the world to entrench multiculturalism in law (Dewing & Leman, 2006).

English and French had been institutionally enshrined in the Official Languages Act of 1969, which educationally ensured that "Canadian students have opportunities to learn both official languages at school, through English or French L2 programs or, alternatively, through intensive or immersion programs" (Duff & Li, 2009, p. 4). Though the Cultural Enrichment Program in 1977 provided modest federal funding towards nonformal heritage language educational initiatives, this support was cut in 1990 (Cummins, 1992). Educators were encouraged to explore ways of promoting the *heritage languages* of Canada's increasingly multicultural population, but cautioned not to do so at the expense of the official languages (Cummins & Danesi, 1990). By separating official languages from those to be maintained informally at home and in the community, the policies of official bilingualism and multiculturalism thus dissociated language from culture and ethnicity, creating a schism in language use and language education.

Kunz (2008) diplomatically states:

> It is believed that Canada's diversity, if properly nurtured, becomes its strength. Canada's approach to ethno-cultural diversity, especially its multiculturalism policy, has won accolades internationally. In practice, however, managing ethno-cultural diversity remains a work in progress subject to the constant evolution of social realities. (para. 1)

Feuerverger (1997) puts this more plainly, stating, "The issue of cultural and linguistic diversity is layered, complex and multiple in symbolic meanings within Canadian society" (p. 40). While English and French are taught across the curriculum via ESL, FSL, French immersion programs, and minority language education—which in official parlance, connotes first language (L1) education in the nondominant official language (i.e., French in provinces other than Québec or English in Québec [Canadian Heritage, 2010; Duff & Li, 2009])—heritage (or international) and Indigenous (or Aboriginal) languages, which are not officially recognized, do not receive the same support. The institution of a *Heritage Language Program* (HLP) in the province of Ontario in 1977 was marked by political controversy; and by the early 1990s, the designation *heritage*, which tied language to derivative culture/s and historical lives, had been replaced by *international*, which detached local languages from the community and repositioned them as foreign.

The multiculturalism policy changed the trajectory of Canada's established reliance on immigration for population growth away from assimilation and towards recognition of cultural diversity. This trend is particularly evident in Toronto, the capital city of the province of Ontario, and the largest metropolitan center in Canada with a population of 5,072,075, according to 2006 census data,[2] of which 2,160,335, or 43%, speak a mother tongue other than English or French. The children of immigrants who have arrived in recent years and are acquiring English permeate the school system at all levels.

From Policy to Practice: Language and Literacy in the Ontario Curriculum

Educational policies, benchmarks and standards regarding language and literacy learning are put and held in place through a complex confluence of political and social factors. In Canada, education is provincially governed. Toronto, the capital of the province of Ontario, is under the jurisdiction of the Ontario Ministry of Education. Thus, the province of Ontario interprets the federal prioritization of English and French into educational aims and objectives.

The Ministry of Education's curricular planning and budgeting decisions predispose the allocation of time, focus and remedial assistance per language and subject as well as influence assessment priorities. There are further spin-offs in teacher education programs designed to prepare teachers to successfully meet provincial standards.

The provincial curriculum is translated into educational practice at the community level, where the school grapples with local demographics that may be at odds with the national languages privileged in formal education. In the case of large urban centers, such as Toronto, local multiethnic communities have developed to accommodate waves of immigrants who arrived both before and after the multiculturalism policy, swelling with reunified international families. Canada also has a historical tradition of welcoming refugees. These populations are glocal (R. Robertson, 1995) communities, speaking the languages of the world, not the languages of the colonial settlement of Canada.

Figure 2.1 depicts the uneasy devolution of the national official languages policy to educational practice at the community level.

In Ontario, literacy is subsumed under the *language* curriculum from Grades 1 to 8. Language means *dominant* language, which is either English or French, depending on the medium of the school. In secondary school (Grades 9–12), this united curriculum is entitled English, expressly treating literacy as written English. There is also a curricular guide entitled: *English as a Second Language and English Literacy Development*, which pathologizes nonnative speakers and readers of English—who constitute nearly half the student body in Toronto—offering explicit remedial help to reach the regular curriculum. There is no ESL curriculum for elementary school learners (Grades 1–6).

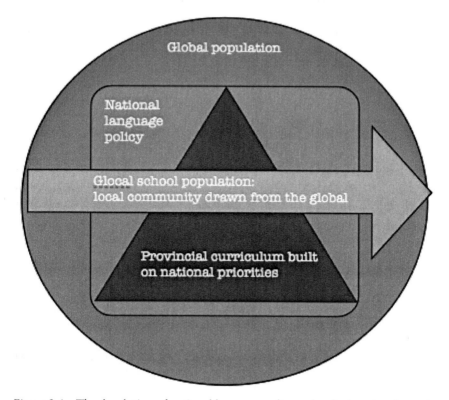

Figure 2.1   The devolution of national language policy to local educational practice.

Languages other than English and French are available for curricular study very selectively at the secondary level. A Native languages curriculum is available for Grades 9 through 12, recognizing "Cayuga, Cree, Delaware, Mohawk, Ojibwe, Oji-Cree, and Oneida" (Ministry of Education, 2000b, p. 3), but the program is rhetorically couched in a protectionist stance for English and French:

> Research on Native education confirms that when students develop the ability to communicate in a Native language, learning that language will reinforce, not interfere with, the learning of English, French, or other languages. (Ministry of Education, 2000b, p. 2)

There is a classical studies and international languages curriculum available in Grades 9–12 whose rationale looks outward towards communicating with those from other countries, rather than inward towards the myriad languages spoken in local communities:

> Courses in classical studies and international languages help students to develop the skills they will need to communicate effectively with people from other countries, and increase their understanding and appreciation of diverse cultures. At the same time, these courses improve students' skills in the English language. (Ministry of Education, 2000a, p. 3)

Language and Literacy Assessment in Ontario

Language and literacy education as defined in the Ontario curriculum is externally assessed by the EQAO, which is an institute established in 1996 by the conservative provincial government to:

- design new tests for grades 3, 6, 9, 10 in reading, writing and mathematics;
- manage the administration of these tests;
- report the results to the public; and
- collect data to help determine the effectiveness of Ontario's education system. (Elementary Teachers' Federation of Ontario, 2010, para. 4)

According to their website, "EQAO ensures greater accountability in the publicly funded education system in Ontario and helps improve the quality of education by providing data on student achievement and by reporting on plans for improvement" (Education Quality and Accountability Office, 2010a, para.1). Literacy is not defined, though the purpose of the Ontario Secondary School Literacy Test (OSSLT) is explained as measuring "whether or not [Grade 10 students] are meeting the minimum standard for literacy across all subjects up to the end of Grade 9" (Education Quality and Accountability Office, 2010b, para. 5). This lacuna reflects Graff's (1987) candid observation that "it is depressing but instructive to note how rarely debates and discussions about literacy levels pause to consider what is meant by reference to literacy" (p. 18).

As Shohamy (2007) makes clear, "Tests are capable of affecting the behaviors of teachers, students, parents and institutions as well as national educational policies" (p. 118). She outlines a significant political shift occurring in language testing over the past decade, that moves language tests "from tools used to measure language knowledge" (p. 117) to "instruments connected and embedded in political, social and educational contexts" (p. 117).

Lotherington et al. (2009) investigated two groups of teenagers who had written the OSSLT, both successfully and unsuccessfully, to tap their assessments of what counted as literacy. Though all participants were proficient and critical consumers of digital media who had creative and sophisticated programming abilities, they found that "none of these skills were tested in the OSSLT, which focused on 'correctness' in prescriptive grammar, multiple choice answers, and rigidly timed, spatially limited essay writing keyed to ad hoc topics of the test-makers' choosing, many of which were found to be irrelevant or boring by the teenagers we consulted" (p. 33). They further noted, "The modern notion of correctness and focus on prescriptive print-based conventions biases against all contemporary learners, but particularly penalizes those for whom English is nonnative" (p. 33).

Fox and Cheng (2007) comparatively examined the accounts of both mother tongue (L1) and second language (L2) users of English on their performance in the OSSLT. Their findings corroborated research indicating "tests such as the OSSLT that are administered to linguistically and culturally diverse populations, but developed and evaluated on the basis of L1 performance, may have lower reliability and validity for L2 test-takers" (p. 21).

The regulatory mechanisms in language and literacy education in the province of Ontario thus equate literacy to written textual English (and/or French), and test curricular delineations of literacy across elementary and secondary schooling in publicly reportable tests that do not validly accommodate the vast cultural diversity of local school-going populations or involve contemporary literacy media. In this way, school literacy agendas, local language capital and social communication practices are at a significant disconnect in the cultural remix that is Toronto.

LANGUAGE EDUCATION IN THE
TORONTO DISTRICT SCHOOL BOARD

Joyce Public School is in the Toronto District School Board (TDSB), which is the largest school board in Canada and the fourth largest in North

America, according to their website.[3] The official claim is that 53% of children across the board speak English at home; thus 47% of school entrants speak a language other than English. Worth noting, however, are the myriad Creolized languages with an English superstrate spoken by students from the Caribbean, in particular, which are typically reported as English, putting Creole speakers needing assistance in learning text-book English grammar in an unreported position. Given that French was listed as the mother tongue of only 58,590 people in Toronto in the 2006 census,[4] which is 1.16% of Torontonians, the percentage of children who enter the school system with a dubious command of both English and French equals approximately half the student body. This percentage indicates the extensive need for language assistance to enable children to function according to the expectations of the curriculum. It does not, however, capture fine-grained information on the degree of children's knowledge of and socialization in English (or French).

There is no curricular mandate for languages other than English or French in elementary school. Heritage/international language instruction, which is governed by continuing education, and taught predominantly in classes held after school and on weekends by teachers who may be uncertified, is regionally dependent and subject to perennially eroding budgets. Nonetheless, both the TDSB and the Toronto Catholic District School Board offer numerous international languages,[5] including a few novel programs integrated into an extended school day.

This means that approximately half of the children entering school in Toronto will need to learn English as the language of schooling. They will have institutionalized support for their home languages only in exceptional cases, limited opportunities for English as a second language support, given the numbers in need, and hit-and-miss opportunities to study the language of their home in multilevel after-school or Saturday classes. Moreover, many of the children who actually do speak English will be what Harklau (2003), writing about the American college context, and borrowing from Rumbaut and Ima (1988), describes as "generation 1.5 students" (p. 1): those who fit neither the profile of the native nor the non-native English speaker.

> Generation 1.5 students are U.S.-educated English language learners. There is great diversity among them in terms of their prior educational experience, native and English language proficiency, language dominance, and academic literacy. Some of these students immigrated to the United States while they were in elementary school; others arrived during high school. Still others were born in this country but grew up speaking a language other than English at home. They may see themselves as bilingual, but English may be the only language in which they have academic preparation or in which they can read and write. At the same time, these students may not feel that they have a full command

of English, having grown up speaking another language at home or in their community. Equipped with social skills in English, generation 1.5 students often appear in conversation to be native English speakers. However, they are usually less skilled in the academic language associated with school achievement, especially in the area of writing. (Harklau, 2003, p. 1)

The high percentage of children in school classrooms across Toronto who are learners of English or generation 1.5 students means that every teacher is teaching a linguistically heterogeneous class in which children's competencies in any language cannot be taken for granted.

LITERACY EDUCATION: A HISTORICAL KALEIDOSCOPE

Graff (2001) frankly admits, "As a student of literacy for two decades, I cannot recall a time when literacy was not in crisis" (p. 3). Literacy is a battlefield. As a facilitating device for archiving human communications, focused, in early textual evidence, on commercial negotiations (e.g., coins and accounting systems), and later, on religious guidance (sacred texts and private devotions[6]), literacy goes back millennia; as a social characteristic, literacy is much more recent. Literacy has shape-shifted and mushroomed over the ages with communicative purpose, political expectations, learning opportunities, textual accessibility, media and changes in the social fabric. As the nature of literacy has changed, so have the needs for appropriate literacy education. The question is: has schooling followed suit?

Literacy and Authority

Throughout its history, literacy has been strongly connected to authority and regulation. Religious texts documenting *the word of God* through the visions of prophets were understood as received learning to be reverentially and scrupulously obeyed. Early religious manuscripts were laboriously handwritten and illustrated resulting in precious tomes such as *The Book of Kells*, circa 800 held by the Old Library, Trinity College, Dublin.[7] Eisenstein (1979) describes the reaction of horror by the Catholic Church in the 16th century that anyone but priests and theologians be entrusted with the word of God, and quotes Reginald Poole during the reign of Mary Tudor direly warning the populace against the subversion of reading the Scriptures themselves (p. 426).

Liturgical texts are still treated with reverence today; in specific cases, proscriptions are still placed on who can access religious material, and how it is to be handled. In the case of Islam, contemporary literature interpreted as affronting the *Qur'an* has resulted in injunctions, riots and even death; as example, esteemed author Salman Rushdie lived in hiding for several years after a religious fatwa was pronounced following publication of his fourth novel, *The Satanic Verses*.

Bäuml (1980) claims that medieval Europe was essentially a literate civilization because "the knowledge indispensable to the functioning of medieval society was transmitted in writing, e.g., the Bible and its exegesis, statutory laws, and documents of all kinds" (p. 237). Clanchy (2002) argues that writing, as the most powerful means of standardization, was the legitimating apparatus of the state in medieval England, offering the *Domesday Book* as the epitome of power through writing, and describing the *Magna Carta* as a document that came to be used as a written constitution. The concept of a constitution today is a decree of superior authority: the ultimate legal touchstone.

Literacy and Culture

Clanchy (2002) proffers medieval precedents to the educational aspirations of the modern state, noting that King Alfred of the Anglo-Saxons in the 9th century, popularly known as Alfred the Great, "was concerned with schooling, cultural definition and the replication of writing" (Clanchy, 2002, p. 69). Nevertheless, from the 4th to the 15th century, the majority of the population was essentially illiterate, including kings as well as peasants. Abbott (2006) describes medieval monks and clerks during the time of King Alfred's rule as readers and writers, but notes that "generals, gentlemen, and kings very seldom [were]" (p. 31).

At this time, the world's oldest surviving dated printed book, the *Diamond Sutra*, a Buddhist tome printed in Chinese in 868,[8] was printed using 9th century Chinese technology: movable carved wooden blocks. This predates by several centuries the publication of Gutenberg's Bible circa 1455,[9] but it was Johann Gutenberg's invention of movable type in Mainz, Germany that kick-started book production and, in Eisenstein's (1979) view, shaped a cultural metamorphosis.

The spread of print shops across Europe affected society in incalculable and complex ways; for instance, the sanctity of religious reading was confronted by the publication of *graven images*, supporting the cause of Protestantism. New ideas were spread, and the reading public expanded, though Eisenstein (1979) cautions this was not a simple historical correlation. She argues that the beginnings of mass culture were in the publication of 16th century incunabula.

With the increasing availability of books arose a concern about how to write well, and rhetorical guides emerged amongst the ideology and the censorship of early scribal culture (see Figure 2.2). Fitzmaurice (2000) describes a push towards fixing a standard for the *best* English, resulting in a proliferation of spellers and grammars following the publication of Samuel Johnson's *Dictionary* in 1755.

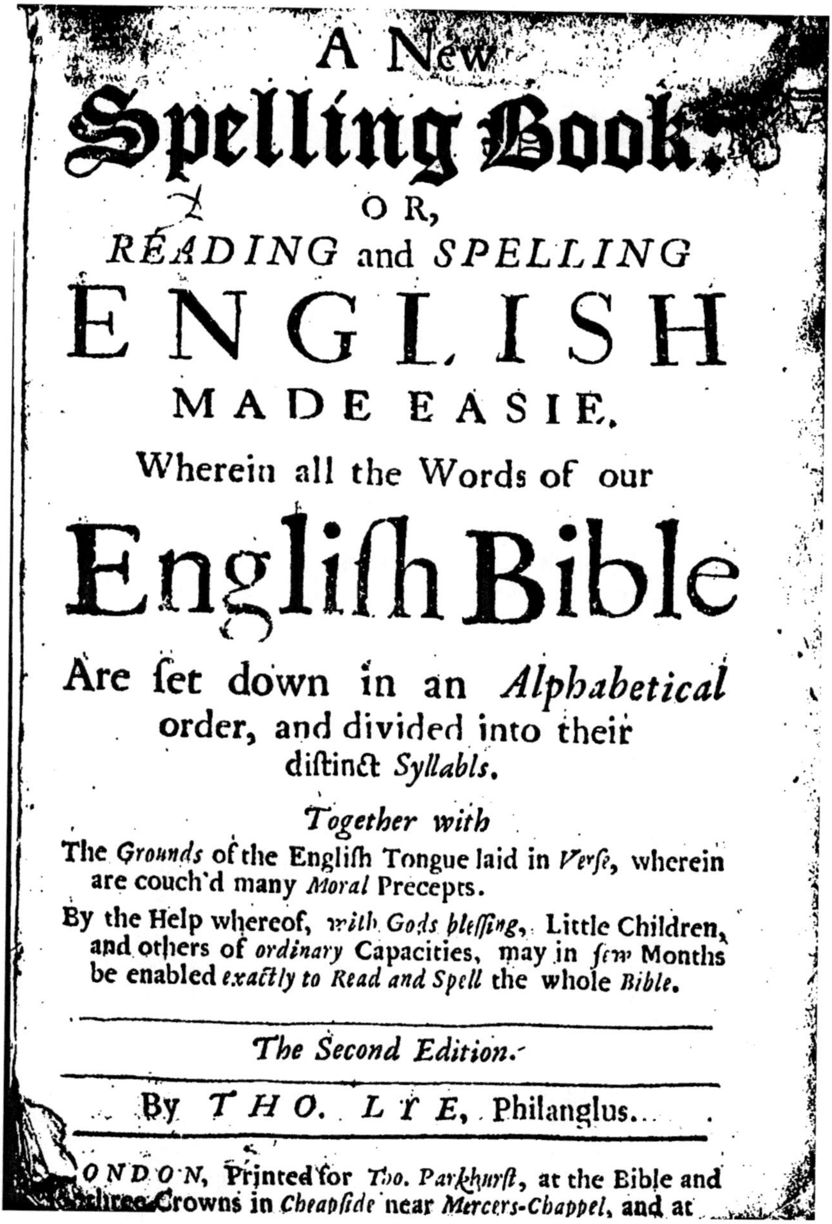

A New
Spelling Book:
OR,
READING and SPELLING
ENGLISH
MADE EASIE,

Wherein all the Words of our

Englifh Bible

Are fet down in an *Alphabetical*
order, and divided into their
diftinct *Syllabls*.

Together with

The *Grounds* of the Englifh Tongue laid in *Verfe*, wherein
are couch'd many *Moral* Precepts.

By the Help whereof, *with Gods bleffing*, Little Children,
and others of *ordinary* Capacities, may in *few* Months
be enabled *exactly to Read and Spell* the whole *Bible*.

The Second Edition.

By *THO. LYE*, Philanglus.

LONDON, Printed for *Tho. Parkhurft*, at the Bible and
three Crowns in *Cheapfide* near *Mercers-Chappel*, and at

Figure 2.2 Thomas Lye's 1677 spelling book.

Literacy as Commodity

In instituting mass production, the Industrial Revolution shaped the conditions for mass education. Mass literacy was the concomitant of mass schooling, which began to gather shape in the early 1800s with the common school whose goals were "to train the rising generation in morality, citizenship, and the basic skills represented by the 3Rs" (Deschenes, Cuban & Tyack, 2001, p. 529). While the evolution of literacy from social exclusion and market niches to public access via mass education was complex and gradual, schooling had mushroomed by the end of the 19th century in industrialized European countries (Maynes, 1985).

Schools became more bureaucratic, reproducing the modern social order as they moved from the one-room schoolhouse to graded classrooms in the latter part of the 19th century with standardized curricula and testing procedures that determined pass-fail achievement (Deschenes et al., 2001). By the 20th century, the meritocratic premise of schooling being the same for all was read as democratic, testing was described as scientific, and students were tracked, normed and labeled according to rigid expectations (Deschenes et al., 2001).

Egan (2000) maintains that modern schooling rests on the 1850s work of Herbert Spencer who saw the curriculum as "an agent of the state in preparing citizens for their future lives" (p. 76), replacing classical studies in the school curriculum with contemporary utilitarian problems. While industrialization relied on skilled workers, Maynes (1985) interestingly argues that changes in education during the 19th century more closely reflected the attitudes of the era than the practical skills—a criticism that can still be made today. Another concordance: mass education in its factory model commoditized literacy, associating it with measurable knowledge and economic growth (Agnello, 2001; Vincent, 2000), a legacy that can be seen today in the rationale for and claims made of standardized literacy tests.

McLuhan (1962) claimed, "Print, in turning the vernaculars into mass media, or closed systems, created the uniform, centralizing forces of modern nationalism" (p. 199). *Modernization*, which developed theoretically in the 1950s, based on the work of German sociologist Max Weber, to justify a model of evolutionary development based on Western industrial history (Agnello, 2001), highlighted education prominently. Indeed the standardization of knowledge dissemination inherent in mass education echoes the essential role of standardization in medieval monopolistic control that Clanchy (2002) asserts was held in place by writing. In a more contemporary setting, McLuhan (1962) states, "The invention of typography confirmed and extended the new visual stress of applied knowledge, providing the first uniformly repeatable *commodity*, the first assembly line, and the first mass-production" (p. 124).

Postmodern Literacy

Contemporary formal language and literacy education are rooted in the knowledge climate of 19th century aims and values. Lyotard (1984) labels as *modern*:

> any science that legitimates itself with reference to a metadiscourse . . . making explicit appeal to some grand narrative, such as the dialectics of the Spirit, the hermeneutics of meaning, the emancipation of the rational or working subject, or the creation of wealth. (p. xxiii)

Modernism ushered in a notion of literacy that was authoritative, linear and paper-based, answering to the educational expectations, models and demands of industrial society. But by the late 20th century, scholars in anthropological literacy were talking about a new literacy based on social practice (Finnegan, 1988; Heath, 1983; Street, 1984, 1995).

Willinsky (1987) links the *new literacy* of the late 20th century paradigmatically to romanticism in its engagement with expressive, whole language in a continuum of complex and transformative learning, understanding of the reader as actively constructing meaning, expectation of environmental influences in literacy learning, and political challenge to modern notions of authority in language and literacy, declaring that those working with the new literacy "are loathe to conceive of the mind as a machine, or of language and learning as mechanical processes" (p. 268–269). In Willinsky's conceptualization of new literacy, the text is not an authoritative automaton but a vehicle for personal engagement, reflection and response, inspiring writing as a more collaborative enterprise. This vision of new literacy confronts modern schooling's aspirations for and expectations of students, teachers, language, literacy and learning.

At the close of the 20th century, the place of literacy in formal schooling and in social practice was diverging significantly and rapidly as society moved increasingly towards what Gee (2004b) describes as "new ways with words, and new ways of learning, afoot in the world—ways not necessarily connected to academics or schools" (p. 1). These new ways with words recollect the 1960s theorizing of Marshall McLuhan (1962), reminding us, "only a fraction of the history of literacy has been typographic" (p. 74). Gee (2004b) continues:

> These [new] ways [with words] are, in their own fashion, just as special, technical, and complex as academic and school ways. But they are motivating for many people for whom school wasn't. At the same time, they may be alienating for many people for whom school ways were motivating. These new ways, though, are just as important—maybe more important—for success in the modern world as school ways. These new ways are the ways with words (and their concomitant ways of thinking)

connected to contemporary digital technologies and the myriad of popular culture and specialist practices to which they have given rise. (pp. 1–2)

By the turn of the 21st century, print was, according to Kress (1997), "literally, being pushed off the page" (p. 2). In historicizing the place of script systems as meaning resources, Kress (2009a) draws a trajectory of the changing relationship of speech and writing between the 19th century when speech was the model of writing and the 21st century, when writing is no longer the sole carrier of meaning. Kress (2009a) maintains that contemporary print has moved from linear to modular presentation, where text is chunked and blocked alongside images that carry increasing meaning-making weight.

As literacy practices have migrated into cyberspace, the predominant media of literacy have shifted from paper and pen to screen and keyboard/mouse, and the assumed pairing of the dominant language and literacy has been seriously challenged. On screens in ever-smaller portable electronic devices, users have dramatically reshaped the materiality of texts; range of meaning-making resources; scope, speed, frequency and nature of interactions; and conventions around linguistic and alphabetic inclusions (Crystal, 2008; Lotherington & Xu, 2004; Tagliamonte & Denis, 2008; Thurlow & Brown, 2003). As digital connection nears ubiquitous availability, we enter what Henry Jenkins (2006) calls *convergence culture*, where the media of communication and the users who control, consume and produce these media have converged. This is best exemplified in collaborative texts enabled by the semantic web, dubbed Web 2.0.

In this climate of collaboration and hybridity in textual production and reproduction, media users construct their identity in online behaviors, and assume far more agency in literacy practices than the passive reading and writing agendas of modern literacy education hold. In this environment, Kress (2009a) asks: "What will writing as a cultural technology look like in the future?" His response is that writing will be a multimodal ensemble in which language will be partial in terms of meaning. To disentangle the modern equation of language and literacy, teachers must ask: What part? What else must now be considered in literacy education? David Olson (1994) reminds us:

> If we regard literacy in the classical sense, as the ability to understand and use the intellectual resources provided by some three thousand years of diverse traditions, the implications of learning to exploit these resources may be enormous. (p. 17)

COMPETING EPISTEMOLOGIES: LITERATE WORLDS

Literacy as Spoken Image

A tautology that Abram (1997) identifies is that "the only medium with which we can define language is language itself" (p. 73). In the human cultural toolkit, language is generally assumed to be a distinguishing characteristic of human development, though research with bonobos indicates these sophisticated apes can competently learn to communicate at a foundational level in a human language system mediated by a complex encoding system as well as spoken English, making them basically capable of human language and literacy (see Savage-Rumbaugh, Shanker & Taylor, 1998). Savage-Rumbaugh et al. (1998) suggest that linguistics has lifted human language from its interactional base and assumed it to be "such a complete system of meta-action and such a complete system of cultural expectancies that generate it that it can be properly studied of its own accord" (p. 192). The objectification and privileging of the language system at the expense of its users has been attributed to the legacy of structural linguistics, which views language as "an abstract, socially disconnected system" (M. Dewey, 2009, p. 67).

Both structural linguistics and semiotics developed from the theorizing of 19th century Swiss linguist, Ferdinand de Saussure, whose *Cours de linguistique générale* was posthumously compiled from his lecture notes by former students, and published. Saussure echoed a curiously Socratic stance in maintaining that signs hold no meaning in and of themselves. He insisted on the primacy of spoken language over written language: meaning was inherent in speech, not in writing, which was simply an image of the spoken form (Allen, 2000; Cilliers, 1998; Saussure, 1916/1974).

Bourdieu (1977) queried the social conditions of production in the Saussurean objectification of language, which removed speech from social exchange, positing,

> a sociological critique subjects the concepts of linguistics to a threefold displacement. In place of *grammaticalness* it puts the notion of *acceptability*, or, to put it another way, in place of "the" language (*langue*), the notion of the *legitimate* language. In place of *relations of communication* (or symbolic interaction) it puts *relations of symbolic power*, and so replaces the question of the *meaning* of speech with the question of the *value* and *power* of speech. Lastly, in place of specifically linguistic competence, it puts *symbolic capital*, which is inseparable from the speaker's position in the social structure. (p. 646)

Olson (1994) challenges the linguistic view that speech is primary, writing, secondary, conceptualizing literacy as an analytical lens not merely a media translation technology, and claiming "that the text provides a model for speech; we introspect our language in terms of the categories laid down by our script" (p. xviii). Ong (1980) promotes the view that literacy is cognitively and socially transformative, distinguishing oral from literate cultures:

> Without writing, the mind cannot even generate concepts such as "history" or "analysis," just as without print, and the massive accumulation of detailed documented knowledge which print makes possible,

the mind cannot generate portmanteau concepts such as "culture" or "civilization," not to mention "macroeconomics" or "polyethylene." (p. 199)

Interestingly, Socrates, who was fundamentally nonliterate, insisted on the analytic introspection of speech, asking students to separate thought and word (Abram, 1997). This we know, as S. Thomas et al. (2007) point out, tongue-in-cheek, through written accounts.

Street (1995) cautions against confounding literacy as a technology with formal schooling, and argues that autonomous theories of literacy manifest a colonial superiority in ignoring the sophisticated ideological and cultural practices of cultures that have alternative models of literacy and learning. Innes (1998) tempers the orality-literacy divide, stating:

> Indeed, the heroic view of a triumphant literacy pushing previous practices aside is being replaced by an understanding of the ways in which oral practices survive the challenge of literacy, and can indeed shape the cultural and social contexts within which literacy is adopted. (p. 4)

Language and literacy are both complex mediating technologies. Neither language nor literacy can be looked at as simple, or removed from context.

Literacy as Alphabetic Competence

The intimate connection of (dominant) language knowledge and alphabetic literacy has remained strong in the public imagination over time—*literacy* is subsumed under the elementary *language* curriculum in Ontario—though many different types of symbolic texts can be written and read (e.g., musical scores, electrical wiring diagrams, maps, blueprints).

In the realm of linguistic communication, literacy offers a means to translate spoken language into written code via different logical systems: syllabaries and alphabets, based on sounds; and logography, based on meaning. At its most conservative level, literacy at school is looked upon as alphabetic encoding and decoding of the dominant language: reading and writing letters, words, sentences, written texts—in English.

There is considerable play in how symbolic systems encode both sound and meaning. Spelling in many alphabetically encoded languages, including English, can be tortuous, revealing historical pronunciation more accurately than contemporary speech, which, in the case of English, has splintered into numerous varieties, each reading sound corresponding to letters within its own phonological framework. The room for interpretation within canonical spelling is inevitable given language change. Furthermore, letter-to-sound encoding is inexact in English because letter combinations hide phonologically conditioned spoken realizations. For instance, the cringe-worthy classroom expectation that the suffix *-ed* can be reliably sounded out creates a great deal of frustration for the child who reads different sound realizations of the cluster in each of *jumped, judged* and *jutted*.

The same symbolic system is exploited to very different effect from language to language. For example, the Roman alphabet used to encode English as well as many other languages creates *taller* which, in English, denotes a comparable degree of height, and in Spanish, a factory. The pronunciation of the same string of letters is unrecognizable from English to Spanish and vice versa. The same principle holds for use of symbolic systems in different genres. In written English, the Arabic numeral representing the number *four* (e.g., 4) optionally encodes the preposition *for*, or a homophonous morpheme, such as be*fore* (e.g., b4) in texting.

The literate interpretation of communication is generically patterned: a letter is not a novel is not a shopping note. But genres are neither static nor leak-proof. A special occasion greeting, such as a Christmas card, traditionally takes the form of a commercial card, with an optional letter that may include pictures. However, it can be composed using other media, such as a software program, following conventions of another genre, and sent via email, such as the joke Christmas card received from a family member (who is an engineer) in which the specifications for the Christmas tree (to fit the space designated), load-bearing roof (to withstand the landing of Santa, his sleigh and eight reindeer), stockings by the fireside (materials and spacing according to fire regulation) as well as a waste management plan (for reindeer residue) were highlighted to comic effect.

Different types of documents constitute intellectual products. A wall post in the John Ritblat Gallery housing treasures of the British Library informs the visitor:

> Historical documents can be any type of text: a note scribbled in a church calendar; a letter; a bill; a diary; a handbill for a meeting. What makes us single out particular texts as historical documents, and view them sometimes as treasures, is our own changing perception of the importance of the people and events with which they are associated. (Public sign, John Ritblat Gallery, British Library, London)

An example of this explanation is the museum's display of the original copy of the lyrics to *A Hard Day's Night* by the Beatles, handwritten by John Lennon on the back of his son Julian's first birthday card.

School expectations of literacy as alphabetic encoding of the dominant language following static generic conventions and standard spelling are, thus, somewhat myopic given the slipperiness of transcription systems and the creative possibilities they invite.

Literacy as Enlightenment

McLuhan (1962) quipped, "By the meaningless sign linked to the meaningless sound we have built the shape and meaning of Western man" (p.

50). Literacy has been lauded as the apex of human achievement. Linguistic encoding systems provide a technology that extends human memory, archiving and transporting theories, languages, history, science and art across time and space. The plays of Shakespeare have been preserved and are available to us through this technology, as are early religious manuscripts in antiquated languages, preindustrial theories of science and indigenous narratives of becoming, to skim just a few topics from the vast literature created with the agency of writing technologies. But are these substantial human accomplishments simply a correlate of learning an alphabet? What is captured in literature is human thought.

According to the *Oxford English Dictionary* (online edition), the term *literacy* appears in the late 19th century as a backformation to *illiterate*, which was the unmarked state of civilization until the advent of mass education. However, the word *literate*, signifying "acquainted with letters or literature; educated, instructed, learned," is first quoted in 1432, when knowledge of letters would have been associated primarily, though not entirely, with clerics and scholars, typically in classical languages worthy of laborious hand inscription, establishing early on an unstated connection between literacy and prestige language norms.

Bruner (1991) reasons that knowledge is culturally invested, and offers a sociocultural point of view, stating, "Originally introduced by Vygotsky and championed by his widening circle of admirers, the new position is that cultural products, like language and other symbolic systems, mediate thought and place their stamp on our representations of reality" (p. 3). He explains that this understanding is behind the theory of distributed intelligence that maintains human intelligence is not self-contained, but influenced by tools, references and collegial input.

One of the proliferating numbers of researchers advocating the complex systems that are today's video games as contemporary literacy learning (see, for instance, Delwiche, 2010; Gee, 2003, 2007; S. Johnson, 2005; Prensky, 2006; Shaffer, Squire, Halverson & Gee, 2005; Squire, 2008), Gee (2007) claims good video games distribute intelligence "between a real-world person and artificially intelligent virtual characters" (p. 326). Digitally enabled game play involves novel immersive mechanisms for distributing learning and situating meaning in a new literacy practice that is, at the same time, educational and *ludic*: play-oriented. De Castell and Jenson (2003) explain the relationship between "play and learning as mutually constitutive, and their conjunction, therefore, as transformative of both" (p. 659).

These sophisticated and contradictory points of view reveal that the nature of literacy is contested and complexly interwoven into epistemologies. Likewise, literacy practices are socially dynamic, and deeply embedded in cultural histories and practices. How has the vast collection of scholarship on literate worlds and possibilities been translated into practice at school?

Literacy as Schooling

Over a third of London primary school children reach the age of 11 without being able properly to read and write, and 20 per cent are still having serious difficulties by the time they leave secondary school.

This is a source of huge economic inefficiency, but in every case of illiteracy we are also talking of a grievous personal handicap. If you cannot read properly, you are more likely to suffer from low self-confidence—and if you suffer from low self-confidence, you are far more likely to turn to crime. (B. Johnson, 2010, p. 16)

This excerpt, from a feature article written by the mayor of London, Boris Johnson, appeared in the Comments and Features section of *The Daily Telegraph* on Monday, July 19, 2010. It reads, though, as a comment from the distant past. Mayor Johnson's article treats literacy as pass-fail alphabetic reading and writing in English, never so much as hinting that in the polyglot metropolis of London, England, that is his political domain, a significant percentage of the city's commerce (and society) runs (lawfully) on languages other than English. Mayor Johnson's feature article presents an oversimplified public attitude to the nature of literacy, and an unsubtle accusation that the educational establishment is somehow holding back on doing the right thing.

The varied forms literacy practices take over time and place are seldom recognized. Literacy and language are typically conflated in both social consciousness and curricular attention at school, where they are treated as an end rather than a means of learning and regarded as portable technologies: a set of encoding-decoding skills that can be isolated from context, taught, learned and applied. Those coming to English from other language backgrounds are pathologized and taught remedially.

As the technologies for encoding communication have expanded over the past 20 years, the ways in which texts are created, accessed and shared have moved decidedly into an era of collaboration and distributed processing. Reliance on the alphabet as pivotal transformer in knowledge building must acknowledge that, more and more, "information comes dressed in many clothes: in numbers, in images, in the binary code of current electronic technologies, and, still, in language" (Kress, 1997, p. 1). As Cope and Kalantzis (2009a) explain, the minimal unit of encoding in literacy is no longer the letter; it is the pixel:

After half a millennium or longer in which written text was a pervasive source of knowledge and power, photographic means of representation (lithographic printing, cinema, analogue television) began to afford greater power to image and comfortably overlay image with written text. The digital accelerates this process as the elementary modular unit of manufacture of textual meaning is reduced from the character to the pixel. Images and fonts are now made of the same raw materials, and more easily overlaid—hence the television screens that stream more and more writing over image, and the magazines and newspapers which layer image and text in a way that was never easily achievable in the era of letterpress printing. (p. 361)

Neither social attitudes to literacy education nor school practices have kept up to date with the changing face of literacy. There have been numerous calls for new thinking about the ways that language and literacy are taught in the contemporary classroom (Ball & Freedman, 2004; Cope & Kalantzis, 2009b; Gee, 2003, 2004b; Kellner, 2004; Kress, 2003; Lankshear & Knobel, 2003, 2006; New London Group, 1996). As Kress (2003) states, rethinking literacy education is not "a project governed by nostalgias" (p. 175). It is a political as well as an educational revision of the curricular agenda in tune with current and future communication needs, media, aspirations and possibilities.

THEORETICAL GUIDE WIRES

Literacy has many faces, and continues to be understood in very different ways. Graff (1987) notes that potential literacy is a void, quoting psychologist M. M. Lewis that "the only literacy that matters is the literacy that is in use" (p. 23). Bazerman (2004) asks, what are "the kind of skills and tasks necessary for people to develop into competent literate participants within the textually dense worlds of modernity" (p. 59)? My year long observation at JPS indicated a number of gaps students had to bridge in order to achieve school literacy acquisition, so there were remedial, facilitative considerations; and there were, importantly, new directions to explore towards developing multimodal literacies more in sync with a globalizing, digitized world. Given the enormous body of work on languages and literacies in social and school spaces, what theories would help to guide our early exploratory research?

Directions for change included ameliorating the poor fit of idealized literacy instruction, and spotty language support to the actual students sitting in the classroom. Students' needs included traditional learning: reading and writing alphabetic print; developing English language proficiency as well as manipulating other symbol sets: numerical, musical, diagrammatic and so forth; learning digital literacies; and acquiring sufficient cultural acumen to successfully navigate institutional assessment. One of the holes in the system was seeing a place in the classroom for the languages spoken in the community. Recognizing these languages is not only supportive of individual children's acquisition of English; it promotes antiracist education by accepting multilingualism as a natural state, and builds into the system preparation for a globalizing world where languages will be of increasing importance not just socially and culturally but economically and politically.

MULTILITERACIES: A BEGINNING

The New London Group was an international collaboration of scholars who met to discuss the future of literacy pedagogy in 1994, and as a consequence of their discussions, crafted a manifesto calling for a new approach to literacy education that was responsive to rapid social changes occurring in the late 20th century, owing to large-scale cultural migration and burgeoning digitization. Their call to action christened this broadened understanding of literacy: *multiliteracies* (New London Group, 1996). Though the context in which they were writing is now outdated—in the mid-1990s Web 1.0 was a relatively static vehicle for document posting and retrieval, and the revolution in mobile devices was in its infancy—their vision of a transforming society outgrowing modern idealizations of literacy, learning and learners was an intellectual landmark that has spawned global research and action for pedagogical and political change.

The *why* behind a new literacy pedagogy acknowledged the rise of a post-Fordist corporate structure in response to the information revolution, the changes in civic engagement with increasing cultural diversity, and the "multilayered lifeworlds" (p. 71) of diversifying private lives (New London Group, 1996). Modern literacy education as it had taken shape since the Industrial Revolution was, quite simply, narrow and obsolescent.

The New London Group's transformative project specifically addressed the *what* and the *how* of a new approach to literacy pedagogy, pointing to new dimensions and designs of learning taking account of multimodality, hybridity and intertextuality. In so doing, they anticipated intermediality (Semali & Watts Pailliotet, 1999), or converging media, and transmodality, or switching from one mode of expression to another, which are concomitants of the semantic web, better known as Web 2.0. They posited a pedagogical framework that called for *situated practice, overt instruction, critical framing* and *transformed practice* (New London Group, 1996). In retrospective writing, Cope and Kalantzis (2009b), members of the New London Group, tap into the enormous changes in digital communications media over the past decade, reiterating, "old logics of literacy and teaching are profoundly challenged by this new media environment" (p. 173), stressing, "meaning making is an active, transformative process, and a pedagogy based on that recognition is more likely to open up viable life courses for a world of change and diversity" (p. 175).

LITERACY AS HUMAN CAPITAL

The multiliteracies project called for a revision in education rooted in modern principles. Agnello (2001), in contextualizing the need for a postmodern literacy policy in contemporary education, indicates that the corporate state's agenda for modern schooling was to manufacture future workers who could follow orders, not to critique the power base of the system.

A human capital theory of literacy has claimed multitudinous socially beneficial if not downright curative effects: Barton (1994) delineates a veritable laundry list of metaphors about *illiteracy*, linked to sickness, handicap, ignorance, incapacity, oppression, deprivation and deviance (p. 13), which literacy has been claimed to fix (and is still being claimed to fix, as Mayor Boris Johnson's 2010 feature newspaper article shows). This stance assumes a state of illiteracy is possible in our print- and media-saturated world where screens scrolling multiple texts adorn elevators, waiting rooms and subway stops; and clothing is riddled with imprinted messages, from subversive slogans on T-shirts to logos on clothing, running shoes and accessories. It also differentiates those who have a categorical and quantifiable skill called literacy from those who do not, rather than constructing a realm of possibility in which there are multiple literacy practices, contexts and purposes. Whatever the social claims made, the modern agenda for the formation of literate subjects is conformist and undemocratic, inscribing power relations in literacy lessons. Writing about the recognition of a new literacy in late modernity, Willinsky (1987) pronounces:

> The danger of teaching by the book, as Wordsworth foresaw it, was a metaphorical reduction of the child from a flower to an engine, all for want of the accidental and spontaneous. For tutors and teachers, having learned how to manage the book, there was the temptation to use it to control and confine those they would instruct. (p. 276)

LITERACY AS CRITICAL AWARENESS

The revolutionary literacy teacher Paulo Freire popularized a Marxist approach advocating critical (adult) literacy education in Brazil in the mid-20th century. Freire (1970/1998) put forward an ideology of education as liberating, rather than subjugating:

> Education as the practice of freedom—as opposed to education as the practice of domination—denies that man (*sic*) is abstract, isolated, independent, and unattached to the world; it also denies that the world exists as a reality apart from people. (p. 62)

He characterized traditional teaching in which information was deposited in students' brains for cataloguing as "the 'banking' concept of education" (1970/1998, p. 53). This he contrasted with "'problem-posing' education" (1970/1998, p. 60) that invited learning as fundamentally dialogic, and raising of critical consciousness: *conscientização*. Reading was not merely decoding a world encoded in print; reading entailed reading the world as well as the word (Freire & Macedo, 1987).

A. Luke and Freebody (1997) extrapolate:

> Although critical literacy does not stand for a unitary approach, it marks out a coalition of educational interests committed to engaging with possibilities that the technologies of writing and other modes of inscription offer for social change, cultural diversity, economic equity, and political enfranchisement. (p. 1)

Critical framing is one of the four fundamentals of literacy instruction in the New London Group's (1996) manifesto. Cummins (2006) glosses critical framing as "a focus on the historical, cultural, sociopolitical, and ideological roots of systems of knowledge and social practice" (p. 54). He acknowledges the New London Group's (1996) reference to transmission pedagogy by naming *overt instruction* as one of the pillars of literacy pedagogy in addition to *critical framing, situated practice* and *transformed practice*, and proposes an elaborated framework that nests transmission, social constructivist and transformative pedagogical orientations within each other, rather than posing them as sequential or contradictory (Cummins, 2006, p. 54), rendering critical literacy a natural component of language and literacy instruction.

Our research aspired to raise critical consciousness, not only in learners, who were being required to fit themselves into the profile of the idealized learner in the Ontario language and literacy curriculum, but also in teachers and, importantly, policy makers.

SITUATED LEARNING AND TRANSFORMATIVE PEDAGOGIES

Appadurai (1996) explains that "the landscapes of group identity—the ethnoscapes—around the world are no longer familiar anthropological objects, insofar as groups are no longer tightly territorialized, spatially bounded, historically unselfconscious, or culturally homogeneous" (p. 48). The linguistic landscape of Toronto reveals a multitude of languages in commercial spaces, such as storefronts, and in municipal signage, such as street signs in designated neighborhoods reflecting local bilingualism (see Figure 2.3). However, in politicized public spaces, official bilingualism predominates (see Figure 2.4). The increasing use of international languages in local spaces is poorly reflected in the curriculum, which, in answering to the national imaginary, promotes the official languages of the nation: English and French. Local languages, despite being welcomed in political rhetoric, are labeled *international* in the curriculum, and assigned a back seat in continuing education.

Figure 2.3   Local bilingualism: English-Chinese street sign in Toronto.

The supportive effects of actively maintaining prior language knowledge and use while learning a subsequent language are well established in the research literature (Cummins, 1981a, 1991, 2000; W. P. Thomas & Collier, 2001). In the early days of experimentation with French immersion programs in the context of Montréal, Québec, Lambert (1974) called for an approach to second language learning that added rather than subtracted language knowledge to the learner's repertoire. Cenoz and Genesee (1998) extended the philosophy of *additive bilingualism* to linguistically complex contexts to promote *additive multilingualism.* Language knowledge, in this orientation to second language learning, is not replaced with one or more new languages in the classroom but added to, positively utilizing extant linguistic knowledge.

Valdés (2004) signals the fact that researchers in literacy and second language acquisition do not have a history of talking to each other because they belong to different communities of practice in academic life. Literacy has been considered de facto tied to the dominant language. In a revised version of a classic 1986 article (focusing on the American context), Cummins (2001a) suggests that the lack of long-term progress in ameliorating the educational performance of linguistically and culturally diverse students is due to social and political failure to renegotiate power relations between teachers and students, and schools and communities. Because of this, students of minority backgrounds must adapt their identities to classroom projections and expectations—a state mirrored in observations that in Ontario, EQAO concurrently tests an Anglo-centric colonial reading of Canadian culture in literacy tests. Cummins (1996) refers to practices that marginalize rather than empower minority language users in the classroom as engaging

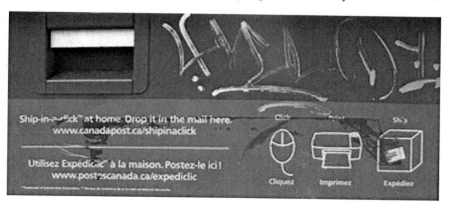

Figure 2.4 Official bilingualism: English-French signage on mailbox.[10]

coercive rather than *collaborative* power relations, serving to reinforce the status quo of unequal access to social power. He frames power in the context of the classroom as *additive* or *subtractive* analogous to language.

Norton (1997) asserts, "Speech, speakers and identities are inseparable" (p. 410), pointing out the shortfall in applied linguistics to socially situate language learners in the classroom. She uses the term *investment* "to signal the socially and historically constructed relationship of learners to the target language and their sometimes ambivalent desire to learn and practice it" (1997, p. 411). In a school-based project to develop dual language books in Toronto, Cummins, Bismilla, Chow et al. (2005) and Cummins, Bismilla, Cohen, Giampapa and Leoni (2005) exemplify *situated practice* and *transformative pedagogy* in the creation of what they term *identity texts* in the linguistically heterogeneous classroom. These are dual language stories created by bilingual children in the languages of the home and school in which they have invested personal identity that is reflected positively in the school environment.

Gee (2004a) notes that "the new capitalism is all about multiple identities, and enacting and recognizing socially situated identities" (p. 283). However, as Allen (2000) argues, quoting Bakhtin, "Identity is only ever achieved in relation to another, an addressee who in answering speech affirms the subject's dialogic existence" (p. 172). The dialogic achievement of identity in classroom spaces where culturally embedded language practices are systematically shaped towards dominant norms translates ultimately into pass or fail; this is existence in school. Valdés (2004) suggests that learners of minority language backgrounds need to develop intercultural literacy so they can comfortably traverse different discourse communities. My argument is that all members of the school community need to develop intercultural literacy, fundamentally recognizing multiple identities in the classroom, in terms of not only ethnic contributions but also cyberspace enactments of identity.

THE DIGITAL DIVIDE

The popular press projects a digital divide that is based on social generation (Barlow, 1996; Prensky, 2001; Tunsbridge, 1995). In an Australian interview published in 1995, John Perry Barlow described those under the age of 25 (ergo, born after 1970) as "closer to being a native, in terms of understanding what [cyberspace] is and having a real basic sense of it" (Tunsbridge, 1995, p. 66), contrasting them with older generations who were more akin to immigrants in the communicative paradigms of the digital era. This was written into *A Declaration of the Independence of Cyberspace* in 1996, as "you are terrified of your own children, since they are natives in a world where you will always be immigrants" (Barlow, 1996, para. 12). The *digital natives-digital immigrants* distinction was popularized by Prensky (2001), who, likewise, relegated comfort with digital technologies and epistemologies to a function of age.

From the vantage point of the second decade of the 21st century, we know that though children born in the digital age are increasingly socialized into a complex mediascape, they are not conversant with digital genres as a function of birthright, any more than those of us, born before the social saturation of digital technologies, are universally struggling to live with them. Social and economic necessities require us to keep abreast of technologically mediated communication. As a business acquaintance recently noted, after having his laptop stolen from checked baggage, "When I asked the airline representative for a form to claim the loss, she directed me to the website; but without my laptop, I couldn't access it."

In 2003, socialization into digital technologies was still at least partly owing to birthright, which positioned computers as typical household appliances to children born in the digital era, just as pop-up toasters were considered standard and ordinary in my generation, but not in my parents' era. There is a clarifying aspect: digital natives had opportunities for comfortable experimental play with technology that allowed them to learn how to successfully manipulate sophisticated computer technology. This put poor children who did not have a computer at home at a disadvantage, though access to learning with technology was, in fact, the community mandate at JPS. Gaining comfort with technology was less culturally comfortable for teachers, though, who were unused to the idea of play, given hectic adult schedules, and unlikely to see a powerful and expensive digital appliance as something to be used for fun. By its very existence in the classroom, the computer challenged teachers' competence as class leaders, causing a general anxiety about instructional use. The principal insisted that teachers each have a laptop computer to play with to learn what they could do with it. Then individual teachers could informally share their learning with other teachers at school.

From the perspective of 2010, Sinclair exposes the gross generalization in drawing a line in the sand between digital natives and digital immigrants on the basis of generation. She offers instead a delineated, experience-oriented description of acculturation into our continuously digitizing world, as *digital aliens, immigrants, adaptives, natives* and *avatars*. Though we did not have access to this sophisticated thinking in 2003, I did realize that wherever individual teachers positioned themselves on a continuum of technological comfort, it did not define the worlds of their peers or their students. This is true now as then.

Multimodality and Digital Media

Gunther Kress, a member of the New London Group, in examining multimodal literacies of the late 20th century, was particularly interested in the reconfiguration of image and print on the page. He advised that "it is now no longer possible to understand language and its uses without understanding the effect of all modes of communication that are copresent in any text" (Kress, 2000, p. 337).

Multimodal texts are not in any way novel; in fact they are very, very old. Rare medieval manuscripts that have been preserved, often in restored condition, and made available for viewing in libraries and museums are multimodal; hand calligraphy is punctuated with ornamented majuscules, and complemented by colorful images and decorative borders (see Figure 2.5 from an early 15th century manuscript of Chaucer's *Canterbury Tales*). These modalities interrelate in complex ways. Subtextual narratives can be painted into the marginalia, depicting scriptural stories or culturally typical chores and games; and mythical and other creatures may frolic inside and around letters (Nishimura, 2009). Images may materially utilize alphabetic text as a design component: the 15th century *Lisbon Hebrew Bible* incorporated Hebrew letters as decorative media;[11] and the mouse in *Alice's Adventures in Wonderland* tells a tale which is written in the shape of a rodent's tail in a complex pun.[12]

With the move from page to screen as the predominant site of literacy, the notion of multimodality takes on new life. Digital media, in which the minimal unit is the pixel rather than the letter or character (Cope & Kalantzis, 2009a), extend and intensify the possibilities of multimodal communication. As Jewitt (2002) points out, "In the move from page to screen a range of representational modes (including image, movement, gesture, and voice) are available as meaning-making resources" (p. 171). Digital mediation introduces interactivity and dynamism in literacy practices, incurring collaboration, which challenges modern notions of authorship as well as text. These semiotic resources in multimodal communication work differently, offering multiple ways of meaning-making, and placing different interpretive demands on learners. Within the viewpoint of multiple intelligences, this means children have more opportunities to find their way into a text. As Gardner (2003) explains:

Figure 2.5   The first page of *The Knight's Tale* of Chaucer's *Canterbury Tales*, from the Ellesmere manuscript, dated early 15th century, held in the Huntington Library, in San Marino, California (MS EL 26 C 9).[13]

Most lay and scholarly writings about intelligence focus on a combination of linguistic and logical intelligences—the intellectual strengths, I often maintain, of a law professor. However, a fuller appreciation of human beings occurs if we take into account spatial, bodily kinesthetic, musical, interpersonal, and intrapersonal intelligences. While we all have these intelligences, individuals differ for both genetic and experiential reasons in their respective profiles of intellectual strengths and weaknesses. No intelligence is in and of itself artistic or nonartistic; rather several intelligences can be put to aesthetic ends, if individuals so desire. No direct educational implications follow from this psychological theory; but if individuals differ in their intellectual profiles, it makes sense to take this fact into account in devising an educational system. (p. 4).

Contemporary interactive digitally mediated literacies, such as massively multiplayer online role-playing games (MMORPGs), are complexly multi-modal, interactive and collaborative. Collaboration is not new, though it has changed considerably in scope with digital mediation. The archaeological find of the *Dead Sea Scrolls*, for instance, as a collection of reconstructed documents written in different languages on different surfaces, including both parchment and papyrus, strongly points to collaborative authorship.

In a guided seminar trip to the Bodleian Library, University of Oxford to view the medieval manuscript, MS. Bodley 764, I learned something of the context of the collaborative production of a secular medieval manuscript. The Curator of Medieval Manuscripts described the mid-13th century bestiary as being, in all probability, privately commissioned for a wealthy family, and produced by a collaborative team including a scribe, an illustrator and a capital letter decorator, working to the instructions of the manuscript director.[14] This is a small-scale publishing company.

So neither multimodality nor collaborative authorship is new; what is new is attending to these frameworks as legitimate literacy activities in school where language in socially abstracted, written form has been habitually singled out for educational attention and assessment, and other modes of communication have been systematically ignored. In an era when none of us can claim to be digital innocents, the multimodal communicational landscape of the 21st century can no longer be neglected. Alphabetic literacy is pedagogically insufficient, and unreflecting of literacy in social reality. We find ourselves caught in Harold Benjamin's (Peddiwell, 1939/2004) colorful parody of education's failure to keep up with environmental change in *The Saber-Tooth Curriculum*, where the faux ice age curriculum is ardently maintained, though it no longer has relevance to the realities of a warmer climate.

MOVING FORWARD

We needed to develop the machinery for collaborative theory-practice exploration in order to move forward with plans to design a pedagogy of multiliteracies. This I saw as requiring an intertwined ideological and pedagogical path. We had established after-school workshops as a default mechanism for meeting. The principal had in mind building a *learning community* as a feature of regular school life, and she strongly supported the development and establishment of our teacher-researcher collaboration. I wanted to merge theory and practice in the development of multiliteracies projects, and though I wasn't quite sure how to go about doing this, I knew that it was the connective tissue between them that would motivate fruitful change. It was important to aim high, but in the back of my mind were the wonderful words spoken by Joshua Fishman on the event of his 80th birthday celebrations at the University of Pennsylvania in 2006, for which there had been a symposium on minority language maintenance attended by many individuals he had personally helped as researchers, including me: "If you aim for the stars, you could fall on your face!" To co-develop new ways of teaching would require fulfilling status quo educational requirements; developing sensitivity to community resources, needs and aspirations; experimenting with contemporary social practices and digital possibilities; and being bravely creative. There would be a lot of balls in the air in this delicate juggling act.

3 Rewriting *Goldilocks and the Three Bears*

FROM *GOLDILOCKS* TO *DREADLOCKS*

In 2003–2004, we decided to try an exploratory intervention. In our conversations and workshops at JPS, I had raised the issue of the popularity of *Goldilocks and the Three Bears* with the kindergarten children. I was mystified. What hooked children into the story? No one in the class had blond hair. Nor did children have access to bears in the city, unless they had been lucky enough to visit the zoo (at the extreme east end of the city). Cottages were places up north that rich kids went to; they were not the high-rise apartments in the city these children knew.

There had to be something in the story that spoke to them. They understand *break and enter* said one teacher, half jokingly.

I proposed to the principal that we try an experiment to help children with some of the challenges they were facing in literacy learning: we would digitally rewrite the story of *Goldilocks and the Three Bears*. Given the school's mandate to explore innovative pedagogies utilizing new technologies, and the literacy gaps children were facing in terms of English language learning, cultural history and literacy socialization, this could be a useful exercise to bring together what children could do well: draw and program, with what they had less experience with: English language, *Canadian culture* and narrative structure. In preparation, the teachers would have to explore available hardware and software to set ideas in motion. This was directly in line with the principal's belief that "you have to put the technology in the teachers' hands." Playing with story retelling in electronic formats was a scribble pad for designing what might be thought of as modal access ports to stories: alternative channels for students to enter a narrative. Digital story rewriting reinforced what My-Linh was doing—putting the children inside their own resources, and it drew on the multimodal composition practices I had observed in classes that implemented varied semiotic resources. It would essentially provide an opportunity for children to learn to read by writing—or rather adapting a story. It turned upside down the traditional *four skills* paradigm of language learning (viz., listening, speaking, reading, writing) and the parallel corollary of literacy learning following sequential skills acquisition (i.e., first listen, then speak [at home], followed by learning to read and then to write [at school]).

To pilot the idea, we tried it out amongst ourselves. Working with interested teachers after school hours, we each did an individualized rewrite of the basic narrative of *Goldilocks and the Three Bears*, inserting our lives into the narrative framework (e.g., *[G]Oldilocks*) and retelling the story via new media to see how we could reshape it.

The collective results of our creative story rewriting were definitely less than prize-winning, but the idea had merit, as we had to think through our writing and media interventions to change the story according to our own preferences. If we could design the pedagogy to introduce children to the basic narrative and guide them to adapt the story to the local context, *Goldilocks and the Three Bears* could become *Dreadlocks and the Three Raccoons*. Why not?

PIONEERING METHODOLOGY

The *Rewriting Goldilocks* pilot research project relied on voluntary participation in keeping with ethical research procedures. A few teachers agreed to meet after school, and we planned how they might introduce the story of *Goldilocks and the Three Bears* in Grades 1 and 2 and then lead the children to adapt the story in such a way that they became a part of it. I applied for and received a small grant[1] to defray basic material costs.

A rich vein of theoretical guidance for our pilot multiliteracies intervention came from the growing body of research investigating aspects of the changing path of literacy in an electronic and swiftly globalizing era, much of which had been galvanized by the New London Group's (1996) call to action to create a pedagogy of multiliteracies (Cope & Kalantzis, 2000; Crystal, 2001; Gee, 2003; Hawisher & Selfe, 2000; Kress, 2003; Lankshear, 1997; Lankshear & Knobel, 2003; Snyder, 1997, 2002). Considering the language and literacy gaps facing children in a high needs area of a large cosmopolitan city attending a school dedicated to innovative technology-enhanced learning and teaching, and pivoting on the curiosity of the kindergarten children's enjoyment of the story of *Goldilocks and the Three Bears*, we rolled up our sleeves to begin to figure out how each teacher could plan a class project to introduce multiliteracies education by digitally rewriting the three bears narrative.

Our research project was approached from the perspective of *action research*, which, as Marshall and Rossman (2006) explain, "seeks full, collaborative inquiry by all participants, often to engage in sustained change in organizations, communities, or institutions" (p. 6). I had previously employed an action research model in qualitative research in a school context (Lotherington, 2003b); but the research had been an evaluation of an experimental program whereas the *Goldilocks* project aspired to novel pedagogical design based on contemporary theorizing, so it had far less structure. Our initial discussions portended the distances we would need to cross to bring together theory and practice in the classroom: to my introductory comments enthusiastically describing the creative possibilities emerging from digitally networked multimedia that could revolutionize the literacy classroom, one of the teachers looked at me and asked, "So what do I do on Tuesday?" It was a sobering moment.

In truth, I had no idea. I relied on the teachers to map out constituent activities for Tuesday and every other day. This moment underscored the delicacy of nurturing what Bakhtin (1975/1981) termed *dialogic learning*, regarding the participatory requirements of action research. It also pointed to the complexity of formal education, which interconnects dynamic systems (Radford, 2006). The teachers had to orchestrate defined schedules, curricular and provincial test requirements, find class sets of storybooks, and timetable access to digital equipment. They were managing classes in which two thirds of the children had questionable levels of English, not to mention issues with regular attendance, behavioral problems and learning challenges. This intervention was a volunteer activity that brought us together after school hours, when teachers were tired and needed to prepare for another day.

Bogdan and Biklen (2003) state that "action research can serve as an organizing strategy to get people involved and active around particular issues; the research itself is an action" (p. 227). It soon became apparent that the anticipated collegial interaction needed to be learned; the teachers expected our workshops to provide *banking education* (Freire, 1970/1998) in that they were willing to try out new ideas but they had less expectation of democratically shaping of those ideas. I frequently got a puzzled head shake with "but I don't know what you want me to do!" We needed to learn to share responsibility in this research endeavor; and I needed to learn as much from them as they needed to learn from me.

Through our rather stumbling early workshop meetings, the principal was always highly supportive of our collaboration in an experimental intervention. She was particularly invested in the idea of working with narrative learning. She perceived our after-school meetings as professional development opportunities offering a research perspective to teacher development. Her unwavering dedication to improved education for the children in her school community together with her visionary management style and administrative experience made her a pillar of support. We would chat about problems and misunderstandings that arose in meetings, which she attended as often and as long she could. She listened, contributing her perspectives and support, never dissuading me. Ideas evolved through these chats, as did structural improvements to collaborative discussions.

Rewriting *Goldilocks*: Emergent Transliteracies

Street's (2000) admonition not to reify the concept of multiliteracies led me to think about our project as the development of *transliteracies*—synergetic literacy practices that revise and reconstruct modern literacies where technologically required, and, where they are still effective, seamlessly integrate appropriate, established literacy practices with postmodern innovations and needs. Our way into this fusion rode on questioning what the story of *Goldilocks and the Three Bears* would look like rewritten through the eyes of an urban child living in a cosmopolitan city in the 21st century.

Since we were working on a small grant, there was no money for meetings during the school day. We met in a series of planned after school workshops, which a small group of primary teachers attended sporadically. We began with a chat about multiliteracies, inviting ideas about how teachers might think about developing (or further developing) emergent multiliteracies in class, brainstorming ideas for adapting *Goldilocks and the Three Bears*. As we thought through the nature and manifestations of multiple literacies, considered cultural pluralism in the classroom and the particular problems that children faced in literacy learning, and shared knowledge of software and hardware, I refined a set of guiding research questions:

1. How can we teach emergent literacy as an inclusive and contemporary process using traditional children's narratives to scaffold learning?
2. How can we include children's cultural and linguistic knowledge in the English language and literacy classroom?

Two contrary points of view arose during our meetings in the fall of 2003 that affected the scope of the project. One of the kindergarten teachers was passionately opposed to the onslaught of technological intervention in literacy education, arguing (quite rightly) that kindergarten teachers were well versed in the use of multiple semiotic resources for classroom learning without the intervention of digital technology, which was seen as a glossy and expensive addition to the inherent multimodality of the kindergarten classroom. Her critical viewpoint provided a test for us. Did we think differently with technological mediation, and, if so, how? We were trying to tap children's cultural and linguistic knowledge in the adaptation and electronic retelling of a traditional narrative. Multimedia meant just that: multiple media. We needed to think more broadly about contributing, facilitating and interacting semiotic resources and representational media.

Another impassioned argument arose from an unexpected quarter. *Goldilocks and the Three Bears* had been chosen for two reasons: (1) the children liked the story, and (2) as a traditional story, it was outside the strictures of copyright. We were legally entitled to adapt it. But one of the teachers, whose introduction to Canada had been as a child refugee, was deeply troubled. The story along with the language had been part of her socialization into a new world of possibility in the *West* where she had been welcomed as an ethnic minority, a child amongst a refugee exodus. To her, Goldilocks was blond because she was Canadian. The character should not be changed.

This comment, which evinced very emotional ground for this teacher, described a postmodern dilemma, following Lyotard's (1984) definition of *postmodern* as "incredulity toward metanarratives" (p. xxiv). For this woman, *Goldilocks and the Three Bears* was an untouchable narrative: a classic that should not be tampered with. She had never queried the origins of a story that had made a profound impact on her conception of Canada and Canadians. This provided powerful support for my concerns about the reification of *Canadian identity* as inherently other to those not of colonial English and French heritages, but it also inspired a third research question about the life history of Goldilocks:

3. Where did Goldilocks come from? Where can we take her story in 2003?

The process we were working out was replete with lumps and bumps, but we had ambitious aims. We wanted to introduce children in the primary grades to *Goldilocks and the Three Bears* in English (as a second language for most children), positively engage their worlds of cultural knowledge and sense of agency to teach an understanding of what a narrative is, and guide the children to update this traditional narrative through their eyes in contemporary urban Toronto. This aim drove the teachers' process development.

I was spurred to investigate the oral and literate histories of the story of the three bears to find out how Goldilocks came into the world of literature, and to think about how we could legitimately adapt her story to this century. This would help thinking about how teachers could work toward an orientation to literacy as contemporary communication, inclusive of multiple languages, semiotic resources and representational media that challenged the assumed synonymy of literacy and written English language, and disrupted the traditional, discrete, *skills-based* approach to reading and writing. This work would contribute to the children's development of a more contemporary and inclusive vision of Canadian culture, moving beyond English-French colonial legacy views of Canada and Canadians towards an embodiment of multiculturalism in a sustained and profound way.

These were big aims to hang on a folktale.

DECONSTRUCTING GOLDILOCKS

During the 2003–2004 school year, as the teachers and I met at JPS in after-school workshops to plan and implement the rewriting of *Goldilocks and the Three Bears* in primary grade classrooms, I looked into the character's past, in response to question 3: Where did Goldilocks come from? Where can we take her story in 2003?

In thinking through how a teacher came to connect Goldilocks with Canada and Canadiana through her refugee journey into Canadian citizenship, I needed to research how and where Goldilocks came into being. How much of the character was fixed on a little blond girl? What was the evolutionary path of the narrative? Could understanding Goldilocks' becoming help us to think about her continuing narrative journey?

I consulted Dr. Leslie McGrath, the head librarian at the Osborne Collection of Early Children's Books, with my query on the origins of *Goldilocks and the Three Bears*. The Osborne Collection, located in the Lillian H. Smith branch of the Toronto Public Library (TPL), is a specialist collection of children's books to the end of 1910 that includes a number of rare manuscripts. Dr. McGrath researched and prepared a chronologically organized collection of critical resources detailing the history of Goldilocks for me, and provided me with valuable historical contextualization of children's literature during Goldilocks' evolutionary journey into her canonical form as a little blond girl (see Lotherington, 2005).

With her assistance, I discovered that one of the Osborne Collection's rare manuscripts was, amazingly, the earliest known text of *The Three Bears* story: Miss Eleanor Mure's (1831/1967) beautifully handwritten and illustrated book, *The Celebrated Nursery Tale of the Three Bears*. Miss Mure's handmade book, which was presented to her nephew, Horace Broke, as a present on the occasion of his 4th birthday on September 26, 1831, tells in verse form a story about three (two big and one smaller male) bears who move into a grand house. They rebuff a nosy neighbor, a little old lady, who makes a social call when they are on their way out for a walk. She, in turn, enters and vindictively vandalizes their beautiful house in the familiar manner. Upon discovery, she meets a grisly end. The familiar refrains of the canonical children's story can be heard in Miss Mure's beautiful storybook.

Elms (1977) points out that *Goldilocks and the Three Bears* is one of the most popular children's stories in the English language, with some 80 publications of the tale between the late 1800s and 1972 (p. 257). Phillips (1954), whose ritual survivalist reading is critically reviewed by Elms, locates possible inspirations for the *Goldilocks and the Three Bears* narrative in a Siberian hunting tradition, where hunters, to give deference to their kill and appease the gods, place three bear skins at a table built in lieu of an alter in a wooden temple (p. 123). Phillips alternatively offers a Norwegian version of *Snow White* in which a king's daughter enters the cave of three bears who are Russian princes in disguise. She eats their porridge and falls asleep under the bed to be later discovered (p. 123).

In another historical trace, Goldilocks' journey into literature began in the oral tradition with the cautionary Scottish folktale of three bears

11.

They went to the drawing-room; where the first bear
Roar'd. "Who, without leave, has sat down in my chair."
The second, astonish'd, more mildly did say,
"Who's been sitting in my chair, when I was away."
The little bear madly cried; "What shall I do?"
"Who has sat in my chair, and the bottom burst thro'?"

"Who has sat in my chair, and the bottom burst thro'?"

Figure 3.1 Page 11 of Ms. Mure's original manuscript of *The Celebrated Nursery Tale of the Three Bears.* Reproduced courtesy of the Osborne Collection of Early Children's Books, Toronto Public Library, Canada.

that eat a she-fox who has invaded their lair (Bettelheim, 1977). In both Eleanor Mure's manuscript and Robert Southey's (n.d./1837) anonymous publication of a collection of miscellanea, *The Doctor*, in which *The Story of the Three Bears* first appears in commercial print (Opie & Opie, 1974; Tatar, 2002), this trajectory explains that the *vixen* is interpreted not as a female fox but as a meddling old woman. Opie and Opie (1974) reference the folktale origins (quoting Jacobs, 1894) as the story of *Scrapefoot*, the fox (p. 199).

The antagonist in the first known three bears storybooks evolves from a spiteful old lady into a mischievous little girl with dark, curly hair, called *Silver Locks*, and the bears morph into a family with the 1856 publication of *The Three Bears* in Aunt Mavor's Picture Books (Anonymous, 1856). Not until 1888 does Goldilocks emerge as a little blond girl in an American version of the story published in New York (Anonymous, 1888).

In the 20th century, the antagonist of the three bears narrative becomes progressively cemented in print as the little golden-haired girl of contemporary recognition, though she is variously named until after the turn of the century (e.g., *Goldenhair* [Anonymous, circa 1901]). Leslie McGrath (personal communication, January 31, 2004) points out that the softening of the harsh penitential ending that befalls the nasty antagonists of early Victorian versions of *The Three Bears*, and the brightening of the character from a vindictive old woman to a curious young girl with golden hair are reflections of the changing era. With the changing audience for fairy tales from adults to children (Zipes, 2007), the dark Victorian tale of victimization and crime develops into a children's story, though it remains a cautionary tale "intended to teach children lessons about the hazards of wandering off on their own and exploring unfamiliar territory" (Tatar, 2002, p. 246). Warner (1994) critically annotates Goldilocks' facelift over the passage of the 19th century from a witch-like character into a blond child in "the conventional fairytale heroic pattern" (p. 366) in which "the legacy of the heroine is passed on in the coin of blonde hair; to generations of listeners and readers, it has naturally enciphered female beauty—inner as well as outer" (p. 366).

These analyses indicated that Goldilocks' embodiment as a fairy tale blond could be legitimately challenged. In fact, Goldilocks was overdue for postmodern updating in our culturally plural, technologically saturated 21st century society.

Media Shifts

The storytelling vehicle for Goldilocks' evolution was critically important to our journey. The story had shape-shifted in terms of characterization, minor plot details and denouement; the media through which the story had been related had changed, too, developing from spurious mixed roots in oral legendry through interpretations (and misinterpretations) and modernizations in print versions from a handmade manuscript to mass produced picture books. How could we retell the story using the storytelling media of the 21st century?

Writing on the future of print, before the digitally networked world we live in today, Walter Ong (1980) theorized a new dimension to oral communication in "a media-conscious world" (p. 203): *secondary orality*, which was mediated electronically and dependent on literary form. As Ong explains:

> There is nothing on radio or television, however oral, not subject to some—and most often utterly massive—chirographic and typographic control, which enters into program design, scripts, advertising, contractual agreements, diction, sentence structure, and countless other details. Primary orality cannot cope with electronic media. (p. 203)

Ong's theorizing of a postliterate orality in an era of relatively unsophisticated electronic technologies illuminates the flawed logic of the traditional linear *oral to written* skills-building progression in language and literacy learning. Building critically on this line of thought, Ryan (2004a) posits that the cultural revolution via electronic communications predicted by both Ong (1982) and McLuhan (1964) produced a *secondary literacy*, in such interactive forms as email, online chats and texting.

Castells (2010) describes the profusion of 21st century communication patterns:

> The shift from a traditional mass media to a system of horizontal communication networks organized around the Internet and wireless communication has introduced a multiplicity of communication patterns at the source of a fundamental cultural transformation, as virtuality becomes an essential dimension of our reality. The constitution of a new culture based on multimodal communication and digital information processing creates a generational divide between those born before the Internet Age (1969) and those who grew up being digital. (p. xviii)

Palfrey and Gasser (2008) mark the dividing line between what Prensky (2001) labels *digital natives* and *digital immigrants* as 1980 (p. 1). My inclination is to move this line closer to the 1990s when the Internet was privatized and began to spread prolifically (Castells, 2010, p. xxv). Wherever the line is drawn, it distinguishes all children in formal education today as born into a digital age. Their world of social communication is networked by mobile communications technologies that have redefined community, culture and literacy. Not only could we legitimately bring *Goldilocks and the Three Bears* into the 21st century, into new media and new story shapes; we had to do this to make the story socially relevant to children's lives.

Goldilocks as Canadian, eh?

There was another aspect of the teacher's assumption that Goldilocks was Canadian that I needed to tackle. Though virtually all traditional children's stories in the Western canon have migrated across space and time picking up bits and pieces as they travelled along trade and migration routes, they have become identified with cultural realizations, particularly, Western European print versions popularized by the Brothers Grimm and Hans Christian Andersen, and American video versions, created by Walt Disney. The character *Cinderella* is recognized in Europeanized form via Charles Perrault's portrait of *Cendrillon*, and to contemporary children in Disneyfied form. However *Cinderella* was told in China a thousand years before European print versions (Lai, 2007; Louie, 1999), where her small feet would have been highly prized as beautiful. Furthermore, Lai (2007, p. 50) posits that the Chinese *Cinderella* story draws on an earlier Egyptian model.

Oddly enough, Eleanor Mure's original three bears manuscript—the first to ever appear in print—had a Canadian twist. Miss Mure's original 1831 manuscript, depicting her father's country home, Cecil Lodge, in Hertfordshire, as the bears' grand house (Mure, 1831/1967), now rests in the Osborne Collection in Toronto, where it was sent in a shipment of rare children's books by Edgar Osborne to the Toronto Public Library in 1949.[2] Not only had the tale of *The Three Bears* that first came to print and was popularized in Victorian England crossed the Atlantic in the late 19th and early 20th century to become an Americanized *Goldilocks and the Three Bears*, the original manuscript had endured a post-WWII immigration journey from England to Canada as a bequest. So, perhaps the teacher was right: Goldilocks did lay claim to Canadian status—as a literary immigrant!

GOLDILOCKS AND THE THREE BEARS REINTERPRETED

Our limited funding reduced our after-school workshops to two per term. I felt that our fall workshops had been fraught with issues and I sensed a general recalcitrance to take on extra work, but a few teachers had soldiered on. I was, however, disappointed in how little most teachers had been able to do over the winter given their heavy regular duties, and the lack of continuity caused by our infrequent meetings. The Grade 1/2 teacher, who was working with *The Velveteen Rabbit* in her class, having children use their own stuffed animals to retell the story, was interested in moving on to *Goldilocks and the Three Bears*. In Grade 5, the teacher was using secret diaries, labeled *do not enter* and *private*, in which the junior students could give their point of view in relating and retelling stories. Only Sandra, in whose kindergarten I had begun this quest, had been thinking consistently about rewriting *Goldilocks and the Three Bears* as a multiliteracies project. She had developed an excellent game plan for her Grade 2 class that we discussed in the meeting at length.

Sandra had started out by reading several versions of *Goldilocks and the Three Bears* to her Grade 2 children. After hearing as many as eight different versions, the children began to work on the concept of *setting*. Sandra had brought along to our after-school workshop several large chart paper illustrations of settings in the three bears story, which answered the question, "Where did Goldilocks go?"

The next step was for the children to make dioramas to illustrate the main story settings in 3D. This would be followed up with small groups of four children adapting the settings digitally, with WiggleWorks chosen as the most suitable design software available to teachers. The principal suggested purchasing cheap disposable cameras for the children to snap their own chairs and beds at home, which could be scanned into the computer. Children could then draw their own Goldilocks character sitting and sleeping on (and breaking!) their personal furniture. This was a wonderful idea to help children develop ownership of the story, but it unfortunately exceeded the limits of our meager budget.

The children would concurrently move into learning about *plot*, thinking about what Goldilocks did. What was verbally repeated from story version to story version? Story webs and journal retelling were discussed. Sandra also planned to videotape children retelling their stories orally to collect data on their story comprehension and progress in learning the elements of a narrative, and for diagnostic purposes in terms of their language learning.

By the end of the academic year in June, our workshops, haphazard and poorly attended though they were, did come to fruition. Two teachers had worked the idea of the intervention into a sustained class activity, and provided a number of children's stories created with software programs available to public schools: WiggleWorks, Kid Pix and HyperStudio.[3] Both teachers had carefully focused the children's adaptations on selected elements of the story after they had learned the basic narrative through immersive exposure. In a primary education model, where elementary narrative analysis consists of *setting, character* and *plot*, the children localized the characters, and adapted aspects of the setting. Sandra interestingly created an alternative denouement to the story that the Grade 2 children had the option to choose.

Grade 1 Versions

In the Grade 1/2 class, the adaptation process started with a focused substitution exercise: children based the antagonists on their own hair types, or in old-fashioned, storybook parlance, *locks*, to create self-as-author characters such as *Straightylocks, Curlylocks, Messylocks* and *Braidy-locks.* The three bears, where reinterpreted, became local animals, such as cats, mice, chipmunks and squirrels. The Grade 1 teacher further steered children into adapting the introduction to the story to provide their antag-onist with a motivation for leaving the house, moving a relatively straight-forward substitution exercise into the domain of much deeper interpretive thought (see Figure 3.2).

The classic chorus refrains of the narrative (e.g., *Someone has been eat-ing my porridge!*) provided convenient pegs for children in the early stages of alphabetic reading and writing to hang familiar foods: soup and peanut butter, for example. In some cases, the foods bore a relationship to the ani-mals characterized. One child wrote about three chipmunks—cute, local animals—whose home had been invaded, and the invader had taken their nuts! In others, the food was ad hoc, or familiar fare to the child though not typical of the characters' diet, as in the case of the three mouses (*sic*), whose roti was stolen while the mouse family was out for a stroll.

This I learned to respect. Wandering around the computer lab one day, I questioned the attractiveness of fish food to a mermaid in a little girl's undersea adaptation of *Goldilocks and the Three Bears.* She looked at me as if I might be a trifle slow, and pronounced confidently: "Well it is a *once upon a time* story. Maybe mermaids like fish food!" Bruner (1991) puts this thought more elegantly: "Narrative 'truth' is judged by its verisimilitude rather than its verifiability" (p. 13).

I was thrilled with the children's adaptations, which provided evidence of creativity and logic above anything I expected of children in the early stages of learning to read and write basic print. In some ways, the stories they created were what I had envisioned: a localization of a traditional narrative that was inclusive of their context enabling them to better iden-tify with the story. How much of this adaptation was a product of the teacher directly interpreting my ideas as class activities, and how much was her development of collaborative workshop ideas was not clear, given the nature of our discussions in optional after-school meetings, the timing of the final products at the end of the school year and the fact that I had not asked teachers to systematically document their journeys in this pilot intervention (for fear that it would be a terminal overload for first time volunteers). The process notes on workshop discussions and class observa-tions were my own. But I had the summer to think about the stories the children had created.

Novel story introductions in Grade 1 adaptations raised questions about children's narrative worlds. As Figure 3.2 shows, the author of *Braidylocks* (after her braided hair, the *i* having got lost somewhere) merged a key ele-ment from *Alice in Wonderland* (e.g., being magically resized) in her story introduction. Such narrative mixing was evident in other stories, with influ-ences from the Disney animated movie version of *The Little Mermaid* being

Once upon a time there was a girl named Bradylocks and her mother sent her out to buy some buttyfull clothes.
On the way home she found something strange.

She said"what does this button do"and she pushed it all the way in. When she opened her eyes every thing was big."Have I sronk" she said."If I can't get home I can't eat and if I can't eat i'll die" she cried. then she found a lovey house just her size so she went in.

Figure 3.2   The introductory panels of *Braidylocks*, Grade 1. Adapted with permission from Lotherington, H. & Chow, S. (2006). Rewriting *Goldilocks* in the Urban, Multicultural Elementary School. *The Reading Teacher, 60* (3), 244–252. Copyright 2006 by the International Reading Association: www.reading.org.

particularly popular. Was this a sign of confusion in separating narratives, or understanding what a story is? Was it an intertextual rendering: two stories merged? This was highly unlikely as an intentional aim, given that it was Grade 1. The children were only 6–7 years old.

Though curious about the influences contributing to their intertextual constructions, I was encouraged and delighted by the interpretive, imaginative and logical thought evident in the Grade 1 children's reinterpreted stories. Beautiful though their stories were, they did not prepare me for the revolutionary rewriting that emerged under Sandra's direction in her Grade 2 class.

Grade 2 Versions

> Papa Alien said, "Someone has been eating my slime." (*Sugi and the Three Aliens*, Grade 2 boy)

Sandra was a wonderfully counterbalancing research partner. In a previous professional life she had been an accountant, and her ability to structure and organize information was a lifesaver to our fledgling research intervention. To my broad vistas of creative possibility, she answered with both feet firmly planted, carefully identifying practical issues that denoted problematic junctures in theory and practice. Though many teachers showed an itinerant interest—and the Grade 1 teacher stuck to it, contributing highly engaging products, though less in the way of process discussion—it was Sandra who took this intervention to heart and paved a path of possibility in the classroom.

Unbeknownst to me at the time, Sandra had introduced the story of *Goldilocks and the Three Bears* to her kindergarten children before my tenure as *the story lady* in her kindergarten in the winter of 2003. The folktale had been used as a diagnostic test mechanism to assess children's knowledge of story structure and English language development. This told me why the children had gravitated to the story: they had been introduced to it before. For some children, *Goldilocks and the Three Bears* appeared to be the only story they knew.

Sandra proceeded in her Grade 2 class by immersing children in the basic narrative, and slowly introducing them to different versions of the story. She conducted activities for familiarizing children with story structure through elementary narrative analysis (character, setting, plot problems, plot solutions) using story mapping, followed by multimodal activities to reinforce key and identifying elements of the three bears narrative: drawing a poster of the setting, creating a diorama and participating in a puppet show to retell the story (see Lotherington & Chow, 2006, for details on the process). At that stage, the children were ready to create their own versions of the narrative. They chose from a list which elements they wanted to adapt:

- the characters,
- the setting and, optionally,
- the story resolution.

Table 3.1 summarizes Sandra's template to guide children through the rewriting process.

Sandra gave the plot a new twist via an optional pro-social ending. The canonical 20th century story has Goldilocks jumping out a window to escape the three bears upon discovery. I had been terribly concerned that localizing *Goldilocks and the Three Bears* to the high-rise apartments that were home to these children would create a suicide mission—hardly the stuff of *and they lived happily ever after* children's stories. Sandra provided a decision point for children to make a choice about the bears' treatment of Goldilocks after she has been discovered in baby bear's bed. The options included an ethical humanist path: to feed the hungry invader.

I had anticipated that a reinterpretation of the three bears narrative would close the gap between a dated Eurocentric folktale bearing no relation to children's everyday existence in inner-city Toronto, and the reality

Table 3.1   Instructions for Writing an Individualized Three Bears Story

1. Introduction	Start with: Once upon a time . . . , One day . . . , One morning . . . , or One afternoon . . . .
	Create a setting (time and place).
2. Talk about your main character	Describe the character's physical appearance.
	Describe the character's personality.
3. Plot: What happens in the story?	The problem: Goldilocks goes into and around the house uninvited.
	The solution: The bears come home, see what has happened, and find Goldilocks.
4. Choose an ending	Goldilocks runs away.
	Goldilocks stays for supper.

Note. Adapted with permission from Lotherington, H. & Chow, S. (2006). Rewriting *Goldilocks* in the Urban, Multicultural Elementary School. *The Reading Teacher, 60* (3), 244–252. Copyright 2006 by the International Reading Association: www.reading.org.

of the contemporary ethnically and culturally diverse classroom. I expected children to insert themselves as antagonist as in *Braidylocks*, depicted in Figure 3.2. My idea was that giving children access to stories they could reinterpret through their own context and culture would help to introduce them to text and to reading by putting them into the story as agentive interpreter. The teachers had warned me that children's ideas about culture would come from mass media and pop culture rather than home customs and languages. Disney, rather than grandma, shaped their cultural contexts and told the stories. They were right; children's sense of culture was shaped through the electronic universe that we were plugging into for retelling.

Most Grade 2 children did not put themselves into the narrative as antagonist. They created or borrowed a character (mostly from popular culture) or even used the same Goldilocks, and then proceeded to map her character logically through the narrative, so their rewriting was not an exercise in substitution but a psychological analysis. Goldilocks was imagined as a ghost, witch, mermaid and vampire among other less obvious media tropes.

Why would Goldilocks enter a home uninvited? What would entice her to eat porridge? (What is *porridge*?) Would bears eat something else nowadays? Would they have to be mean and horrible or could they be nice to Goldilocks? Would a child today enter a home uninvited to eat porridge or would a more age or culturally appropriate food be more tantalizing?

FROM BENEVOLENT BEARS TO SHARKY

Figures 3.3 to 3.6 present collages of selected slides[4] from four original hypertext stories written by Grade 2 children in Sandra's class. These stories were programmed using an old version of HyperStudio that is no longer playable on current hardware.

In Figure 3.3, the antagonist is a rather pathetic creature, *Stinky Robber*, whose name clarifies his motivation for entering the house: to rob it. Why the robber is stinky is up for grabs: is he a neglected child or just a bad guy, or a bit of both? The house he invades belongs to three bears that look more like cuddly toys than ferocious animals. They have a reasonably healthy diet and have left their soup out to cool, which Stinky Robber helps himself to. Stinky Robber goes through the canonical plot, trying all and eating baby's soup, breaking baby's chair and sleeping in baby bear's bed. But this author, who has not strayed far from the original narrative outside of the main antagonist, chooses an ethical ending to his story: Stinky Robber is indeed afraid, and the bears, sensing this, offer him some soup, to which Stinky Robber finally shows some manners in reply. The bears here are a civilizing influence; the antagonist, a neglected kid who has gone bad, but is not beyond redemption.

In Figure 3.4, Goldilocks is interpreted as space explorer, *Sugi*, who invades the UFO of three aliens. Sugi is the brother of Yugi, manga hero of *Yu-Gi-Oh!* fame, and so is suitably drawn as an adventurer who is bravely searching out new worlds, not a vandal. The aliens' food, left out conveniently for Sugi to try, is suitably gruesomely appealing to a 7-year-old boy: slime (perhaps a reference to porridge through a child's eyes?), taffy with nails (possibly attractive to superhero explorers who need to be brave?) and, the ultimate reward for a kid: Jell-O, a culturally relevant treat. Sugi tries on three masks and then finds the three beds which have odd problems—the first one is sticky, the second wobbly. When discovered by the three aliens, he beats it out of there, never to be seen again, super-hero status deflated.

Figure 3.5 profiles a Goldilocks who has not changed much physically but has developed a personality as a neglected little girl who is in need of guidance, rather than a mischievous child committing a juvenile break-and-enter—at least this is the interpretation of the bears upon finding her. They are, again, drawn benevolently as teddy bears that smile and, clearly, watch their weight. The story resolution in this version of *Goldilocks and the Three* (socially conscious!) *Bears* is touching: the bears are concerned that no one is looking after this child. They feed her, walk her home, supervise her homework and then, a year later, baby bear goes to her house for a reciprocal sleepover. This is a neat twist on the fear factor driving the traditional narrative. Kids can be helped, and a little attention goes a long way.

Sharky, whose story ending is shown in Figure 3.6, is arguably the most convincingly redrawn Goldilocks. Created by a sweet little 7-year old girl of Vietnamese descent, Sharky is a bully through and through, invading the home of three fish that have gone for a swim. Sharky goes for the jug-ular—it is papa's food (little fish versus seaweed and little bugs), chair and bed that he takes, not baby's. No small place in the universe for Sharky; he eats the three fish when they come home to discover they have an unwanted guest! He then has the audacity to live happily ever after.

All rewritten *Goldilocks and the Three Bears* stories were beautifully drawn and many were brightly colored, illustrating the importance of visual design to children's expression. Each story had a distinct style as well, addressing Mitchell and Reid-Walsh's (2002) concern:

with the idea of the unique standpoint or perspective of the child in researching children's popular culture. We offer that because so much of children's popular culture is highly visual, ranging from the artifacts of popular culture themselves in all their "larger-than-life" forms of plastic, frequently brightly colored and so on, to the packaging that is specially formulated to attract the child, to methods of play, it lends itself to being explored visually. (pp. 81–82)

Figure 3.3   Stinky Robber and the Three Bears. Adapted from material published in Lotherington, H. (2008) Digital Epistemologies and Classroom Multiliteracies. In T. Hansson (Ed.) *Handbook of Research on Digital Information Technologies: Innovations, Methods, and Ethical Issues* (pp. 261–280). Hershey, PA: IGI Global. Copyright 2010, IGI Global, www.igi-global.com. Posted by permission of the publisher.

Figure 3.4   Sugi and the Three Aliens. Adapted from material published in Lotherington, H. (2008). Digital Epistemologies and Classroom Multiliteracies. In T. Hansson (Ed.) *Handbook of Research on Digital Information Technologies: Innovations, Methods, and Ethical Issues* (pp. 261–280). Hershey, PA: IGI Global. Copyright 2010, IGI Global, http://www.igi-global.com.www.igi-global.com. Posted by permission of the publisher.

Figure 3.5   Goldilocks and the Three Bears, socially conscious version. Adapted with permission from Lotherington, H. & Chow, S. (2006), Rewriting *Goldilocks* in the Urban, Multicultural Elementary School. *The Reading Teacher*, 60 (3), 244–252. Copyright 2006 by the International Reading association: www.reading.org.

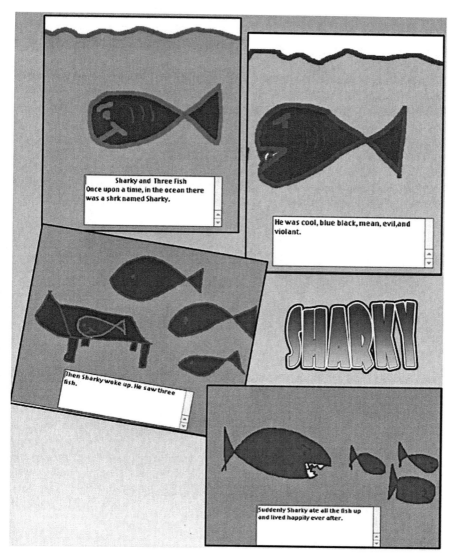

Figure 3.6   Sharky and the Three Fish. Adapted with permission from Lotherington, H. & Chow, S. (2006), Rewriting *Goldilocks* in the Urban, Multicultural Elementary School. *The Reading Teacher,* 60 (3), 244–252. Copyright 2006 by the International Reading association: www.reading.org. The figure also includes material published in Lotherington, H. (2008). Digital Epistemologies and Classroom Multiliteracies. In T. Hansson (Ed.) *Handbook of Research on Digital Information Technologies: Innovations, Methods, and Ethical Issues* (pp. 261–280). Hershey, PA: IGI Global. Copyright 2010, IGI Global, www.igi-global.com. Posted by permission of the publisher.

WHAT DID WE LEARN FROM REWRITING *GOLDILOCKS*?

Our guiding research aims for this collaborative intervention had been to introduce children in the primary grades to *Goldilocks and the Three Bears* in English (as a second language for most children), positively engage their worlds of cultural knowledge and sense of agency, teach an understanding of what a narrative is and update the traditional narrative through their eyes. These aims focused our trial development of multiliteracies pedagogies.

The children's exercise in multiliteracies learning by retelling *Goldilocks and the Three Bears* across different media using their own creative ideas certainly fulfilled our research aims. They developed and illustrated their learning of narrative structure, analyzed a traditional story and retold it creatively utilizing new media in a format that included multiple means of representation as well as alphabetic writing of English. They developed character and setting, importing pop culture tropes, and recreated the antagonist and protagonists, who, in turn, motivated twists in plot actions and reactions. Their stories surpassed everything I imagined the children might achieve. But the stories also held a number of surprises.

Cultural Inclusion

You don't watch YTV?!!! (Grade 2 boy, 2004)

The children's retold stories unwrapped what *Goldilocks and the Three Bears* looked like through the eyes and in the hands of young children living in a cosmopolitan city in the 21st century, given the scaffolding to be creative and to experiment with multiple media. True to teachers' predictions, the children engaged a torrent of pop culture knowledge in their cultural reinterpretations, but not the kind of grounded cultural heritage I had anticipated, verifying Wark's (1994 cited in Beavis, 1997) claim that "we no longer have roots, we have aerials; we constantly download culture" (p. 241). This was wonderfully captured in the incredulous response of a little boy to my candid admission that I did not normally watch YTV[5] in the afternoons, and was not actually familiar with the superhero he declared to be his inspiration.

Adapting a story requires understanding and respecting the essential narrative. In transforming Goldilocks into pop culture figures, the children ran into intriguing confusions. Ariel, the protagonist in Disney's film production of *The Little Mermaid*, currently popular with children, showed up in numerous rewrites as Goldilocks, but her storyline also butted into Goldilocks' adventures in a way that made it apparent that learning a story is a very complex thing to do. Carmen Luke (1995) suggests,

> Television shapes the child's entry into narrative and consumption by being
> located in the center of family life (however families may be constituted),

and by assimilating and cross-referencing to other narrative forms such as movies, stories, comic books, video games, music videos (often movie soundtracks), of which toys are an integral extension. (p. 28)

In a couple of the children's retold stories in our project to rewrite *Goldilocks and the Three Bears*, there was evidence that narrative fragments were cutting across children's understanding of plot, supporting the New London Group's (1996) assertion that children are learning stories from commoditized fragments in "TV, toys, fast-food packaging, video games, T-shirts, shoes, bed linen, pencil cases, and lunch boxes" (p. 70).

Under careful guidance, the children acquired the agency to retell their versions of a story their way, imprinting their cultural stamp. The option to treat benevolently the hungry vandal maximized children's control on an otherwise threatening set of events, and offered an ethical choice as a possible conclusion, illustrating Egan's (2001) hypothesis that narratives are a tool to orient the emotions.

Narrative Discoveries

Narratives, in Bruner's words, deal "with the vicissitudes of intention" (1986, p. 17). In the examples of children's work discussed and illustrated here, and in other Grade 2 children's stories, Goldilocks was reborn, not as an image replacement, but as a rebuilt character who, herself or himself or itself, had agency to act in ways that the author wrote into the narrative. Propp (1968) asserts that motivations are relatively unstable elements in a story that contribute "a completely distinctive, vivid coloring" (p. 75), though the majority of characters are naturally motivated by the turn of events in a plot. Villainy, however, as the basic function of tales, needs "supplementary motivation" (p. 75). This requires careful scheming!

The story-rewriting project opened multiple entry points to learning a narrative for children, and they had clearly succeeded in understanding narrative shape, though, in some cases, it got tangled in curiosity-raising ways. Children's access to Disneyfied narratives in their lives outside of school hours ran unintended interference with their retold narratives that raised essential questions: What is a story? What can be changed in an adapted version? But their imaginative stories were testament to their development of agency in *writing*, and by all accounts, they enjoyed the process. Their hypertext stories were printed and bound into books that were taken home and presented to dad for Father's Day.

Curricular Learning

The creative unfolding of their retold stories illustrated the multifaceted literacy learning of 7- and 8-year-old children of diverse language backgrounds, still unsteady on their alphabetic feet. At the same time, it was important to keep track of Ministry expectations of literacy development; we were aiming to help children bridge gaps in literacy learning through multimodal project work, but teachers and children still had to meet Ministry requirements. How did their agentive learning stack up against the learning objectives set out in the literacy curriculum?

Literacy is subsumed under *language* in the current Ontario Ministry of Education curriculum document (Ministry of Education, 2006). Knowledge and skills are delineated for purposes of assessment in terms of knowledge and understanding, thinking, communication and application (pp. 20–21). Assessment is based on individual performance within the expectations of four skill-based learning strands: oral communication, reading, writing and media literacy (pp. 9–14). The grade expectations for each strand set out achievement objectives.

Literacy, thus, is written language. Nonetheless, the inclusion of oral, written and digitally mediated language indicates a synesthetic approach to literacy. However, the separateness of the strands is a hindrance, and further examination of the strand expectations indicates that *language* is limited in ways that are unhelpful to JPS (and other urban) students. For example, the Grade 2 expectations for oral communication set out that children will learn to:

1. listen in order to understand and respond appropriately in a variety of situations for a variety of purposes;
2. use speaking skills and strategies appropriately to communicate with different audiences for a variety of purposes;
3. reflect on and identify their strengths as listeners and speakers, areas for improvement, and the strategies they found most helpful in oral communication situations. (Ministry of Education, 2006, p. 50)

Language, according to this description, is the socially appropriate use of oral English in public circumstances. These expectations contain a hidden curriculum for children who are not, or are no longer, or who were never designated as ESL students. This takes in the majority of students at JPS who speak a language other than English (or French) at home.

The literacy agenda set out in the Grade 2 curricular expectations focuses teachers' attention on media literacy, reading and writing. Media are interpreted in these aims, though, as mass media forms to be learned, rather than as popular media forms to be created and remixed. The writing aims for Grade 2 anticipate children learning to:

1. generate, gather, and organize ideas and information to write for an intended purpose and audience;
2. draft and revise their writing, using a variety of informational, literary, and graphic forms and stylistic elements appropriate for the purpose and audience;

3. use editing, proofreading, and publishing skills and strategies, and knowledge of language conventions, to correct errors, refine expression, and present their work effectively;
4. reflect on and identify their strengths as writers, areas for improvement, and the strategies they found most helpful at different stages in the writing process. (Ministry of Education, 2006, p. 55)

Though the placement of commas in this description could be debated, the aims logically lead children to write a short text according to a modernist model. This is a worthy learning objective, though unnecessarily exclusive and problematically limiting, reinforcing skills mastery, banking education (Freire, 1970/1998) and passive learning of content knowledge. Children are directed to reflectively measure themselves against extant models of print and media texts created by (mature, successful) native speakers, but not encouraged to play across semiotic resources and media for creative expression. Critical analysis is applied to personal attainment of established standards, not to those standards themselves, or the power base they assume.

The centralization of the curriculum means that it cannot cater to local populations, bypassing variation in what children bring to school from their diverse cultural and linguistic backgrounds. Standards are thus generalized to a population that may be more a statistical ideal than human reality. However, Allan Luke (2008) warns:

> Where language and literacy education fails to engage with local material conditions, and with the complex community and institutional ecologies of practice . . . it risks contradictory effects: first amongst them, a recolonisation of the local under the auspices of scientific pedagogy and economic development. (p. 249)

The single strand approach of the *language* curriculum limits children's pathways for telling stories to past print models in a language most are in some stage of learning, and focuses both teacher and students on perfecting grammar and spelling, not on critical interpretation or creative reinterpretation. In short, it is entrenched in a modernist literacy agenda lacking in critical inquiry, creative energy and synergetic possibility. Worryingly, it projects no sense of space for creative play—which easily and naturally includes literate and cultural exploration—so important for children at this age (Dyson, 1993, 2003; Marsh & Millard, 2000; Vygotsky, 1978).

MOVING FORWARD

We posed the following questions to guide the pilot collaborative intervention of rewriting Goldilocks:

1. How can we teach emergent literacy as an inclusive and contemporary process using traditional narratives to scaffold learning?
2. How can we include children's cultural and linguistic knowledge in the English language and literacy classroom?
3. Where did Goldilocks come from? Where can we take her story in 2003?

The pilot intervention indicated that, in answer to question 1, we could teach emergent literacy as inclusive and contemporary process based on narrative retelling. This we accomplished more by luck than good management, truth be told, through collegial discussion and planning to merge theory—in terms of ideas generated from the research literature on multiliteracies—with practice—in terms of what happened in the classroom when these ideas were translated into practical application. The nature of our meetings suggested that our teacher-researcher team needed more time together, better continuity and connection, and more experience and structure to grease and organize theory-practice discussions.

One of the solutions to the awkwardness in finding convenient meeting times after school was to open a gateway between the TDSB Intranet and the York University Faculty of Education Intranet, which used the same software program: First Class. This opened up a pathway between two protected systems using the same sophisticated conferencing software that provided us with a space for discussion, questions, meeting agendas and publications.

In response to question 2, we were able to tap children's cultural knowledge, though in this round we did not find access to children's multilingual knowledge. This lacuna stimulated us to think about how to do that. I realized my folly in assuming a grounded notion of culture in a digital project. The major influences motivating children's ideas of culture clearly came from pop culture, just as teachers suggested.

In answer to the third question, Goldilocks was deconstructed historically in terms of her place in the narrative of *The Three Bears*, the media shifts through which the traditional story has been carried and the international voyages the narrative has taken to give it its characteristic shape of three protagonists in the form of an anthropomorphized bear family, and an antagonist frozen as a little blond girl who is inexplicably walking alone in the woods and wandering into strange cottages.

To develop our pilot intervention into a reproducible pedagogy of multiliteracies required more experimentation in the classroom and better organized sharing and discussion sessions. Our pilot had stimulated thinking about language support, cultural development, technological possibilities (and problems), the narrative as an organizing structure in learning, and educational frameworks generating and shaping language and literacy aims.

Our intervention to rewrite *Goldilocks and the Three Bears* was a good kick-start despite the steep learning curve. The principal had been both directive and supportive of our fledgling *learning community* as she called it: a community of practice for research-oriented, multidirectional learning, though our structure had been more or less organic. We had succeeded in mobilizing collaborative path finding via action research, though, at the time, it didn't feel like it. We had much to do to refine our process.

The principal had been insistent on one aspect of the research design: that it be focused on narrative learning. This had been a fundamental requirement and it built beautifully from my curiosity about the kindergarten children's fixation on the story of *Goldilocks and the Three Bears*. The use of traditional children's stories gave me a strong push to learn more about narratives and children's literature.

The choice of the story of *Goldilocks and the Three Bears* got a useful critique from the teachers in terms of suitability for interpretation as a multiliteracies project. The story had a complex setting moving from room to room in a family dwelling, which provided a lot of useful vocabulary, but it also created an unnecessary complication for adaptation. The idea of changing only certain elements of the story opened up many questions. What could be changed without losing the basic narrative thread, and how much adaptation was useful? What did children have to keep in the story to be able to adapt it? Indeed, thinking through what made a story identifiable as a story was a conundrum in many ways. These questions and ideas together with the remarkable stories the children created led us into the next year.

4 *Goldilocks* Revisited
Telling Old Stories in New Ways

GOLDILOCKS REVISITED

Our pilot intervention to work with children to rewrite *Goldilocks and the Three Bears* as an introductory team effort to create multiliteracies pedagogies had met with the approval of both the principal and teachers, despite our figure-it-out-as-you-go-along approach to bringing theory and practice together in after-school workshop sessions peppered throughout the school year. Following our elementary methodological pathfinding in *Rewriting Goldilocks*, I searched for funding to help us further our research, but came up flat. The principal, though, thought we should continue so our efforts did not go cold; several teachers showed interest and members of the original team very altruistically stated that they hoped to continue. So we did.

My continued search for funding got a positive response from the Faculty of Education at York University[1] who supported dissemination of our pilot multiliteracies development in a teacher-oriented workshop. With this assistance, we were able to continue to refine the methodology we piloted in *Rewriting Goldilocks*. *Goldilocks Revisited* was opened to interested teachers who agreed to develop a multiliteracies project with support, and document their learning journey over the year. Our culminating goal was to mount a spring workshop to share our multiliteracies pedagogies development at Joyce Public School with teachers in the Toronto District School Board. Our project aims focused on continuing to experiment with and refine the pedagogies pioneered in the pilot *Rewriting Goldilocks* study, explore children's ideas of culture and think about spaces for community languages in the literacy classroom. These aims were distilled into the research question:

1. How can we teach traditional narratives using digital resources that would facilitate children writing their cultural and linguistic realities into the story?

Seeds of a Learning Community

Our seed funding limited us to after-school workshops again, but our pilot experience provided a useful template for *Goldilocks Revisited*. Our workshops grew an infrastructure as the teachers, who were used to structured periods, brought materials in process with them and suggested ways of organizing our discussion and their follow-up action. Sandra created a project calendar so we could schedule our workshop meetings, track project expectations and progress, and plan the shape of our spring workshop. From these discussions, a structural framework for our workshop took shape as:

- *learning*: sharing theoretical information on multiliteracies education, technology and education, and second language learning;
- *planning*: putting theory into practice by discussing, and suggesting ideas for class project design, scaffolding project development, and taking up emergent concerns, problems and issues;
- *sharing*: demonstrating software, sharing technological knowledge and ideas, troubleshooting problems, and sharing teachers' and children's progress.

We were beginning to function as a *community of practice*, in which "the shared learning and interest of its members are what keep it together" (Wenger, 1998, p. 4).

Our immediate mission was to create a professional workshop for teachers in the TDSB to share what we were jointly learning around multiliteracies pedagogies and narrative learning, but our meager funding limited the number of meetings we could have, and provided little in the way of

Table 4.1   Scheduled Story Adaptation Procedure Across One School Term

2005 agenda	Goldilocks revisited *projects*
January	• choose a story to adapt • brainstorm ideas about taking the story in new directions • gather resources • indicate software knowledge, needs, and learning-sharing agenda
February	• consider the stories both historically and in terms of digital innovations • introduce the basic narrative for retelling in oral and written versions
March	• introduce variations on the story • guide class/individual variations
April	• make rough copies for interpretation in selected media • develop in selected media
May	• work on multimedia versions
June	• show and tell!

material support for project interventions. The principal came to the rescue with supplementary support. We met informally after school in the fall, beginning *Goldilocks Revisited* in organized earnest in early January 2005 with a scheduled morning of professional development (see Table 4.1 for our story adaptation schedule). With this opportunity to mobilize, we were able to move on to follow-up meetings after school, which developed organically in keeping with Wenger's (1998) description of communities of practice as "fundamentally self-organizing systems" (p. 2).

Telling Old Stories in New Ways

Sandra had found *Goldilocks and the Three Bears* to offer an awkwardly complex setting for young children that required conceptualization and artistic representations of three rooms in a house: the kitchen, living room and bedroom. In consultation with two primary grade teachers interested in the idea of telling old stories in new ways, she selected *The Little Red Hen* to use in her Grade 2 class because it had a simpler story line and setting, and gave a clear message. Sandra's aim was to streamline and build on the adaptation process she had piloted in the *Rewriting Goldilocks* experiment, and to ensure that class production was on target so they were not all in a rush to finish in June. Sandra and two other primary teachers set out to retell the story of *The Little Red Hen* in kindergarten, Grade 1 and Grade 2, imbuing the recalcitrant barnyard animals with a more ethical sense of participation, and giving the little red hen the option for a more humane and forgiving response to her fellow creatures. To do this convincingly, they engaged the children in updating the animals and the setting and creating culturally relevant food choices.

Two other traditional stories were chosen in other primary classes. Michelle chose *The Gingerbread Man* to introduce the concept of story to her kindergarten children. Her particular aim was to take on the challenge of localizing the story. Shiva decided on *The Three Little Pigs* for her Grade 1 class, which offered a convenient vehicle for the holistic teaching of art, math, language, social studies, science and technology. The wolf's ability to blow down the little pigs' first two houses tied in with science objectives to learn about the qualities of different materials. Shiva was also keen to bring children's parents and their home languages into the story production process. When I asked whether she was concerned about some parents' cultural recoiling at the idea of pigs as subject matter, she said no. Given that Shiva also held a position as teacher of Farsi in an after-school heritage language program, and was of a Muslim background herself, I was interested to see how she handled this sensitivity.

The teachers shared their software knowledge and access, indicating programs they wanted to know more about, and incorporated into their lesson planning process ideas on how to use what software for the ends they wanted to achieve. The stories were to be adapted into multimedia productions not because the software was there, but because the ideas were there; the role of technology was supportive and facilitating, not directive.

NARRATIVES AS A FRAMEWORK FOR CLASSROOM MULTILITERACIES PROJECTS

Our research agenda to develop multiliteracies in the primary grades was framed around narrative development. Narrative learning was of intrinsic interest to the principal, a key stakeholder in the research, who pointed out that great teachers across the history of time have relied on stories to communicate their ideas, including religious prophets who spread their word in parables.

Gubrium and Holstein (2009) ask, "What are stories? Do they have borders?" (p. 225). Narratives are many things to many people: literary genus, memory structure, living history, cultural link, psychotherapeutic tool, ethical lesson, religious parable and educational vehicle. Livo (1994) states that what a story is depends to an extent on the listener as audiences relate and react differently to stories. Stories have multiple potential values to the reader; they

- make us more human,
- help us to live more lives,
- develop our compassion and insight,
- help us to see the world from the perspectives of others,
- illuminate the present through the past,
- help us to entertain new ideas, and
- develop the imagination. (p. xvii)

Grubium and Holstein (2009) describe borders of "stories, storytelling, and accountability" (p. 226) in terms of:

- a discernable topic: the story must be about something;
- emplottedness, typically scaffolded as beginning, middle and ending;
- a theme underlying the surface text of the story; and
- narrative environment. (pp. 225–227)

Ryan (2004b) pulls this together, describing the narrative text as one that "brings a world to the mind (setting) and populates it with intelligent agents (characters). These agents participate in actions and happenings (events, plots), which cause global changes in the narrative world" (p. 337).

Labov's foundational linguistic analysis distinguished two functions of a narrative: referential and evaluative (Labov & Waletzky, 2004). As Bruner

(1986) puts it, Labov's early work looks at "what happened and why it is worth telling" (p. 12). In Labov's (2006) thinking, all narratives are generically bound by "the inverse relations of reportability and credibility" (p. 44) that impel storytellers to recursively negotiate causality. Traditional folk and fairy tales are based on binary opposites: "powerful conflicts between security and danger, courage and cowardice, cleverness and stupidity, hope and despair, and good and evil" (Egan, 1993, p. 121) that put children in decision-making positions.

Davis, Sumara and Luce-Kapler (2008) provide a psychological explanation for the time-tested practice of using narratives for instructional purposes. They distinguish two types of long-term memory structures: the *episodic* memory, which is "event-based, autobiographical, and narratively structured" (p. 13); and the *semantic* memory, which is "fact-based, rote, and often lacking an integrated structure" (p. 13), pointing out that episodic memory is both the more stable form, and comparatively better at facilitating recall.

Bruner (1986) distinguishes narrative learning, or story, and factual learning, or argument, describing them as distinct ways of knowing with different modes of cognition and design principles. Arguments, he states, "convince one of their truth, stories of their lifelikeness" (p. 11). He explains that whereas argumentation relates the paradigmatic thinking of abstraction, logic, mathematics and scientific reasoning, stories narrate the psychosocial world of intention and action. Narratives have a complex grammar:

> The story must construct two landscapes simultaneously. One is the landscape of action, where the constituents are the arguments of action: agent, intention or goal, situation, instrument, something corresponding to a "story grammar." The other landscape is the landscape of consciousness: what those involved in the action know, think, or feel, or do not know, think, or feel. (Bruner, 1986, p. 14)

Egan (2001) credits the essential conflict-complication-resolution structure of the narrative with providing a sense of security by imposing on the otherwise randomness of life events an ending: an assured conflict resolution.

In Ryan's work (2004a), narrative study transcends media to embrace "language, image, gesture, and further, spoken language, writing, cinema, radio, television, and computers" (p. 1), as well as traversing disciplines. In the elementary school context, narrative learning provides an ideal scaffold for language and literacy across the curriculum. Stories weave together different sets of constraints on reality (Bruner, 1986), creating problem-solving opportunities. They engage children in the word and the text, whether written or spoken, and involve them as readers in ethical conflicts and social consequences. A typical traditional tale brings in perspectives that include a variety of subjects: mathematical problems are stories requiring conflict resolution using the universal language of numbers; history and social studies tell the stories of people in particular times and places; musical genres from opera to the blues tell stories.

The important place of stories in early educational experience is undisputed. Narratives are a major social genre for knowledge and cultural transmission from nursery rhymes to advertisements. As "privileged forms of discourse which play a central role in almost every conversation" (Labov, 1997, para. 3), narratives are socially ubiquitous. In our exploratory research, traditional narratives formed the structural backbone for pedagogical experimentation in multiliteracies development, and the peg for specific curricular teaching aims. What the children were to do with the narratives they revised would not only showcase their learning processes, collaborative skills, developing voice and creative product but raise awareness of their fears, concerns, biases, ethics, emerging identity and sense of fun.

Folk and Fairy Tales

Propp (1968) categorizes traditional tales into three types: "tales of fantastical content, tales of everyday life, and animal tales" (p. 5), and notes that there is much in the way of crossover: animals can have fantastical properties, for instance. Briggs (1970) differentiates "folk fiction, told for edification, delight or amusement," (p. 1) and folk legend, which "was once believed to be true" (p. 1). She explains that fairy tales are "those folk fictions of which magical or supernatural episodes are a necessary part" (p. 113), noting, "a difficulty arises when these tales are handed on by people who no longer believe them, for entertainment or as curiosities. Then they begin to be embellished with picturesque touches, new circumstances, and the legend becomes a fiction" (Briggs, 1970, p. 1). But as Bettelheim (1977) reminds us, "fairy tales, like all true works of art, possess a multifarious richness and depth that far transcend what even the most thorough discursive examination can extract from them" (p. 19).

Learning folk and fairy tales is an assumed rite of passage in childhood though most of what we think of as traditional children's literature was once intended for adult education (Zipes, 2007). Folktales are all fundamentally educative in intent; explicitly so in the case of the fable, which states a direct moral lesson through the safe remove of the actions of anthropomorphized animals. The fairy tale is a modern construction (Opie & Opie, 1974, p. 14), containing an element of enchantment. Even though it may not be about fairy folk, the fairy tale takes events out of human control. This is in contrast to the fable, which pokes fun at human frailties through animal voices.

The Little Red Hen, The Gingerbread Man and *The Three Little Pigs* are folktales based on hunger, a stark reality of life, and its solution: food, essential for life sustenance and once a much scarcer commodity than present day children surrounded by fast food might imagine. All three stories rely on anthropomorphized animals, a characteristic of fables, to illustrate the need for human agency in feeding oneself and, in the case of *The Little Red Hen*, which is the most explicitly didactic of the three, in feeding the community.

The three folktales chosen by teachers for children's creative retelling were constructed with educational intent, directed to developing communal responsibility (*The Little Red Hen*), ensuring mutual safety and security (*The Three Little Pigs*) and self-preservation (*The Gingerbread Man*). Folktales, as Rodari (1973/1996) reminds us, entered the literary world as raw material from the oral tradition. The three stories selected by teachers all rely on a chorus refrain to clarify and reinforce the didactic purpose of the story, though these take different viewpoints. In the case of *The Little Red Hen*, the repeated message: "Who will help me plant the seeds / cut the wheat / bake the bread?" is explicitly directive. In the case of *The Gingerbread Man*, and the big bad wolf in *The Three Little Pigs*, the refrain is an antagonistic challenge, sportingly so by the cheeky gingerbread man; but more threatening in nature from the big bad wolf, whose figurative reality—the wolf at the door—may or may not resonate with these urban children who, though they might be poor, receive subsidized healthy school snacks at recess and are monitored for general health and care at school. In all cases, the refrains provide easily memorized pegs to hang learning on for children in the very early stages of learning to read connected prose, and as such they function as a kind of advance organizer (Ausubel, 1960) facilitating predictive reading.

THE LARGER NARRATIVE

Clandinin and Connelly (2000) ground the life of the educational researcher in a larger narrative set in an educational landscape populated with individual and institutional lives:

> For us, life—as we come to it and as it comes to others—is filled with narrative fragments, enacted in storied moments of time and space, and reflected upon and understood in terms of narrative unities and discontinuities. (p. 17)

This was a helpful perspective as our fledgling learning community took its own narrative turn when unmet demands in the elementary teachers' union culminated in a work-to-rule campaign in March 2005.

Public elementary school teachers at 18 Ontario school boards began a work-to-rule campaign on March 21, thus increasing the number of Ontario school boards working to rule to 30, leaving only 2 school boards not involved in the action. The teachers, members of the Elementary Teachers' Federation of Ontario, are demanding more classroom preparation time. As a result of the job action, they are not performing administrative, secretarial-clerical or custodial functions, organizing any new field trips or attending staff meetings. (International Committee of the Fourth International, 1998, para. 3)

D. Johnson (2009) describes work-to-rule as "a common strategy where teachers come to school but do not perform any duties beyond the limited duties very specific in their contracts" (p. 1). All after-school programs were cancelled immediately, and teachers were required to leave the school grounds within 15 minutes of the final bell.

The project we were collaboratively engaged in relied on voluntary participation during after-school hours, putting it into the after-school program category for union purposes. We were now in contradiction of union action; our workshops went on hold until the labor dispute was settled. Many in the educational community were charged and angry; and teachers were torn by their allegiances to the children, the school community and the union, whose action was in the best interests of education despite the obvious inconvenience to everyone. The cessation of our multiliteracies project workshops meant that teachers were on their own with their individual class projects; worse, the narrative projects, which were technically outside of normal teaching requirements, were not sanctioned classroom activity under work-to-rule. In this way, a political action out of our individual control obstructed our collaborative research project by effectively banning our learning community—a group comprising teachers affected by union action, and administrators and researchers who were not.

There was one piece of good news during this period: the numerous grants the principal and I had applied for working in her office after school hours had paid off. We received a 3-year standard research grant from the Social Sciences and Humanities Research Council to continue our research from 2005 to 2008.

DIGITAL NARRATIVES: A NEW PERSPECTIVE ON STORYTELLING

The TDSB negotiated an agreement in the late spring politically enabling us to move forward with the workshop we were preparing for teachers across the school board. However, the work-to-rule campaign had blocked my opportunities to collaborate with participating teachers, jeopardizing their progress, and it had quashed the time and space for collaborative reflections on participating teachers' journeys through their multiliteracies projects, which affected the scope of what we could confidently present in our workshop to teachers. We focused on the collaborative theory-practice interface that we were developing, and illustrated our project with children's digitally retold stories from *Rewriting Goldilocks*. Though the workshop had been advertised to the TDSB family of schools in the northwestern region of the city, it drew teachers from numerous school districts in the GTA and beyond, with one teacher driving for several hours from another city to reach us. Despite the seeming death knell of a labor disruption deeply affecting research progress, we managed to meet our obligations and presented our multiliteracies research to an audience of interested teachers who engaged in lively discussion.

E-Learning From the Inside Out

The digital age had made its mark on teachers' consciousness, and they were hungry to learn about the project work we were engaged in and to take it back to their schools. Concerns focused around access to digital know-how and equipment, and structuring pedagogical support for conducting innovative multiliteracies projects.

The question of software availability was relatively easy: the Ministry of Education had licensed a growing list of educational software which was available to schools through the school board, whose IT division controlled distribution and installation. Though teachers were normally unauthorized to directly download software onto school computers, they could look up available software on the website of the Ontario Software Acquisition Program Advisory Committee (OSAPAC) and go through a request process for software titles of interest. In those days, programs were downloaded from CDs; nowadays most of the licensed software is web-based, requiring a user ID and password.[2] So if teachers wanted to use specific programs for particular learning ends, and these programs were available on the website, they could make an IT request through school board channels. This access I have come to realize is a relative luxury not necessarily common to teachers in other countries.

Other queries about incorporating digital technologies in project-based multiliteracies teaching needed both historical contextualization and direct problem-solving. All teachers needed access to hardware on which to run licensed software. There was baseline school board support for this, but JPS had applied for grants to use technology for teaching and learning and so had been awarded funding for purchasing hardware. This, however, did not alleviate the embedded problem that dogged all teachers and all schools: how to build sufficient technology support to facilitate teachers experimenting with technology-enhanced learning—both in terms of machine maintenance and in terms of pedagogical development. Without a support network, teachers became frustrated by the constant threat of computer crashes and breakdowns, which made avoidance an attractive path.

Technology at JPS was not synonymous with computers: it referred to an array of digital equipment, including scanners, digital cameras, camcorders, USB flash drives and smart boards, as well as older equipment, such as photocopiers. In contemporary society, it is the rare home that does not have a family computer, and digital *access* now connotes knowledge as much as, if not more than, hardware availability. But in the late 1990s and early 2000s, the idea of the digital divide referred to hardware access.

Joyce Public School had acquired its equipment through ingenuity and developed its technological savvy from the ground up. Given that the JPS building, an artifact of the 1960s, had been constructed in an era when there was neither room nor money for expansive sports ovals, swimming pools and shiny school band instruments, the administrators had reasoned that computers could be their special focus, and applied for numerous grants to acquire hardware. Focusing on *technology* was envisioned as an equity boost for a school community with limited access to computers in the home, and as a conduit to mobilizing parent involvement in schooling.

A mandate to push for children's digital literacy in a high needs inner-city school was avant-garde at the turn of this century. But the local children lacked the cultural capital of more established Canadian families, and their parents, as newcomers to the country, lacked the socioeconomic clout to lobby for educational options, or to pay for private lessons. Focusing on technology-enhanced learning would provide children with a competitive educational base for middle and secondary school when they would be in classes with children from upper-middle-class neighborhoods whose elementary education had been in public schools where there was a learn-to-swim program, a school band or track and field meets in the local sports oval. The focus on technology encouraged learning differently, and sharing learning throughout the community.

The principal candidly describes the arrival of early hardware purchases at the school: "We opened the boxes together, plugged in the machines and pressed buttons to see what happened." Learning which cables worked with which machines was a challenge at first. Sharing was local, teacher-to-teacher:

> We used a number of strategies with the staff to make people more comfortable with technology. Though it currently is called "co-teaching," at that point I realized that I put most of the technology expertise in the librarian. I needed to spread it through the school. So I had

him co-teach with a number of staff who were not as comfortable. So they co-taught and used different curriculum units—language, literacy, or social studies. And this helped the teachers become more comfortable with the technology. Another thing we did is we would champion teachers any time we went around and we saw an effective use of technology to support curriculum. And the bottom line again here is always curriculum. Is this going to help the child learn better? Is this going to help the child learn more clearly? Is this going to help me teach it better? When we identify those [strategies], we would bring them up to staff meetings and show people, because I think people have to see a vision of how this could happen. I think the collective intelligence of the whole staff began to show, expand the actual potential possibilities of how technology could support curriculum. And it was very interesting. We had an awful lot of very strong staff members who had very different points of view and you put them together. It was a joy to watch really. I'm so proud of my staff. (C. Paige, personal communication, February 8, 2010)

The principal has a firm belief that technology must be in the hands of the teachers who need to play with the machines to learn how to use them so they can think about classroom applications. The encouragement of a discovery method of learning and sharing in the elementary school not only put the technology in the teachers' hands, it gave them the agency to experiment, to think collaboratively about pedagogy and to bypass the dominant transmission model of learning to create a school culture of 21st century learning. The school's technology mandate transformed how teaching and learning were approached. Teachers worked collaboratively so they could economize on learning—Sandra had begun using HyperStudio, which she shared with other teachers. They played with programs on the Mac mobile lab laptop computers the school had been awarded: My-Linh learned how to use iMovie; Leon, Comic Life; Anthony, GarageBand. In learning the programs, they found applications they could share with others. Teachers became mini-specialists, and each knew who to go to for help with a specific software program.

Hardware maintenance was another thing. Though schools were acquiring computers (normally housed in a remote lab with scheduled access separate from classroom learning), they had little in the way of in-house infrastructure for keeping the machines in good running order. A computer lab in an elementary school suffers from sticky fingers on screens, too many keys pushed at once and programs not properly closed. The JPS solution was to make strategic hires as and when the budget allowed, looking for professionals with an interest in technology and e-learning. A stroke of luck had brought a young man interested in technology into the school in the late 1990s as a volunteer to help children with desktop publishing. When a position for educational assistant (EA) opened up, he was offered the job, and he left the business world to work with children full-time. Brian was a flexible person who had good social as well as technological skills. He quickly became an indispensable member of the school community, immersed in collaborative discussions and plans, and up to his ears in wires that did not match.

The principal had encouraged a culture of research internally, and she extended this vision to external researchers, inviting a number of university researchers into the school. I had walked into the school at the right time: our project had become one of several collaborative research ventures taking place at Joyce Public School. But as educational researchers know, schools do not always roll out the welcome mat for research liaisons. Learning at Joyce Public School was an inherently collaborative and cooperative experience.

This history did not provide direct advice to workshop participants but it described a model of how to create a culture of collaborative learning in your own school, working from the inside out.

ADAPTING OUR RESEARCH STORY

In our own narrative unfolding, put into a political context not of our choosing that had maimed our research plot, we had to rewrite our roles. Stories fashion ways to do this, as Zipes (2004) recounts:

> Stories help us navigate ourselves and locate ourselves as we interact with others in our endeavor to create ideal living conditions. They help map out the terrain of utopia. They reiterate messages that we sometimes forget. In our most common stories, the utopian tendency is constituted by the actions of an ordinary, quite often naive character who manages to overcome obstacles or an adversary to achieve some kind of success. (p. 3)

The teachers at JPS had been socialized into a climate of do-it-yourself experimentation, and supported in their efforts to try out new ways of learning and teaching that served the students. Their dedication to their students, their passionate involvement in teaching well and their ingenuity in juggling conflicting demands paid off. Working largely on their own in internal collaborative groups over the spring period when guidance to tackle problems and keep on schedule was critically needed, several teachers completed all or part of their class projects working creatively around the labor injunction. The principal understood our research project as working hand in glove with the demands of the curriculum: class narrative projects were tied to curricular aims, though approached with a narrative lens in a multiliteracies orientation. We were not legally entitled to continue face-to-face after-school discussions, but we still had a digital channel open for questions and discussions, and the teachers were not restricted from teaching in a different way if they were teaching curricular objectives. And so we proceeded as best we could.

Michelle: *The Gingerbread Man*, Kindergarten

How do you teach narrative shape to children who cannot yet read or write? How do you teach a story (in English) to a class of 23 children who speak a total of 16 different languages, and come to school with broadly varying cultural experiences with picture books, storytelling and children's literature? These were issues Michelle had to grapple with to conceptualize her story retelling project.

One early source for the first known published story of *The Gingerbread Man* in 1875 is a story about a runaway pancake that avoids being eaten by its makers—three old women in a German tale called *The Thick, Fat Pancake*—and outruns a sequence of hungry animals only to offer itself to three hungry children at its conclusion (Ashliman, 2004). Interestingly, this cumulative tale has grown less altruistic over time, with the gingerbread man now ending up in the mouth of a wily fox who transports it across a river.

Michelle introduced her kindergarten children to the story of *The Gingerbread Man*, and as they became familiar with the story line, she documented them photographically as they experienced the story from the inside out by stepping—unawares—into the plot as characters. The children became the adaptation and their school became the setting for the gingerbread man's marathon escape, and ultimate end.

Students made their own gingerbread men in class, and with the teacher's help and guidance took their cookies to the staff room to be baked in the oven. When the gingerbread men had been baked, they were taken out of the oven to cool, but when the children returned to the staff room to get their gingerbread men, they discovered that they had all run away! The gingerbread men had vanished, but they had carelessly left a trail of crumbs to follow, a neat borrowing from another traditional children's story in which the protagonists must use their wits to avoid being eaten: *Hansel and Gretel*. Michelle's kindergarten class had to recognize the shape of the story to find their gingerbread men by following a cookie crumb trail to trace their naughty runaway gingerbread men, and by looking for notes on which the gingerbread man's cheeky refrain read: "Run, run, as fast as you can. You can't catch me! I'm the gingerbread man!" By the time they wound back to the kindergarten classroom, they found their runaway gingerbread men at their own desks, and they—together with their freshly baked gingerbread men—got their just desserts. Interestingly, Michelle reports that some of the children scolded their cookies before eating them!

Michelle captured the children's multimodal narrative adventures decorating, baking, finding and eating their own gingerbread men in photographs, which she programmed into a PowerPoint accompanied by a description of the children's progressive actions. *The Gingerbread Man at Joyce Public School* reads as a localized retelling of the classic story that positions the children as protagonists in the story and tells it from their point of view (see Figure 4.1).

The gingerbread men's escape at Joyce Public School required the kindergarten children to consult their understanding of the story plot and predict appropriate actions, and to decode written clues on which the gingerbread man's catchy refrain was repeated; the escape also led the children to a computer screen in which the naughty gingerbread man was dashing through a hybrid photo-animated cyberscape familiar to them: a shot of their school computer lab complete with their classroom EA, Brian, carrying the gingerbread man on his back (on page 2 of *The Gingerbread Man* at Joyce Public School), paralleling the role of the fox carrying the gingerbread man across the river. This is a 21st century gingerbread man who understands that digital space is essential to contemporary literacy education.

The gingerbread man is an escape artist of the fanciful type children aspire to when they are caught in a disciplinary net. At the same time, the gingerbread man is recognizably running on fear, a staple of folktales. His trust in the fox is unfounded and he is outwitted. However, in the 19th century German forerunner of the contemporary storybook plot of *The Gingerbread Man,* the pancake offers itself to hungry children at the culmination of its run. In a parallel mode, the children's gingerbread men find themselves back in the hands of the children who made them after their sporting run. The ending is happy for the children, though not so for their disobedient gingerbread men!

To introduce her multilingual kindergarten class to a traditional tale in English, a second language for most children, Michelle provided multiple avenues for accessing a text: familiarity with the plot in which they found themselves, knowledge of the setting (the school), predictable clues on paper, complicit helpers in real and digital space. Each of the children in Michelle's kindergarten walked into a localized version of the traditional story in a literary as well as physical role as creator of the gingerbread man, and, ultimately, his nemesis. The multimodal text of *The Gingerbread Man at Joyce Public School* offers a retelling of their version of the traditional story, in which they figure as protagonists, and their own gingerbread men are the antagonists. They learn the story from the inside out by predicting the actions of the gingerbread man, tracing his steps in physical as well as digital space with help from teachers, written notes and each other, and they reap the reward in more ways than one. Michelle's goal to localize a traditional story was brilliantly accomplished.

The gingerbread man at joyce public school

by room 102 kindergarten

Once upon a time the children made a gingerbread man.

The children put the gingerbread man in the oven.

The children went to get the gingerbread man from the oven

Run! Run! As fast as you can! You can't catch me I'm the Gingerbread Man!

The gingerbread man was gone. He left a message. Run, Run as fast as you can! You can't catch me, I'm the Gingerbread Man.

Figure 4.1   The Gingerbread Man at Joyce Public School.

Shiva: *The Three Little Pigs*, Grade 1

Despite the labor injunction and lack of guidance in her first attempt at designing a multiliteracies approach to narrative learning, Shiva drew her Grade 1 class into the story of *The Three Little Pigs* in a number of experiential ways, and emerged with products, and more importantly, ideas.

The children saw cookie crumbs on the ground. They followed them to the library.

The children saw Brian. They asked if he saw the Gingerbread Man.

The children saw Mr. M. and asked, "Did you see the Gingerbreadman?" Mr. M. saw the Gingerbread Man. The Gingerbread Man said, "Run, Run as fast as you can. You can't catch me I'm the Gingerbreadman!" The children ran on.

Brian said he saw the Gingerbread Man. Brian said the Gingerbread Man jumped on his back! Poor Brian! The Gingerbread Man said, "Run, Run as fast as you can. You can't catch me I'm the Gingerbread Man." The children ran on.

The children went to the office. Gingerbread Man going into ro

The end/

The children went to room 102 and saw the Gingerbread Man on the table. They decorated him and ate him up!

Figure 4.1 (continued)

After familiarizing the children with the basic story, she surveyed the class to learn about variants of the story known to the children in other cultural guises. In class she carefully led the children into the anatomy of a story through storyboarding, and analysis of the characters, action and setting. The children embarked on a variety of hands-on simulations, making houses of different materials using paper and shoeboxes, and test-driving their constructions to explore the link with science materials.

On visiting Shiva's classroom in June after the labor disruption had been resolved, I found beautiful storyboards of *The Three Little Pigs*, with examples of rewritten versions as well as two translations: one in Cantonese (see Figure 4.2); a second in Japanese. This is the first time a teacher has been successful in bringing local languages into the classroom, and Shiva's pioneering work towards developing multilingual versions raises questions about process and access to language support that push our multiliteracies agenda forward. How and where in the story rewriting process can we introduce languages into a story? How we can combine different languages into multilingual versions? How can we facilitate parents sharing their language knowledge in the classroom? Where can these trial stories take us?

Sandra: *The Little Red Hen*, Grade 2

Sandra was interested in refining the methodology she had piloted the previous year. Having gained experience in the first complete run-through of a narrative rewriting project using digital mediation in *Rewriting Goldilocks*, she steamed on, looking to improve the learning benefits of the process for her students. Her experience and efficiency paid off, and her class finished their digital stories in early May. As work-to-rule legislation was still in force for the TDSB, banning our after-school meetings, she took her project to another level on her own, moving children's digitally retold stories into plays and then into iMovie productions.

Sandra began the process in her Grade 2 class by exposing children to the canonical story of *The Little Red Hen*, rereading it to them over time until they recognized the basic narrative. The children then were able to plot the story using story maps and plans. At that point, she moved on to reading the children quirkier versions of the narrative, enabling them to grasp the essentials of the plot. The students compared story versions using a variety of graphic organizers, such as Venn diagrams.

After the children had accomplished an oral retelling of the story, they storyboarded the narrative pictorially (see Figure 4.3). Using procedural writing, they developed individual versions of the story, making their own choices of setting and characters. They illustrated their new settings using Storybook Weaver, a children's educational software program that provides a set of graphic tools for illustrating storyboards. A final multimedia version was programmed using HyperStudio. These were completed in May, when work-to-rule was still in effect.

To extend their project into plays, Sandra introduced the procedure of democratic voting. The children listened to and selected by ballot their top three favorite individually retold versions of *The Little Red Hen* for dramatization and presentation. When I rejoined their project in process in late May, the children had formed teams, each transliterating one of three top

斜狼用梯從

煙囪爬入第三隻

小豬的屋但被

煙囪裡的火燒到

斜狼的腳.

Figure 4.2   *The Three Little Pigs* with parent's Cantonese translation.

Figure 4.3　Child's storyboard of *The Little Red Hen.*

voted story versions into a play. Each child on a team played a role in the production: as actor, narrator or stage manager. They created their own costumes and sets, found or made the props they needed and selected music for the two intervals between the three plays. They presented their plays to parents and to every class in the school.

I volunteered to be the videographer on a day in late June, when the children's plays were being performed throughout the day for JPS classes on the half hour. The suite of three plays took about 20 minutes including stage changes, which were very professionally conducted with the stage managers organizing the props and changing the sets to rousing music. As a first time videographer, I am learning as we go along, and am grateful for the constant repetition. The three dramatizations include:

Title: *The Birthday Party*

Setting:　　A castle in the woods. A digital screen projects a forest created in HyperStudio in which an animated butterfly flutters around. There is a cardboard castle on stage that the characters can hide behind until they are called, and a cardboard stove/oven for baking the cake. Various fake ingredients do double duty for the third play in the suite.

Characters:　Princess Cinderella, Prince Chamy, cat, dog and the narrator.

Costumes: Prince Chamy is dressed in a cape, and he carries a large
              tinfoil covered cardboard sword at his side. The actor got his
              ideas of what a prince wears from a storybook. Cinderella is
              a princess amalgam who wears a beautiful dress and a tiara.
              The actress got her model for princess clothes from the Dis-
              ney film version of Snow White.

Plot: Princess Cinderella is helped to make her own birthday cake
              from scratch by a very cooperative Prince Chamy who takes
              well to his supportive role. Everyone, animals included, helps
              to make the cake, which they mix from scratch according to a
              recipe in a real cookbook. They all sing *Happy Birthday to you*,
              audience included, when the cake is taken out of the oven.

Comments: Finnegan (2005) notes that performance art is typically
              bypassed in analytical discussions of literature. This perfor-
              mance is highly informative, particularly vis-à-vis the chil-
              dren's naming and portrayal of their characters.
                  The children's evident dependence on media tropes, partic-
              ularly Disneyfications, in their character portrayals supports
              Carmen Luke's (1995) assertion that childhood is played out
              in an "intertextual network between TV and commodities"
              (p. 27), where narrative encounters are patched together from
              fractured and commoditized fairy tale representations in
              toys, games and clothing (New London Group, 1996). Marsh
              (2005) notes that studies of 3- and 4-year-old children in a
              London nursery school indicated children "were most often
              engaged with those texts and artefacts which linked with
              their popular cultural and media interests" (p. 27), and that
              parents tended to buy merchandise inscribed with children's
              favorite story characters. Hamer (2009) describes how books
              for the preadolescent market (ages 8–12) are often part of
              branded multimedia franchises that range from video games
              to cosmetics (p. 121). The New London Group (1996) warn,
              "Teachers find their cultural and linguistic messages losing
              power and relevance as they compete with these global nar-
              ratives" (p. 70). I question, however, whether in unearthing
              such culturally appropriated stereotypes in these children's
              story adaptations, and bringing them into the classroom, are
              we not meshing children's popular culture knowledge with
              imaginative and agentive scholarship?
                  Phonologically, I am also intrigued: is Chamy a misinter-
              pretation of Charming? The story rewriter tells me no, it is a
              rhyme. So what is a rhyme to this English language learner?
                  I must admit Prince Chamy cuts a dashing figure. He is
              a short, chubby fellow of Chinese descent with a fabulous

costume, who accidentally situates himself in front of the screened backdrop in just the right place to get a thin fluorescent green moustache from the bottom of the set projection. He is about half the size of the princess, who is a tall and elegant girl of South Asian background, but he exudes gallantry with his tinfoil sword at his side, and he helps his tall princess make a birthday cake, following real cookbook instructions which are well above the level of Grade 2 reading materials. There is none of the essential conflict and villainy of narrative structure here, but everyone enjoys his or her role, including the audience, who gleefully participate in singing *Happy birthday to you* when the characters sit down to eat the cake they have made together.

§

Title: *In the Desert*

Setting: A desert is painted on a mural held up against the board with magnets.

Characters: Ann,[3] tiger, camel, eagle and the narrator.

Costumes: The children have applied makeup to simulate their animal characters. The camel has a large fake bump, and the eagle wears a beak and mouth with tongue hanging out and large wings strapped to her arms. Ann wears a scarf to protect her (sensibly) from the desert sun.

Plot: Ann is in search of water and needs help to get it into a cup. No one wants to help but she gives everyone some of the water when she finally scoops it up.

Comments: The tension of conflict is left in this plot enabling the protagonist to show humanity above the call of duty towards her fellow creatures. The essential story line, that all living things need water to survive, is well conceived, and there is no Disneyfied pop culture in character portrayal. The costumes suffer a little as the day goes on, unfortunately; the eagle's wings start to unravel, and the animals' makeup gets rather weary under the constant lights.

§

Title: *The Cake Party*

Setting: The stage set is an underwater scene depicted on four large blue cardboard stand-up panels on which are pasted sea patterns and green streamers.

Characters:	Stinky the starfish, crab, fish, jellyfish and the narrator.
Costumes:	The costumes are paper designs for fish, starfish and crab, but jellyfish has a pillow-like blob over her shoulders with streamers.
Plot:	Stinky the starfish, so named because if you don't wash your hands after you use the washroom, you will have stinky hands, makes a cake underwater with her fellow sea creatures. Crab reads directions from a cookbook but jellyfish keeps bringing the wrong ingredients. Fortunately, Stinky the starfish knows the correct ingredients.
Comments:	Despite the fact that the plot has an intelligent intervention based on accuracy in literacy as well as a health-related subtext about cleanliness and food handling, there are a number of unpredictable moments, which mar the children's obvious educational intent around health and cooperation. The question of how one bakes underwater is not taken up, but as in all *once upon a time* stories, the unreal is permitted. The narrator has rather unfortunate timing in one set when she urgently needs to make a trip to the washroom and the teacher has to step in for her. Stinky gets a bit shy as the day wears on when the audience laughs at her name, clearly a reaction she had not anticipated. There are minor costume malfunctions; most noticeably, jellyfish's streamer costume falls progressively off her shoulders in one set. I guess even jellyfish have bad days.

The videotaping of the plays helps to preserve them, but without the use of microphones on the stage, the sound recording is poor, and the children's voices are muffled. To fix this, Sandra decides to transfer the videotaped movie to iMovie so the children can do their own voice-overs. At this moment, I see where we could record multiple voices on different sound tracks in iMovie to create multilingual versions.

MOVING FORWARD

Egan (1993) applies Bruner's theorizing on narratives to educational infrastructure positing that "focusing on the mind as a narrative concern" (p. 119) can guide thinking about teaching, learning and curriculum structure. The basic plot of *Goldilocks Revisited* had been upset by an unexpected turn in the political setting of education in Ontario. Though far from the villain of the classic fairy tale narrative, the elementary teachers' union had developed into an antagonist in our research story action. Our fledgling learning community had been dented but not destroyed by this action. In fact, we had adapted our own roles, using the time during which we were unable to openly communicate as a group to experiment in class to plan for the 3-year study to begin the following year. The stories that survived the change in the basic plot of our research plan were successful in providing directions for thought and action. Importantly, this success included those classroom projects that were not completely finished.

Our project extension, nicknamed *Goldilocks Revisited*, was scheduled over a half-year period and based on the discoveries and research relationships we had formed in the pilot year of *Rewriting Goldilocks*. The question driving us forward was:

- How can we teach traditional narratives using digital resources that would facilitate children writing their cultural and linguistic realities into the story?

Digital Facilitation of Children's Cultural and Linguistic Contributions

The classroom multiliteracies projects were highly instructive, but in different ways, consistent with teachers' aims and interests, and curricular objectives. All interventions, however, supported Garrison and Anderson's (2003) claim that "with the expanded capabilities and choices that e-learning presents, it is natural to shift towards an interactive and inquiry-based approach" (p. 64). Each classroom project was a narrative journey in itself.

LOCALIZING A STORY: *THE GINGERBREAD MAN* AT JOYCE PUBLIC SCHOOL

Michelle introduced her kindergarten children to the story of *The Gingerbread Man* as multimodal play. They learned the story from the inside out by walking through the narrative as adventurers in a storyscape. The children became familiar with the concept of narrative by literally doing narrative: they were the characters of a known narrative in a new setting.

Michelle's digital photo capture of the children's participation in the story, using a simple and inexpensive technology, facilitated programming the children's localized version of a classic story: *The Gingerbread Man at Joyce Public School*. This process normalized a digitally captured multimodal product as a way of telling stories to primary school children, and provided a playful mixture of media to help children acquire alphabetic print literacy and narrative knowledge through interaction with:

- alphabetic print in story books, on the gingerbread man's handwritten notes and in the captioned PowerPoint story;

- a tangible antagonist: a gingerbread man who was made and eaten by each of the children;
- photographs of the children's story actions that were organized according to story structure, uploaded, programmed as a PowerPoint presentation and captioned to document the children's narrative experience;
- a known, concrete setting to negotiate on the strength of written clues and known plot;
- spoken assistance in tracking the runaway gingerbread men.

Emergent literacy is semiotically complex. In this engagement with language and literacy acquisition, literacy was not limited to print, nor did it move from one mode to another in a linear process that pinned written acquisition on oral proficiencies (or ignored digital programming as literacy). Children's encounters with narrative were both transmodal and multimodal, moving purposefully across meaning-making resources to track the runaway gingerbread men. Michelle's project put children squarely inside the story they were learning as participants in narrative production. It opened up a dialogic learning space that merged the fictional with the real, and it provided a menu of communicational media for children to tap in problem-solving.

TRANSMODAL LITERACIES:
PERFORMING *THE LITTLE RED HEN*

Sandra had ventured into transmodal interpretation as an opportune time-filler, given the larger narrative of the labor disruption. The children's dramatic transcriptions and performances of the three most popular adaptations of *The Little Red Hen* created a plethora of pathways for bouncing a narrative across and through different media so children had more opportunities to understand and manipulate narrative structure, and to express and enact their vision of the narrative. This active transmodality, though essentially linear in progression, from rewritten stories to transliterated plays to performance to iMovie production and postproduction, offered children multiple channels for interacting with the narrative they were learning.

The transmodal orientation created flexibility in how the canonical *language skills* demanded of the curriculum could be remixed within the realities of contemporary media. It succeeded in merging popular and school cultural representations of literary folktale characters, responding to Carmen Luke's (2000) recommendation that "preschool and primary media must now be expanded to investigations of how the mythical worlds of fairy and folktales are constructed in other media forms" (p. 99). Multiple dialogic learning spaces were created in this project: children wrote individually, transliterated collaboratively and performed with the clock-work interaction of a professional troupe. Sandra's project introduced transmodality as genre-bending; performance as an old and a new way of putting children inside the story; and, as is often the case, in an attempt to correct something that had not worked out well, illuminated a direction for utilizing a programmed soundtrack to record multiple voices. This would emerge in our work as an enormous stride forward.

BUILDING HOME-SCHOOL BILINGUALISM INTO A CLASS STORY: *THE THREE LITTLE PIGS*

Sandra's experimenting with genre-bending created an entry for where Shiva's class left off. Shiva was new to the research project, and as the first participant who had a professional investment in multilingualism as a teacher of Farsi herself, she had interesting ideas on including the many languages spoken in her classroom. However, the labor action had effectively cut her off from lifeblood support in pursuing multilingual inclusion. Bravely moving into accessible spaces, she invited parents to assist in their children's imaginative work, and discovered not only positive reactions but also willing cooperation from parents who were happy to add a multilingual dimension to a traditional story that included their voices, too.

Sandra's utilization of iMovie had opened a space for documenting those voices though we were yet to figure out quite how to use the resources available to us. Though Shiva's stories had not all been completed, they had given us a clear direction for moving into complex and dynamic multilingual texts. We could include community voices through local participation, and we could capture them in educational context through digital programming.

Building a Learning Community

I was frustrated by the fact that the conditions for our small study could be so fatally disrupted by events out of my and the school's control. In conversation with the principal, I learned an important lesson: we needed the funding to make teachers' classroom interventions a part of the regular school day. Funding for in-school workshops was vital to valuing our collaborative relationship and research aims. If our group met during school hours, the work teachers were doing in their classrooms could not be construed as external or extracurricular, and our learning community could be built into the structure of a school day.

Our plan to develop a pedagogy of multiliteracies was evolving (see Figure 4.4). Crystal ball gazing was beginning to reveal real visions for real classrooms.

Though the literacies of the future were still a beacon to our imaginations, the languages through which I imagined children could express those

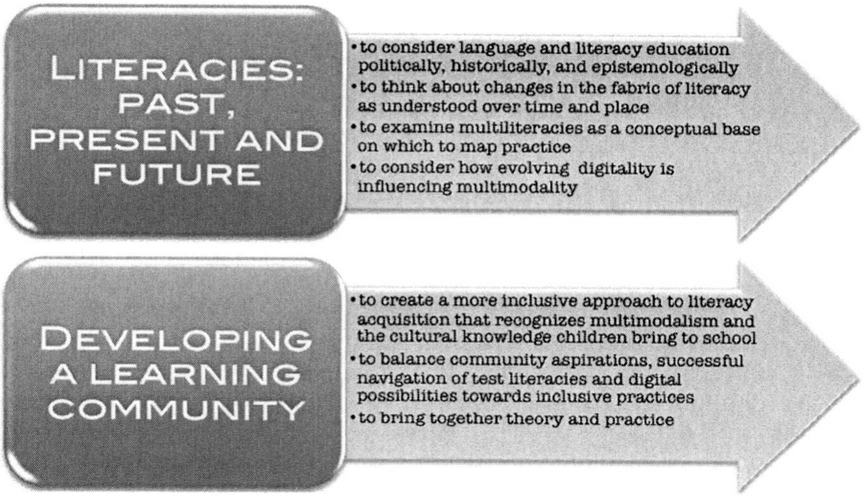

Figure 4.4 Our evolving multiliteracies journey.

literate practices were very much with us, and Shiva had developed the first channel for multiple bilingual story versions in the Grade 1 children's unfinished rewritten stories of *The Three Little Pigs* that brought parents into the classroom and into the multiliterate development of their children. Though these bilingual story beginnings had not moved into digital space, they presented us with real possibilities that could be programmed into multilingual productions, using voice-overs, which Sandra's Grade 2 children had done to repair the poor audio quality of their videotaped performances. If they could add their own voices to an iMovie, why couldn't we add more channels for more voices in different languages?

We needed more time per project, better organization for our workshops and more cooperative planning opportunities. But we were in motion, despite the disruption of the labor injunction. The teachers were developing multiliteracies pedagogies in primary classrooms. They were creating novel transmodal and multimodal access to language, literacy and narrative structure; and they were putting children, the school and community members into the stories they were learning and teaching in their classrooms. In so doing, they were making exclusive resources inclusive for their learners. The teachers had engineered multiple dialogic learning spaces from the starting point of a curriculum favoring teacher-centered banking education (Freire, 1970/1998), discrete English language skills and alphabetic literacy. Our educational pathfinding was on training wheels, but we were moving forward.

5 Genre-Bending
Transcoding Narratives

Jewitt (2009) ascribes the turn to multimodalism in the 21st century to the increasing democratization of knowledge in a networked society, which has challenged modern configurations of truth and authority, such that knowledge is no longer the stable commodity it was once assumed to be. Lyotard (1984) described this social condition as *postmodernism.* Our project to develop postmodern multimodal literacies for the unfolding information era coherent with the culturally diverse school population and the technologically infused social world they lived in was set, of necessity, within modern institutional education, which has been constructed and refined towards the preparation of an industrial workforce that no longer exists. The stable and singular account of literacy on which modern schooling is based has become something of a saber-tooth curriculum for a fishnet generation (Peddiwell, 1939/2004).

Kellner (2003) describes the rupture between children's life experience and schooling in:

> a global economy marked by constant restructuring, flux and rapid change, and novel material conditions and subjectivities. Students coming into schools have been shaped by years of computer and video games, television, a variety of music technologies and forms, and new spheres of multimedia and interactive cyberculture. Moreover, the steady jobs that were waiting for well-disciplined and performing students of the previous generation are disappearing, while new jobs are appearing in the high-tech sector, itself subject to frenzied booms, busts, and restructuring. (p. 59)

We had been successful in our application for national funding[1] for a 3-year study to develop emergent multiliteracies at elementary school. Our context, Joyce Public School, was an urban public school noted for technological innovation and open to positive change. The student body, comprising just over two thirds English language learners, was taught and tested according to the Ontario curriculum and the external EQAO assessment structure, which was geared to individual print literacy in English.

Working with a visionary principal who sought to advantage a population who entered public school with little in the way of cultural capital allowed us to band together in structured discovery. Nonetheless, teachers did have a set curriculum to teach, learning benchmarks to meet and critically important examinations to prepare children for, which provided the larger backdrop to our exploratory and interventionist inquiry.

EMERGENT MULTILITERACIES IN THEORY AND PRACTICE

Our 3-year project was rooted in an evolving theory of multiliteracies that highlighted how late 20th century global migrations and digital innovations in information and communications technologies had significantly changed the tapestry of literacy possibilities and practices. The nature of these changes in literacy practices, which were constantly evolving with rapid progress in the development and cost of digital devices, defied definitive theorizing and had been poorly integrated in educational practice. Our research project aimed to contribute to the development of emergent multiliteracies in theory and practice. To do this, we would collaboratively design processes for creating economically, pedagogically and linguistically sustainable literacy resources for culturally diverse elementary school children.

The vehicle for experimentation was narrative structure, which is an important touchstone in elementary learning. Our focus was on traditional stories: folk and fairy tales, myths, legends and fables. The questions framing our project were practical:

1. How can we create sound educational multiliteracies practices that support:
   a. old (paper) and new (digital) literacies;
   b. multicultural perspectives; and
   c. multilingual acquisition and maintenance?
2. What might these resources look (and sound) like?
3. How can we facilitate the teaching of contemporary reading and writing through new narratives?

Our incipient learning community was the glue for our explorations.

Shaping a Learning Community

The construction of a learning community, a community of practice geared to mutual learning such that it benefited the teachers, the children and the school in general, had been the principal's vision: our research collaborative provided the raw material to shape that vision. Wenger, McDermott and Snyder (2002) describe three fundamentals of a community of practice: "a *domain* of knowledge, which defines a set of issues; a *community* of people who care about this domain; and the shared *practice* that they are developing to be effective in their domain" (p. 27). Our domain was the development of multiliteracies pedagogies for elementary school children; our community was a school-university research collaboration seeking mutual understanding and advancement in multiliteracies teaching, focused on the development of young children in a culturally and linguistically diverse urban community; the practice was the development and understanding of contemporary multimodal literacy.

Receiving external funding gave us the capacity to structure our collaborative workshops within school hours. This was organizationally very important: we were conducting our research within the confines of the curricular day. Our discussions were a component of daily education, not something extracurricular to be tacked on after hours. My role in the school was as legitimate contributor to the educational mission, not visiting observer.

Reason and Bradbury (2008) describe the potential of action research as follows:

> Good action research emerges over time in an evolutionary and developmental process, as individuals develop skills of inquiry and communities of inquiry develop within communities of practice. Action research is emancipatory, it leads not just to new practical knowledge, but to new abilities to create knowledge. In action research knowledge is a living, evolving process of coming to know rooted in everyday experience; it is a verb rather than a noun. (p. 5)

The emancipatory capacity of action research in schools develops from open, critical discussion that is interpretable as classroom practice. Gayá Wicks and Reason (2009) speak of "opening communicative space" (p. 243) in action research, which they base on Habermas' conceptualization of communicative action, which concerns the co-ordination of discursive actions and orientations. They describe Habermas' concern with negotiating "boundary-crises in systems and life-worlds" (p. 246), where systems refer to economic and administrative structures addressing material social reproduction, and lifeworlds refer to the commitment and affirmation of community values. Action research provides a critical space to explore the juncture between community values and the colonizing, regimenting influences of economic and administrative systems: space to play with what literacy should and could be and is evolving into in social life, and how it is conceived and bolted into place in official educational documents.

As Gee (2004a) explains, participation in a community of practice moves on a give-and-take of knowledge, which is "distributed across people, tools, and technologies, not held in any one person or thing" (p. 185). Everyone has specialist knowledge and no one owns or legislates a totality of knowledge. Each teacher in our group was, in essence, conducting an

They intuitively chose modes that scaffolded learning aims, answering: How can children learn this story? What new ways of telling this story can I try? How can I move this child from outside the text to inside the story? The media they gravitated to:

- supported rather than drove their pedagogical aims;
- were accessible physically and pedagogically;
- were friendly to periodic scheduling and classroom importation.

Literacy as Programming

Literacy is programmatic in school: literacy programs are big business, as phonics wars attest to. But researchers and practitioners alike were beginning to speak publically about the need to understand literacy as *programming*, in video game play (Gee, 2003), graphic layout (Kress, 2003) and cell phone customization (Prensky, 2006). Prensky (2008) provides an explanation:

> I believe the single skill that will, above all others, distinguish a literate person is programming literacy, the ability to make digital technology do whatever, within the possible one wants it to do—to bend digital technology to one's needs, purposes, and will, just as in the present we bend words and images. Some call this skill human-machine interaction; some call it procedural literacy. Others just call it programming. (para. 4)

Programming lay at the heart of early research discussions disguised as trying to figure out how to use available software programs for specific teaching aims. In the early years of the 21st century, before the semantic web opened up participatory possibilities, big business monopolized digital learning via software products that have shaped many current digital practices and expectations (e.g., Microsoft Office products: Word, PowerPoint, Excel). Brunelle (2003) explains:

> The modern free-software movement exists for the simple reason that some programmers felt that the licenses imposed on users by companies selling software were too restrictive. Some people wanted to fix their own problems, some people were curious, and some people felt they were unfairly shut out of a process in which they had intimately been involved. (p. 109)

The principal had early discovered that technology must be put into teachers' hands for exploration. Participating teachers were each supplied with a laptop; for some, this was a new laptop bought with scarce research funds; for others, a machine reallocated from school resources. For the children, though, teachers had limited resources at their fingertips: a school desktop lab, an aging mobile lab of Apple 3G clamshell laptops and a couple of desktops in each classroom. They also had a few cameras, a couple of scanners and a photocopying machine: resources often overlooked by educators, but that were appreciated, well used and incorporated in classroom teaching and learning at JPS.

As a group, we had to address platform differences, program incompatibilities and frequent technical problems. Learning how to work with system translations and incompatibilities was fundamental to planning, and propelled teachers into exploration on an unanticipated and somewhat veiled programming level. Brian, the EA who had come into the school from a major computer firm, was indispensable to discussions; he had to understand what teachers were doing to help when things went wrong. But we all had to learn to cope with minor problems as they arose. Necessity was the mother of invention, and the lack of resources, both human and physical, moved us into highly collaborative learning. Our learning community, though often characterized by anxious troubleshooting, began to turn naturally into multidimensional learning.

LEON: *CHICKEN LITTLE*, KINDERGARTEN

Leon, an immensely talented, experienced senior teacher-librarian at Joyce Public School, had won numerous prestigious awards, including *Teacher of the year* for the province of Ontario, and had been seconded to the Faculty of Education at York University in Toronto. His expertise was focused on literacy, early reading intervention and technology, and his research interest followed naturally: the move from page to screen as the primary site of literacy for children in this day and age. His position was flex-time librarian and technology facilitator, and he worked with small groups of children who needed special attention in literacy acquisition.

One of these groups comprised a number of children from Marion's joint junior and senior kindergarten class (J/SK), who were newcomers to Canada and nonnative speakers of English. Leon, in facilitating these young children's precarious introduction to school in Canada, began to think about how stories could help children to deal with scary, deep-seated emotions, focusing on psychological fears, such as children's nightmares, as well as culturally intruded fears, such as Muslim children's negative reactions to dogs, which, in Toronto, are viewed as family pets. Given that children at this age do not have the means for conflict resolution, could stories be used to benefit their psychosocial development in understanding and confronting fear?

According to Livo (1994), stories can help children face their myriad fears. Leon chose the fable *Chicken Little* for the small J/SK pullout group. *Chicken Little* is a study in panic and doomsday fear mongering, whose lessons are to check your sources and make logical deductions. Sandra joked that *Chicken Little* as a character over-reacted hysterically, but this was the point: it was a perfect story to use to help children talk about and work with their fears.

Bettleheim (1977) makes the case that "deep inner conflicts originating in our primitive drives and our violent emotions are all denied in much of modern children's literature, and so the child is not helped in coping with them" (p. 10). In this view, children benefit from traditional stories that address their deep, unspoken inner anxieties. Working with scary stories helps children to build resources for coping with difficult problems.

Leon's plan was to lead children into the fable of *Chicken Little*, and then towards storying their own fears. Children in J/SK cannot yet write; they are 4–5 years old, and just being introduced to the structure of formal schooling. These children were second language learners of English as well. Leon introduced preinformation and communication skills, building concepts about narratives, and beginning with a variety of stories students were familiar and comfortable with. He used large book formats, and focused on the setting and the characters to build children's knowledge about narratives. To introduce the idea of plot, he moved to *Chicken Little*, which he saw as a fable rich in repetitive detail that he felt students could access and use for building predictability.

The children then drew the story characters, which Leon arranged along a clothesline to illustrate the progression of the narrative line. Having learned to map the sequence of events in the story, the children placed the pictures in order in a little eight-page paper doll booklet created from a sheet of paper folded into quarters and snipped at the top.

Narrative plot mapped out, the children discussed the lesson of the story to think about how the problem was resolved. The students mentioned fear continually, leading beautifully into discussing their own fears. The class moved on to creating their own stories, beginning with each child relating a story in which fear was a motivating force. These were recorded on chart paper. Children then revised their stories, so that they, as the main character in their evolving story, resolved their fears in a pro-social manner, guided by Leon. In one scary story about kidnapping, though, two girls working together decided to finish their story on a happy note, and resolved their story on their own without the teacher's intervention.

The stories revealed children's deep-seated fears, from bugs to big dogs to nightmares to abduction. The stories were drawn in children's own eight-page paper doll books. Leon transcribed their narrated text, typing stories out and cutting each line according to the illustrated story page for children to paste into their little books beside the appropriate picture. Figure 5.1 captures two pages from one little boy's story about a big dog that frightened him.

In and of itself, this is a remarkable journey for very young, immigrant children. But for the children in Leon's pull-out class, the voyage was just

Figure 5.1   Two pages from *The Dog Was Chasing Me.*

beginning. They then learned how to use the scanner to transpose their hard copy picture books into a digital format. The translation from page to screen captivated them; they now had a digital object: a programmable reproduction of their original work on paper.

Children were presented with a choice of software that they could operate: PowerPoint, Kid Pix and iMovie (see Figure 5.2). Though children's storybook pages were transposed verbatim from page to screen, the edges of those narratives had changed and expanded in digital translation, enabling children who were preliterate on paper to manipulate menu driven software that drove preprogrammed moves.

Most of the children chose Kid Pix with its cute frame choices (see Figure 5.2 for example). The multimedia capabilities of each program enabled students to produce complex modal blends including those used on the bimodal page: image and print, with new digital possibilities: voice, sound and movement. Leon remarked that children showed considerably more ease and control manipulating the screen than they did the printed page. Following his modeling, children went on to edit their stories, and add voice-overs and visual effects. These were presented to their fellow classmates for self and peer assessment.

Literacy Learning in Atoms and Bits: Transmodality

Leon's small pullout kindergarten class can be described as having learned about literacy in the world of *atoms* and in the world of *bits*, using Negroponte's (1995) metaphor for the physical-digital divide. The work of these kindergarteners indicates that young children can program—at a very elementary level—before they can write alphabetically. Indeed, navigating a screen extended their world of print. Multimodal

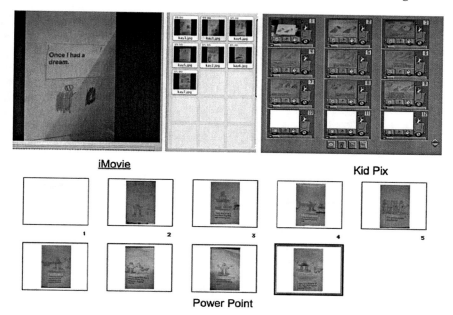

Figure 5.2 A choice of digital slide trays for Kindergarten children, adapted from material published in Lotherington, H. (2008), Digital Epistemologies and Classroom Multiliteracies. In T. Hansson (Ed.) *Handbook of Research on Digital Information Technologies: Innovations, Methods, and Ethical Issues* (pp. 261–280). Hershey, PA: IGI Global. Copyright 2010, IGI Global, www.igi-global.com. Posted by permission of the publisher.

complexity was, thus, not complicating but facilitating of emergent print literacy acquisition.

This is a wake-up call to those in formal education who prioritize alphabetic literacy in the physical world over digital access, treated, so often, as an add-on. The fact that the children manipulated iconic programming with considerable agency and independence, but required carefully scaffolded intervention to understand the alphabetic text of the story, indicates that policy makers as well as teachers need to rethink the prioritizing of alphabetic print as the primary, or worse, the exclusive interface to emergent literacy learning.

In telling their own fear stories, the children in Leon's pullout group played with communicative modalities in two ways: sequentially in moving from one mode to another, or *transmodally*; and in complex bundles, or *multimodally*. S. Thomas et al. (2007) describe these possibilities with the term *transliteracy*, which they coin as a backformation from transliterate, and define as "the ability to read, write and interact across a range of platforms, tools and media from signing and orality through handwriting, print, TV, radio and film, to digital social networks" (para. 3). They claim, "Transliteracy is an inclusive concept which bridges and connects past, present and, hopefully, future modalities" (para.16), pointing to both diachronic (historic) and synchronic (occurring at the same time) relevance in that transliteracy relates to the simultaneous engagement of multiple media in communication, as well as to mode-switching, or moving from one modality to another.

Nearly a decade earlier, Semali and Watts Pailliotet (1999) developed a discussion around the idea of *intermediality* that addressed eliminating "the inequalities of learning and instruction that have made their way into classrooms based on social class" (p. 2). Their conceptualization was oriented to critical media literacy, and illumination of the mediating potential of texts, whether print, visual or electronic.

Working with elementary school children in the early part of the century, I proposed the idea of emergent *metaliteracies* (Lotherington, 2003a) to describe the facility children needed to navigate contemporary literacy environments. Leon's class learned a single alphabet and concentrated on a single language (though we saw in hindsight how and where bilingual intervention could be very helpfully worked into the process for the children and their families), but chose among three software trays that offered similar menus but went about connecting the raw material children input in different ways. This is another side to complexity. Children are learning to navigate different software programs and to choose which principles are transferrable and how.

The children's individual creations were preserved online in a form that made them easy to improve, embellish and share. The digitization of their handmade books opened new spaces for the development of voice: children narrated their own hand-drawn stories using the software they chose (from three options), creating personalized talking books. We would work to enlarge these opportunities for developing voice to create bilingual and multilingual talking books.

SANDRA: *OLD MAN YU MOVES THE MOUNTAIN*, GRADE 4

Sandra had moved from primary (i.e., K–Grade 3) to junior education (i.e., Grade 4–6) with a Grade 4 class. She chose a story that was not from the Western literary canon: a traditional Chinese folktale, entitled *Yu Gong Yi Shan*, which translates literally as *The Foolish Old Man Removes the Mountain*. Her choice was motivated by several factors: she, as a Chinese Canadian, was familiar with the canonical story and liked its moral message; the story would appeal to children in the class with Chinese backgrounds who might be familiar with the story, if not the language in which it was being told; all children would broaden their horizons with a story that had an important lesson for education.

Sandra read a couple of versions of the folktale, settling on a storybook in English translation, entitled *Mr. Yu Moves the Mountain*. The story is about an old man named Yu Gong (foolish Mr. Yu) who decides to remove the large mountains blocking the path from his house to the village. Though the task seems very foolhardy, Mr. Yu gathers his sons and a number of others to help him to move the mountains by taking the earth away to the sea. When, en route, he is confronted by a wise man scoffing at his foolish actions, Mr. Yu speaks to the Chinese values of hard work and task persistence towards a defined goal, assuring the wise man that though it may take many generations, even a mountain can be moved.

The lesson that determination, courage and hard work can (figuratively) move mountains was used as a springboard for ethical education. Sandra wanted children to think about what they were gaining from the story and how they could apply this knowledge to craft their own entertaining but instructive stories. The project offered many junctures for collaborative problem-solving.

Sandra chose to approach the project as a class reinterpretation so the story writing would be shared across the whole group. Some of the children had been in her Grade 2 class 2 years ago, rewriting *Goldilocks and the Three Bears*, so they were familiar with the idea of story retelling; others were not. The children brainstormed wish list ideas, and voted on the suggestions for their story line. They settled on the specific aim of attending the 2006 winter Olympics in Torino, Italy, to watch the gold medal hockey finals, with hopes of seeing Canada win,[2] They then developed the setting, and two characters who would inhabit the story canvas: Puppy and Horse, who were avid hockey players. This was an interesting choice. Motivating story action through animals is typical of fables, which are explicitly moral in intent. By utilizing animals to speak and act as humans, children can examine human actions from a safe remove.

The children began to think about how Puppy and Horse could get themselves to the Olympics: they could fly in an airplane, or build a bridge from Canada to Italy and drive there, or row across the Atlantic in a boat. Each travel path posed particular difficulties that the children had to decipher and iron out. They settled on earning the money to buy an air ticket to travel to Torino, Italy, to watch their national teams play hockey as providing the most plausible action for their characters to take. Having made this decision, they discussed different methods of earning enough money to buy an air ticket, and decided they should sell lemonade. Their research assignment took them to the Internet to look up recipes for lemonade.

The essential story line built, problem democratically voted on and resolution collectively decided, the children then began the interesting work of storyboarding their narrative. Sandra expressed interest in using a dynamic platform for this story retelling, so I called on Professor Jennifer Jenson at York University whose specialization in technology, gender and pedagogy, with a particular interest in digital gaming, made her an ideal consultant.

Jen was working on a large pedagogical gaming project that employed a programmer and involved graduate students in building a storyboarding tool that used Lego³ animation, which they called *legomation*. Sandra and Jen negotiated using her Grade 4 class as guinea pigs to test out the lego-mation tool, which provided them with a sophisticated web environment to create mini-animations, fitting to a tale where characters took a lengthy journey to watch a dynamic sport. The format provided the class with a web-based simulated handheld game device (see Figure 5.3), creating a trendy youth culture medium.

The children sculpted their characters first in modeling clay. Sandra pho-tographed and scanned these to the web designer, who programmed the clay figures into the website, and provided digital versions of the originals and legomation clones. The web designer then sent the children individual passwords to the website on which their characters were stored, facilitating programming the class story in smaller groups. At this point, teacher and students alike were provided with a new digital medium to explore, which Sandra told her students, was a joint research project: they were all trying to figure out how to use this medium together. The children were very excited about being innovators in a brand new learning environment and working collaboratively with game designers. They learned how to manipulate the characters for their story, organized the sets and backdrops needed, and designed the necessary props from available characters. In Figure 5.3 their innovated hockey puck, fashioned from a miniaturized black legomation horse, is visible on the main screen.

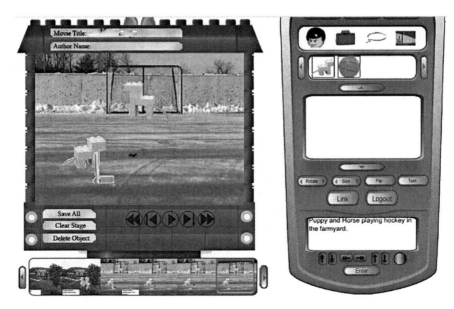

Figure 5.3   Puppy and Horse Go to the Olympics.

The webmaster and a doctoral student thus became involved in the children's pedagogical journey from a Chinese folk tale to a class shared writing project to a contemporary story programmed by small groups of students in handheld device format, stretching the collaborative learning community to surprising levels, where the children were able to inform the web designer of bugs in the system affecting their character actions. This provided a tremendous learning opportunity and confidence booster for the children, fitting of the lesson of the Chinese story they began their learning journey with (i.e., goal-directed, collaborative work and perseverance pay off). The children had grown from storybook readers to designers of web-based animations.

The project had another interesting, though unincorporated dimension. Sandra was still playing with the linguistic aspect of the story. Beginning with a Chinese story was a wonderful idea not only culturally, but also linguistically. English is not neutral or baseline; it is one of many, many languages on this earth. We thought about the idea of spiraling the story from Chinese to English where it was transformed by the children and back to Chinese again. Tapping community assistance, Sandra had the Grade 4 children's story of *Puppy and Horse Go to the Olympics* translated back into Chinese.

Literacy and Play: Digital Puzzles

Gee (2008) claims:

> Something very interesting has happened in children's popular culture. It has gotten very complex and it contains a great many practices that involve highly specialist styles of language. (p. 316)

This complexity is evident in the playful transmodal retellings Sandra was pioneering with her elementary school classes. The previous year, her Grade 2 class not only redrew the context and the characters of *The Little Red Hen*, but transposed their reinterpreted stories into other genres, moving from story → play → performance → video, all of which had different demands on children's participation in the story. Sandra adventured further into transmodalism with the progression in *Mr. Yu Moves the Mountain* which took two metamorphosing pathways as depicted in Figure 5.4, one a translation in language, culture and narrative shape that happened on the page (following the modal translation from oral folktale to storybook page); the other an exploration in narrative shape from page → screen, requiring programming for animation: an essential literacy skill that continues to fly under educational radar in terms of recognition and assessment.

The children moved pedagogically from learning a traditional story from a different culture to engaging in a familiar shared story writing exercise in the classroom to programming an animated narrative into a digital handheld game format in the school computer lab that required playful

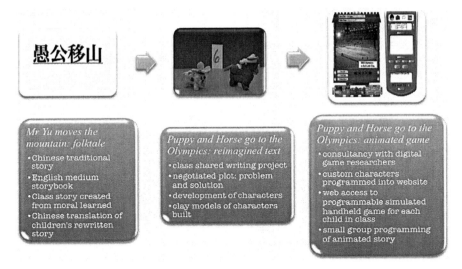

Figure 5.4   Transmodal processes in *Puppy and Horse Go to the Olympics*.

exploration. Burn (2009) makes the point that reading and writing are assumed to be flip sides of the same process in the world of print literacy and given complementary time in the classroom. In the world of digital literacy, this is not true, with reading media far outstretching creating media texts. He suggests that making media is about representation, combining ideas "that represent the world in some way and the material substances—of language, image, music, dramatic gesture—which make it possible" (p. 1). This aptly describes the vision of multimodal narrative learning that Sandra successfully guided her Grade 2 and 4 students through.

Creating the stories in small groups incurred playful design, and playing animated stories in a simulated game device is culturally appropriate play. De Castell and Jenson (2003, 2007) take up the notion of *serious play* in children's education. Taken into digitally supported environments, they see play as a powerful, connective learning mechanism in "the emerging global technoculture" (p. 2).

Gee (2003, 2007, 2008), a strong proponent of video games for learning, criticizes the elementary readings that children get in school as less demanding than the pop culture games they engage in. He assesses young children's *Yu-Gi-Oh* cards, which he points out are banned from some schools, as being "in complexity . . . far above the language many young children see in their schoolbooks until they get to middle school at best and, perhaps, even high school" (Gee, 2008, p. 317).

Mateas and Stern (2007) identify the paradox of the narrative game, questioning whether the linear narrative of a story line is compatible with the multilinear interactivity of a story space in game play. In answer to this question, de Castell and Jenson (2007) explain that in digital play models, narratives move from a simple linear to a "multi-level, hybrid, open-ended structure in which characters and players have 'conversations' both inside and outside the game" (p. 4). Though these projections speak to far more sophisticated game play than that in which children were engaged in their Grade 4 classroom, the discussion indicates that to keep up with contemporary digital play, education must engage new story shapes and interactions, including familiar possibilities, such as the branched story ending, and new twists, such as student programmed screen-controlled animated sequences.

MOVING FORWARD

My original observations about gaps needing bridging in order to facilitate urban, multicultural children's literacy development targeted:

- home, community and school languages,
- social and school literacies, and
- cultural understanding across
  - o *Canadian* and home cultures, and
  - o school, pop and digital cultures.

These problems led our evolving collaborative research group into a plan for developing multiliteracies pedagogies (see Figure 4.4). To understand

- future literacies so we could anticipate social trends likely to stick,
- ways to support languages in the linguistically heterogeneous classroom to help children with the language learning and language valuing they needed to do,
- connections between the global and the local in education in a globalizing era, and
- a more inclusive Canadian identity, to do justice to the society we had created,

we had to get involved in trailblazing an ecological approach to language and literacy education that accommodated:

- positioning local languages as global assets,
- developing multimodal texts,
- creating an inclusive notion of culture, and
- narrative development.

So where were we?

There were three main issues at stake: making a more facilitating link between the languages of the community and those of the classroom for children, which in itself linked the local and global and impacted on how we see ourselves as Canadians; developing multimodal texts utilizing digital technologies consistent with social resources and trends that could extend the boundaries of literacy and the limits of learning currently encoded in curricular documents; and building new pedagogies to do this. Our mechanism for working on these aims was the development of a learning community towards action research in the classroom to experiment with small cross-curricular, multilingual and multimodal projects based on narrative learning.

Lessons From the Learning Community

Over the course of the year, our learning community had matured into a working group that complained of not having enough time to work on class projects rather than not knowing what to do. Our annual projects were showcased at our June show-and-tell mini-conference for participating teachers. In addition to the projects completed by Sandra and Leon, Shiva's Grade 1 class produced three-dimensional versions of *The Three Little Pigs* that were transformed into claymations, using clay storyboards and iMovie; and Michelle and Helen created short curve narratives (title page + beginning-middle-end) with kindergarteners based on Aesop's fable, *The Lion and the Mouse* that included multilingual PowerPoint retellings of considerable imagination and power, tapping the language resources of both the community and the teaching assistants (for details, see Lotherington, Sotoudeh, Holland & Zentena, 2008).

Teachers' multiliteracies explorations, which, though remarkably protean, were defining modal complexity along three axes:

- a *paradigmatic* axis, regarding selection of appropriate meaning-making resources for the content and communicative intent: *aptness* following Kress (2010);
- a *diachronic* axis, to map out sequential modal transformations: *transmodality*; and
- a *syntagmatic* axis, to consider modal complementarity and complexity: *multimodality*.

These incubating conceptualizations present practical decision-making junctures in teaching:

1. *paradigmatic*: modal choice/aptness
   a. How can I tell this story? What work does this meaning-making resource do to tell this story?
2. *diachronic*: transmodalism/transmodality

    b. What comes first? What do children need to know before they can transform this story? How can these transformations be pedagogically linked?

3. *syntagmatic*: modal complexity/multimodalism/multimodality

    c. Can I combine different ways of telling this story for better effect? How do these modes work together to tell this story?

Multimodal exploration was moving along very well, showing teachers and children to be full of imaginative directions and surprises. Children were expressing their overt interest in doing these projects—a substantial indicator of success in my books. However, community language inclusion was proving to be more slippery. A number of teachers had produced beautiful bilingual and multilingual texts using community know-how. Yet in these projects, the languages were illustrative of available linguistic capacity rather than facilitative of language learning or language maintenance. Realizing that videos could be narrated in multiple sound tracks was fantastic, but when Shiva tried to do just that, she discovered that she could not identify where the English and the Yoruba versions said the same things: the languages had to be co-programmed. This Michelle did with her children's versions of *The Lion and the Mouse* retold fables in kindergarten, but that was with adults who were actually in the classroom.

We had bargained on investigating translation software, which in the early days, seemed to be an excellent idea. However, we quickly realized that translation is an art as well as a science when demo software turned out howlers in languages members of our learning community could follow. So we found that translation software offered good comic relief, but a poor resource for our educational purposes.

The failure of translation software to translate children's stories into multiple languages spoke to several problems, both with the rapidly spinning engineering cycle in digital technoculture and with software marketing. The idea of machine translation is a wonderful time and money saver. But who will buy it? The languages offered for translation reflect business markets. Ergo, Guyanese Creolese is not targeted, though Japanese and German are, so many of the languages we needed help with were not available to us in any case. The languages we could access were only partially translatable. The reality of machine translation is that artificial intelligence cannot accurately simulate the fuzzy logic of the human brain; the complexities of human social communication outstrip the binary processing of machines despite sophisticated algorithms. Moreover, software innovations may have *bugs*, or technical glitches, that disrupt the translation of intention into product. Furthermore, as Venezky and Davis (2002) comment:

One of the major frustrations of modern schooling is the impermanence of innovations. What is here today may be here tomorrow but the likelihood of this occurring seems to depend on how compatible any new method is with what teachers traditionally do and believe, upon the context in which the change has occurred, and on the support system for the teachers. (p. 35)

Technologically driven solutions do not have children's learning in their sights so much as company profits, so the technological determinism of using software to effect learning is backwards: learning aims must come first. Supportive resources then follow. Nonetheless, we were on the right track: it was not the software we needed: machines do not translate languages, people do. We needed facilitative connection to humans for language sharing and translation; we needed to establish digitally connected as well local community support. Given the ease with which interactive technologies open communication lines, this seemed to be straightforward. But it wasn't, as we were to find out.

6   Creating Dialogic Spaces for Learning

INSIDE THE (SCHOOL) BOX

Our learning community was gelling nicely around the narrative project focus in developing multiliteracies pedagogies. However, the benefit of being positioned as a part of the school day, which was critical for breathing life into a multiliteracies orientation to language and literacy pedagogy in the classroom, also meant that we had to work within the spatial and temporal boundaries of the school system.

Formal education in Ontario is structured in terms of atomistic subject areas, though holistic connections are suggested in curricular documents. Grade progression proceeds along a linear path towards achievement of curricular objectives in defined subject areas. *Learning* is defined in terms of successful achievement of curricular goals as assessed both internally and externally over the course of the school year. Modified progress is determined for students with suspected and demonstrated exceptionalities as set out in individual educational plans (IEP).[1]

This compartmentalized, linear trajectory of learning within disciplinary walls favors transmission pedagogy so students can get from point A to point B in a quantifiable way. Learning in this ideology takes place through mental filing of inert information that has been structured according to external logic—what Freire (1970/1998) described as: "the 'banking' concept of education" (p. 53).

The temporal packaging of the learning process has a spatial analogue: the specialized learning environment. Schools are walled edifices. Entrance into a school is always carefully monitored; insiders and outsiders are marked. This, in itself, is not exceptional: corporate and national spaces alike are monitored for security purposes, and entrants are documented. This security measure is particularly salient in a school where children are in loco parentis, requiring responsible care and protection. Though not a consistent feature, classrooms are normally walled, as are libraries, gyms, computer labs and music rooms. Learning is linked to physical spaces (e.g., band in the music room, physical education in the gymnasium, Kindergarten in the Kindergarten classroom).

Robbins (2002) laments, "Design is rarely viewed as an essential force in making and remaking our society, and too often, social needs, education, and innovative design are perceived as separated by unbridgeable gulfs" (p. 1). Upitis (2004) sums up how the architectural organization of the school reinforces compartmentalized learning:

> Public schools have been built largely as a reflection of the factory model for learning: put a homogeneous group of children in a confined space (called a classroom), process them for a year (fill them with knowledge), make sure they have learned the set and predictable curriculum (test them according to established standards), move them to the next processing container (another classroom), and continue the cycle until they have reached the age at which they are deemed ready to leave (and enter the workplace). (p. 20)

Our collaborative experimentation with learning and teaching multimodal literacies required breaking this mold. The spatial and temporal boundaries around modern factory-model learning needed to be dismantled so that teachers and university researchers could share and discuss ideas across a table, teachers could interact with each other in the classroom as well as the lunchroom, parents could contribute meaningfully to classroom projects, and children could question their place in learning and add their perspectives in ways that were valued and valuable, not simply external to the structure of the curriculum. In order to invite the languages of the community into the classroom, we needed to open the classroom to the community, both local and digitally connected, and to link interests across artificial borders in subject disciplines so that conversations could traverse English and science, math and art, Grade 2 and Kindergarten.

Outside the Box: Project-Based Learning

The mission of education in Freire's (1970/1998) vision is to stimulate critical consciousness, not to reproduce the status quo. He characterized the student-teacher relationship in transmission teaching as fundamentally narrative, describing education as suffering from "narration sickness" (p. 52) in which the teacher as the narrating subject expounds tediously to students who listen passively. The transmission of knowledge as some sort of absorbent quality lacking human mediation inspires neither creativity nor transformation. Freire labeled his fix to the dehumanizing and oppressive banking approach to education, *problem-posing education* (p. 60), which "breaks with the vertical patterns characteristic of banking education" (p. 61). Problem-posing education invites active learner investment in the learning process; it transforms, not transfers, thinking. Problem-posing education is fundamentally dialogic; students are cognitive actors in the educational process, not empty vessels.

Though a project-based orientation to learning was not characteristic of curricular subject and classroom bound teaching agendas in the context in which we were working, project-based learning is neither new nor has it been ignored in primary education. Indeed Katz and Chard (2000) advocate project-based learning specifically for the primary classroom, describing a project as "a piece of research about a topic—one that may be related to a larger theme—in which children's ideas, questions, theories, predications, and interests are major determinants of the experiences provided and the work accomplished" (p. 5). This is fundamentally problem-posing education.

Leo van Lier (2006) traces project-based learning to the "experiential and action-based learning" (p. xi) advocated by John Dewey in the early 20th century, but notes myriad antecedents in European educational thought from Jan Comenius in 17th century Prague to Maria Montessori in early 20th century Italy, and Lev Vygotsky in Soviet Russia, whose theories of learning as socially scaffolded have contributed substantially to contemporary thought, specifically to educational activity theory. Van Lier (2006) warns, though, that project-based learning is sensitive to systemic demands, so despite the facilitating positive contribution of project-based multimodal affordances to language learning opportunities, the approach tends to get shelved under pressure of standards-based education driven by external tests.

Bereiter and Scardamalia (2000) find antecedents to their "collaborative knowledge building" (p. 1985) approach to education in problem-based medical education, and identify pedagogical commonalities in derivative approaches to learning. These include: dialogic learning, collaborative problem-solving, small group interaction, procedural investigation and distributed learning with the ultimate aim of learning over production. Collaborative knowledge building fosters the construction of problem-centered theory in which educational technologies function to support the learning process. In this contemporary conception of education, the classroom is not physically walled—it is a digitally connected community; and the role of the teacher is not as knowledge broker, but as facilitator and co-investigator.

Sawyer (2008) reminds us that students have lives; they do not enter the classroom as tabula rasa. No teacher should be *operating under erasure* (Ibrahim, 2004, 2008). Sawyer (2008) identifies creative thinking as key to education for the innovation economy, and promotes digital technologies as supportive of educational customization in the classroom, where the standardizing approach of modern factory schooling has failed to stimulate deep thought. Interestingly, creativity, along with authentic experience, intense engagement and improved language and collaborative skills, is at the top of the list of benefits Stoller (2006) attributes to project-based learning in language learning contexts.

Sawyer's (2006, 2008) vision of education for the innovation economy has in common with Bereiter and Scardamalia's (2000) collaborative knowledge building, collaborative and distributed learning in small groups, problem-solving with diverse resources and, though unspecified, the classroom as digital community rather than physical enclosure. The teacher in this classroom is a critical knowledge worker who is creative and resourceful; and teaching is an improvisational act (Sawyer, 2006, 2008).

In the project-based approach we were experimentally implementing at JPS, education is emancipatory for the teacher as well as the student. Gramsci (1971) referred to "the living work of the teacher" (p. 35) in connecting instruction and education. Our learning community rejected the notion of the teacher as modern functionary meeting curriculum objectives—and in so doing, inviting in what a Freirean analysis describes as narration sickness and banking education—for a respectful stance towards the teacher as knowledgeable, reflective practitioner who utilizes education and professional commitment to orchestrate discursive, inclusive, exploratory learning. I am reminded of this continually as our learning community grows in confidence. Teachers, at first slow to speak out, cross that they "didn't understand what I wanted" and worried that they somehow had the wrong idea or answer, were incrementally discovering that their ideas were not only professionally provoking contributions—but embryonic hypotheses saturated with rich knowledge-building implications about learning and teaching affecting not just this school and these students, but the educational community at large.

Dialogic Learning

Socrates promoted dialogic learning in ancient Greece. His method was based on oral question and answer dialogue; what exists of his work comes through the written accounts of others, chiefly Plato. For Socrates, knowledge was virtue (Benson, 2000); learning required attentive listening, critical analysis, careful reflection and argumentation.

Socrates' aim is described as "testing those who profess to care about 'wisdom, truth, and the best possible state of their soul'" (Benson, 2000, p. 32). His method, *elenchos*, translates as "'refutation', 'test', or 'cross-examination'" (Benson, 2000, p. 32), suggesting that the shape of the oral dialogue was formatted, though soul-searching towards wisdom remains a laudable educational aim—one not prominent in a modern monologic curriculum favoring teacher presentation to students (Guilherme, 2002).

For Vološinov (1929/1973[2]), writing in Soviet Russia in the early 20th century, language itself was a dialogic tool. Vološinov promoted a process view of language as verbal social interaction, cautioning against static structuralist orientations to language as a collection of typologically classified signs. He viewed consciousness as internal to the individual, but socially constructed through human verbal interaction in shared *"interindividual territory"* (p. 12), stressing that it is human communicative interaction that links one individual consciousness with another.

In Socrates' dialogic method, definition was a preoccupation (Benson, 2000, p. 13). Vološinov (1929/1973) understood the word as a *"two-sided act . . .* determined equally by *whose* word it is and *for whom* it is meant" (p. 86). His formative work on language as a dialogic tool stimulates penetrating questions about formal language learning: whose word is *right* in the classroom, and conversely, *who* has the right word to use? In a monologic curriculum, it is the teacher who has the right word, which the child passively integrates and inhabits. In a dialogic view of learning, words must be viewed more equitably and hospitably. This requires revising how learning is formally construed in educational practice. Whose words are used? Whose words can be used?

In the context of contemporary schooling, Landay (2004) questions whether, how and to what extent schools promote learning through social interaction, motivated by Bakhtin's (1975/1981) theorizing that all aspects of language are dialogic:

> Dialogism is . . . central to all interactions between speaking subjects. Every utterance a person speaks is oriented toward an anticipated response. Individuals frame what they say by a foreknowledge of who will hear it, what they imagine listeners are thinking and might reply. Thus, dialogism is embedded in all meaning; and constant interactions between meanings affect and shape a single instantiation of meaning in a given utterance or word. (p. 109)

Janet Maybin (personal communication, November 12, 2010) comments that a Bakhtinian sense of social communication not only anticipates future responses to an utterance, but also includes a backwards dimension, responding to past utterances, including the speakers' own voice. Communication in the classroom is thus socially embedded in complex, multilinear patterns.

Vološinov's theory of language as a consciousness-raising dialogic tool resonates in Freire and Macedo's (1987) view of literacy as cultural politics, and their insistence on the learner's own language in the classroom towards emancipatory learning, rather than reproducing colonial discourse. However, in the case of contemporary urban spaces where students of diverse cultural origins and languages meet, how is that to be done? How can dialogic learning involving multiple voices be developed in the heterogeneous language classroom?

THE DEVELOPMENT OF *VOICE* AT SCHOOL

An important part of my stake in our collaborative research agenda was to develop and extend notions of *voice* in dialogic learning to include multiple languages and modes of communicating in the classroom. However, working with *voice* is conceptually complicated by the fact that the term is used throughout language, education and linguistics both specifically and generally to refer to distinct phenomena including, but not limited to, semantic and pragmatic aspects of grammar, anatomically produced vocal qualities, politically representational participation, simulated speech in software development and individual expression inside and outside formal learning environments. Though researchers and educationists alike use the term *voice* in respect to classroom learning, the concept is slippery.

Maybin (2009) has identified four distinctive ideological interpretations of *voice* in language study that will be considered in turn:

- authorial presence on the page
- representative point of view
- the freedom to make oneself understood
- speaking consciousness (dialogically constituted). (p. 3)

Authorial Presence on the Page: Being Read

Donald Graves uses the term *voice* extensively in his work as a leading advocate of process writing, an approach to writing that moves the writer recursively through multiple drafts of a composition with the supportive assistance of others, including peers. He describes voice as:

> the imprint of ourselves in our writing. It is that part of the self that pushes the writing ahead, the dynamo in the process. Take the voice away and the writing collapses of its own weight. There is no writing, just words following words. (Graves, 1983, p. 227)

Graves' (1983) push for self-expression through writing connotes the writer's voice as primary motivator. Voice in Graves' work emanates from the ego of the learner and is tied to the development of authorial vision: "The voice shows how I choose information, organize it, select the words, all in relation to what I want to say and how I want to say it" (p. 227).

A problem with this approach to voice as unassailable and identifiable authorial presence on the page is, as Maybin (2009) points out, whether that voice is read and recognized as authorial. She cautions that the impetus for individual expression is tempered by entrenched canonical language expectations in formal schooling that color educational contexts, in some instances encouraging the student to experiment with personal voice, and in others, leaving little room for responses not cohering to school expectations of what Bourdieu (1991) calls *legitimate language* (J. Maybin, personal communication, November 12, 2010).

What, then, marks a voice as authorial in the academic context? An examination of a publicly available essay-marking rubric for the OSSLT, which defines literacy attainment for all secondary school students across the province of Ontario, offers little hope that individual voice is recognized much less credited. The Education Quality and Accountability Office (2011) essay-marking rubric grades two aspects of composition:

1. *topic development*, specifying the degree to which: "the response is related to the assigned prompt. A clear and consistent opinion is developed with sufficient specific supporting details that are thoughtfully chosen. The organization is coherent demonstrating a thoughtful progression of ideas." (Code 60, para. 2); and
2. *use of conventions*, specifying the degree to which "control of conventions is evident in written work" (Code 40, para. 3).

Development of an ego-driven voice in writing would appear to be a substantial deviation from the accomplishment of conventionally correct, topically relevant, coherent and logical prose referred to above. It is important to note, of course, that process writing does not in any way neglect or negate relevance, coherence, internal logic and conventional correctness. Indeed, Graves and Kittle's (2005) straightforward advice for teachers on writing addresses the internal consistency focused on in the EQAO marking scheme in tandem with the value of individual voice:

The writer should:
1. Write frequently.
2. Concentrate on main ideas.
3. Reread what one has written.
4. Organize one's writing.
5. Support claims with supporting details.
6. Use a distinct and recognizable voice. (p. 3)

Maybin (2009) critiques the interpretation of voice as authorial presence as a culturally specific judgment, noting that it may act to disadvantage rather than empower the individual. If to be recognized as a voice on the page requires competently reproducing extant models, graded in terms of adherence to writing conventions, as is suggested in the EQAO essay question marking guide, then authorial presence is recognized through social reproduction. Bourdieu (1991) refers to normalized, standardized language as *legitimate language*, which confers *symbolic power*. The aim of achieving symbolic power through social reproduction is the mission of transmission pedagogy, or *banking* education (Freire, 1970/1998). Voice in this reading is not creative but regurgitative of social competency models.

Bakhtin (1975/1981) distinguishes between and contemplates the interplay of *authoritative discourse*, which refers to "the discourse of tradition, generally acknowledge [*sic*] truths, the official line, the voice of authority" (Landay, 2004, p. 109), and *internally persuasive discourse*, which is "the discourse of our personal beliefs, the ideas that move us, that shape us and create the stories we tell ourselves about the world and who we are" (Landay, 2004, p. 109). *Authoritative discourse* reflects Bourdieu's (1991) *legitimate language*: sanitized, economically viable and nationally standardized, describing what the EQAO favors in its essay-marking scheme; *internally persuasive discourse* describes Graves' (1983) somewhat romantic notion of voice as the egocentric driving force behind individual expression.

Though the educational value of developing a coherent and identifiable authorial voice seems intuitive, this may not be officially recognized as authorial, or authoritative, if marking rubrics for conservative formal assessment systems are to be attended to. The downfall of this is abandonment of originality and creativity in favor of social and cultural reproduction in the language classroom. This is not the emancipatory self-discovery through multilingual voices that our project envisions. But efficient negotiation of authoritative discourse must be part of language competencies, too.

Voice is, thus, subtle and complex, navigating a political-cultural tension, referring to past utterances and anticipating future responses. The development of voice is the development of a strategic capacity, not a singular, simple or neutral proficiency. To achieve a personal yet recognized authorial presence on the page demands a polyphonous range, shaped by context, purpose and culture.

The implications of this complexity go two ways. How do we teach literacy as culturally complex, politically strategic, expressively competent polyphony? Moreover, how do we encourage the imprint of ego-driven authorial voice on the sanitized, standardized prose desired in authoritative discourse—and tests of language and literacy competency?

Representative Point of View: Being Heard

Voice as representational point of view refers to political participation and the concomitant development of agency. Flutter (2007) promotes the development of student voice as a strategic mechanism for agentive educational participation:

> Pupil voice can be seen as nested within the broader principle of pupil participation, a term which embraces strategies that offer pupils opportunities for active involvement in decision-making within their schools. The basic premise of "pupil voice" is that listening and responding to what pupils say about their experiences as learners can be a powerful tool in helping teachers to investigate and improve their own practice. (p. 344)

Delpit (1988, 1995) applies voice to the context of racially representative political participation in American classrooms, with the mission of "identifying and giving voice to alternative world views" (Delpit, 1988, p. 282).

She grounds the concept of voice in racial politics and the culture of power that has unstated rules validating participation in public learning spaces. Being denied access to public participation is seen as political invalidation that is tantamount to silencing.

Lo Bianco (2001) points out that language policies in state texts silence as well as give voice. Freire's (1970/1998) agenda to release and develop the voices of students towards agency and self-realization developed in response to classroom learning as the disempowering reproduction of colonial discourse. His approach was a political dialectic, encapsulated in the title of his well-known book: *Pedagogy of the Oppressed.*

Spivak (1988), writing on the politics of interpretation, cautions that ideological agendas may advance generalities that exclude or appropriate homogeneous notions (e.g., of women). This is a critique of voice as representational point of view that Maybin (2009) also makes: there is a neutralizing, homogenizing tendency in sweeping political statements on group identity. The resolution to silencing may, thus, take the form of tokenism and manipulation rather than fundamental change in dominant group values.

Nonetheless, the politics of dominance and exclusion provide an important backdrop to considerations of voice in contexts of cultural and linguistic heterogeneity. In the linguistically plural classroom, cultural diversity disintegrates too easily into symbolic tokenism (e.g., the term *allophone* is commonly used in Canadian publications on official bilingualism as a blanket category for those who speak neither English nor French as a mother tongue[3]), and the languages and knowledge children bring to the classroom become marginalized, supplanted by the *legitimate language* (Bourdieu, 1991), which is precisely the agenda of ESL, and of tests such as the OSSLT. This marginalization is politically implemented, difference sinking under the dominant political voice that confers symbolic power.

Giroux (2000), in discussing critical multiculturalism, asks "who has ownership over the conditions for the production of knowledge" (p. 62). In our context, political notions of *Canadian identity* impose a colonially manufactured identity thread through essay questions in official language and literacy assessment instruments. Santa Ana (2004) describes the linguistic ideology that oppresses multilingual children in American classrooms as being as old as colonialism itself, embodying a Eurocentric project of supremacist racism that denies indigenous ways of knowing—and speaking.

Voice in the context of political participation may be more recognizable not as representative point of view, but as silencing. But gaining a political voice only breaks the surface of the status quo and the language expectations underpinning it. How do we engender tolerance for developing voices, nonstandard voices, polyphony? How—and what—can we learn about expression and legitimacy from these voices in development?

Capacity for Expression: Being Functional

Blommaert (2005) states, very practically, "Voice stands for the ways in which people manage to make themselves understood or fail to do so" (p. 4). Hymes (1996) in considering linguistic competence in the social context of the United States identifies two kinds of freedom addressing linguistic inequality and discrimination: freedom to use language in whatever form, and freedom to explore it imaginatively. He compounds these freedoms in a concept of *voice* as: "freedom to have one's voice heard, and freedom to develop a voice worth hearing" (p. 64). Blommaert (2005), following in this tradition, frames voice functionally as the "capacity to generate an uptake of one's words as close as possible to one's desired contextualisation" (p. 68). Hymes (1996) asks big social questions around functional language:

> What counts as a language?
> What counts as a language problem?
> What counts as proper use of language?
> What counts as a contribution (about language) to linguistics, to soci-
> ology, etc.?
> What will count in changing the above? (p. 65)

Voice in this view is socially indexical: the speaker reveals and wields (or not) social mastery through voice, bringing the facilitating efforts of education into focus. However, an interesting educational paradox is revealed: Whose voice is taught if social navigability is the aim? Is a personal voice educationally developed, as in the Freirean agenda, or is access to the dominant voice demystified and shared?

Speaking Consciousness: Being and Becoming in Social Context

> *The organizing center of any utterance, of any experience is not within but outside—in the social milieu surrounding the individual being.* (Vološinov, 1929/1973, p. 93)

Interpretations of voice as individually constructed, culturally appropriated or silenced, or developed within or against sedimented historical expectations view language as (reasonably) socially stable. Vološinov (1929/1973), though, conceives of the word as "*the product of the reciprocal relationship between speaker and listener, addresser and addressee*" (p. 86). Bakhtin (1975/1981) explains:

> Language, for the individual consciousness, lies on the borderline between oneself and the other. The word in language is half someone else's. It becomes "one's own" only when the speaker populates it with his own intention, his own accent, when he appropriates the word, adapting it

to his own semantic and expressive intention. Prior to this moment of appropriation, the word does not exist in a neutral and impersonal language . . . but rather it exists in other people's mouths, in other people's contexts, serving other people's intentions: it is from there that one must take the word, and make it one's own. (pp. 293–294)

The view that voice is dialogically constituted provides another lens through which to examine authorial representations of voice: as the voice examined for logic and coherence, which the EQAO is grading (though bereft of personality), developed with the rhetorical control functional approaches to voice aspire to. Language, as speaking consciousness, is socially multilayered. The rigidity—or perhaps absence—of expressive style recognized in the OSSLT marking guide speaks to a standardized language—what Bourdieu (1991) calls *legitimate language*—which is "impersonal and anonymous like the official uses it has to serve" (p. 48). Holquist (1981), clarifying the alterity in language that Bakhtin addresses, explains:

There is no such thing as a "general language," a language that is spoken by a general voice, that may be divorced from a specific saying, which is charged with particular overtones. Language, when it *means*, is somebody talking to somebody else, even when that someone else is one's own inner addressee. (Introduction, p. xxi)

Maybin (2009) points out that dialogicality is bidirectional, extending inwards as listening, and outwards in speech communion, transforming and reaccenting voices in the process. This is ideally what learning is. As Bakhtin (1975/1981) puts it, "Understanding and response are dialectically merged and mutually condition each other; one is impossible without the other" (p. 282).

Heteroglossia and Polyglossia

Language in the Bakhtinian view is complexly layered with the intentions of all members in the speech community, thus:

there are no "neutral" words and forms—words and forms that can belong to "no one"; language has been completely taken over, shot through with intentions and accents. For any individual consciousness living in it, language is not an abstract system of normative forms but rather a concrete heteroglot conception of the world. (Bakhtin, 1975/1981, p. 293)

As Holquist (1981) explains, context takes primacy over text: "All utterances are heteroglot in that they are functions of a matrix of forces practically impossible to recoup, and therefore impossible to resolve" (p. 428).

A standard national language is, in Bakhtin's (1975/1981) view, a centralized verbal-ideological system, stripped of the layered social realities of its speakers. This notion of a stylistically impoverished language is mirrored in Bourdieu's (1991) description of the sterile legitimate language; and it responds to those whose interpretation of voice as political representation addresses real people who feel politically silenced because they speak everyday, unsanitized language.

The utterance in a heteroglossic world cannot be monologic; it is dialogic: an act of co-authorship. The *correct form* of conventional language tested in the OSSLT essay question is impoverished and unimaginative, and though it feeds political access aims, it offers only its own internal logic, and does not tap the thought system of the speaker-writer. Heteroglossia invites social argumentation in a plurality of voices; it imagines language as elastic and pliable, inviting depth, growth and artistic license through hybrid interpolation.

But what are the spaces available to a social unit functioning in a multiplicity of languages? Bakhtin applies the term *polyglossia* to a number of languages; *heteroglossia*, to social and stylistic variation. In the metropolitan cities of the 21st century we work within, diversity is normality. Our classrooms are culturally plural and linguistically global. Furthermore, the world we teach and reside in has a digital portal connecting and extending us in ways that hybridize language and introduce other communicative modalities.

The heteroglossic nature of the contemporary classroom has grown more complex: we work with a panorama of communicative possibilities that extend to globally transplanted languages and new semiotic modalities. The notion of supporting the developing voices of children, always ideologically complex, is now a much more challenging venture. How do we work supportively with voice in a polyglot context? In a multimodal context? How is voice projected in other modes? What and where is individual voice in collaborative and remixed texts where authorship has dissolved into a mixture of voices?

DEVELOPING SPACES FOR MULTILINGUALISM IN THE CLASSROOM

In discussing conceptions of academic language and the kinds of academic language we can teach in school, Valdés (2004) queries "the voices available to second language learners in both their communities and their schools" (p. 67), noting that "what is missing from a number of professional and scholarly discussions focusing on academic language is a Bakhtinian view of the types and range of experiences and interactions that must surround minority youngsters if they are to acquire the kinds of language proficiencies considered desirable by educational institutions." (p. 67)

This view is important: children must recognize and be capable of participation with an enabling social voice. At the same time, this aim has historically involved social reproduction with concomitant cultural and linguistic erasure, constituting oppressive and constraining rather than liberating and empowering education. Our project's express aim was to collaboratively create sound multiliteracies practices that invited multicultural perspectives, and supported multilingual acquisition and maintenance in a broad conception of literacy. There was no question but that acquisition and ability to fluently navigate the majority voice, academic English, was a critical aim—but not under conditions of erasure (see Ibrahim, 2004, 2008). The wealth of languages that constituted the contemporary classroom was a benefit: a gift of our diasporic population. This gift gave our school, tucked into a northwestern corner of quasi-industrial Toronto, a passkey to the whole world. I was not going to throw it away.

Parents, though, do not always understand that they might be doing just this. As the principal of JPS recounts:

> I think sometimes [parents] think they should be teaching their children English, and we've been really trying to get the message across—[your home language] is a gift you have to give your children. We want you to give this gift, and we will give them the gift of English, but you give them the gift of your language. And because of that, we've opened our doors to international languages after school, and the teachers have opened the classrooms to that. With respect to the parents, they were educated in different countries. So their expectations as to what they believe is good education can be somewhat different than ours. (C. Paige, personal communication, February 8, 2010)

Good intentions notwithstanding, we had walked into a gulf between inviting languages into the classroom and implementing meaningful multilingualism in literacy education. The problems were multiple: children's (and parents') reticence to offer their home language use as relevant to schooling, which behind brick walls was officially (and punitively in terms of assessment) channeled into English; difficulty in locating reference sources for all languages in a classroom that included uncommon and creolized languages; utilizing technology for translation which did not work according to plan; and teachers' problems incorporating languages—in which they had no proficiency—in multilingual texts, both written and programmed. To support a language that is resource poor in society requires ingenuity. Singh (2009), in discussing language policy and education in South Africa, isolates how easily lost in translation supporting minority languages can be in the classroom despite the good intentions of official policy. She makes the point that "the languages of instruction should facilitate effective educational development and not obstruct it" (p. 281).

We began the planning phase of the project where teachers considered what narratives they would use, to what curricular purposes, and how they could involve the languages of the community in the classroom. I took responsibility for the theoretical rationale and support to stimulate ideas on inviting classroom languages into the classroom, but the mobilization of those ideas rested on teachers' ingenuity and practical opportunities. Our beginning phase offered past models which illustrated how multiple voices could be distributed over soundtracks and modes of expression, and asked teachers to think about story, genre, technology-modality, languages and scheduling, framed around:

1. the story and ideas for children's creative textual reinterpretations:
   a. the retelling process involved,
   b. the learning development to accomplish this process;
2. the languages to be involved, specifically:
   a. origins of the focus languages:
      i. home,
      ii. community,
      iii. class membership,
      iv. tied to story project,
      v. anything we can translate with resources available;
   b. where the focus languages enter the story rewriting process:
      i. the story introduction stage (translation from X),
      ii. the creation stage (bilingual or trilingual development),
      iii. the finished text stage (translation into X);
   c. access to language support for bi- or multilingual story rewriting process:
      i. locate bi- or multilingual story,
      ii. use parents, volunteers at school or cross-age groups to help translate story while rewriting it:
         1. teachers and staff members at school,
         2. after-school international language teachers,
      iii. use children, parents, volunteers or translators available through online connections to translate children's rewritten stories:
         1. develop partnering possibilities with schools in other countries;
      iv. spiral stories from L1 into English, rewrite, translate back into L2 and others;
3. supplies and technological assistance needed.

We invited in speakers to discuss multilingualism in the community, how the community could be tapped for multilingual resources, how the Ontario school system treats languages in and after school, and ESL recognition and support. The real work was then put into the teachers' hands.

Mike with Shirley and Helen: *The Little Red Hen*, Kindergarten

The Berlin Wall is gone but we still have so many walls here. (personal communication, Mike Zentena, June 28, 2007)

Mike was uneasy about two aspects of our experimental multiliteracies project. Firstly, he was unsure of how to implement *technology* in a way that made sense to his style of kindergarten teaching and did not intrude into pedagogical planning as something extra he had to think about. Certainly seeing technology as an add-on was anathema to our thinking about communicative modalities opening up new pedagogical possibilities. *Technology*, in our understanding, facilitated narrative expression and linguistic inclusion; it was not a hindrance. New (and old) technologies were woven into educational vistas to extend teaching and learning capabilities—indeed, to extend the borders of the classroom itself. But Mike's concern was important; it stumped him where I envisaged a license to be creative. This provided one of what became several moments that propelled us into ensuring that each rewriting project was conceptualized, developed and conducted collaboratively. At this point we were cooperatively planning and troubleshooting projects, but most projects were still being taught/explored solo by teachers in their own classrooms.

Secondly, Mike was of the opinion that what we were aspiring to—creating a culturally and linguistically inclusive classroom that welcomed children's home languages into formal learning—should be how things are done in school, not just the objective of an experimental project. With this, I could not agree more, but to convince policy makers, school administrators and external testing bodies to change their ideology required models and evidence of success from the kind of microcosmic explorations in which we were engaged. To Mike, who received children in their first year of formal schooling, the classroom needed to be a welcoming environment, not one of exclusion. Acknowledging and finding accommodating spaces for the real lives of children in the classroom was an aim, not a problem to be off-loaded onto parents, as the curriculum does in assuming parents naturally prepare their children for school by reading stories to them (in English), modeling writing in their own activities (which occur during children's waking hours) and providing coloring books and other such literacy socialization materials (that cost money). Parenting style, free time, cultural socialization and financial implications notwithstanding, school is an idealized institution that few new immigrants to the country know much about. Many are afraid of school and of teachers, having suffered failure, corporal punishment or exclusion in their own schooling in other countries. Many immigrants elected to bring their families to Canada so their children would have a better life. This long journey towards success begins in the school system.

The story project Mike created was motivated by his desire to make the kindergarten class a welcoming introduction to formal schooling. In his view this introduction included embracing the languages used in the community, and he was concerned with working constructively with social and cultural differences that motivated moments of bullying in his classroom. One of his ideas was to include parents in cooking or baking activities at school, so they could narrate the processing of foods that were familiar to them. This he saw in relation to the teasing children received over lunches that were perceived as different. As Mike put it, he wanted to address the issue of the ethnic foods kids brought to eat at school, which may not always be well received by other children.[4]

The population of JPS is highly culturally diverse; two thirds of the children attending JPS in any one year speak a language other than English in the home. Though this statistic varies slightly from one yearly intake to another, the community is characterized by high cultural and linguistic density, and low socioeconomic status; over 90% of parents are recent migrants to the country, not long-settled Canadian citizens whose ancestors, of no matter what cultural origins, have been here for generations. Some children may speak little or no English on school entrance.

With this in mind, Mike wanted to change the typically negative reactions of children to those who did not know enough English to participate actively in class. Believing strongly in equity, he was appalled at the tendency of children to point and laugh at those using a community language in school spaces, taunting, "you don't even know English!" Following Shiva's practice of encouraging children to answer the roll call in their home language, he implemented places for multiple bilingualisms in his class. He encouraged comparative learning, asking, "How do you count to ten in your language?" In short order, he had changed the culture of his classroom vis-à-vis difference from one of mockery to pride, instituted a parent-child link in schoolwork, and encouraged a culture of inquisitive learning. Children pestered their parents and grandparents to teach them how to count to ten in their home languages, and excitedly recited their numbers in a panorama of languages to the class.

Mike's actions worked to legitimate polyglossia in small classroom polylogues, rendering language diversity a facet of normal human communication that was welcomed in the space of the classroom, and overwriting the limitations of the normative code, while not negating it. Kids became curious about others' languages, and proud to show off their own. In this way, being able to use a language other than English or French added to children's cultural capital; and using their "own languages" was received by classmates with enlightened tolerance rather than mockery.

Kindergarten classes in Ontario have educational assistants (EAs) who help the teacher to cope with high needs learners and provide on-the-ground support for very young children. Mike had two assistants in his class. Like the teachers in the school, many educational assistants and volunteers were, themselves, of diverse ethnic backgrounds. In Mike's class, where the children were beginning to use their languages in ways that demonstrated competencies, reinforced their learning in English and created a culture of language awareness and anti-racism through active curiosity, Mike and his EAs were using English. He decided that they could also contribute their language knowledge to the class.

The story Mike chose to use was *The Little Red Hen*, which uses repetitive language in dialogue format, and illustrates procedure in food production. He taught the story as a hands-on project: the children added pictorially to an expanding interactive word wall depicting the story, pinning up the cat, dog and pig in the appropriate places. The EAs added to the growing narrative, using their languages both orally and in writing: Cantonese and Vietnamese. *The Little Red Hen* grew into a trilingual story in English, Chinese and Vietnamese, with the language contributions of the EAs, who, like many of the children, had learned English subsequent to their first language. The trilingual story was displayed on an interactive felt board as a multilingual word wall, the narrative pinned semantically into place with the craft pictures added by the children (see Figure 6.1).

Mike explains how important it is for children to be exposed to language visually so they can link the spoken and written word. His multilingual word wall was visually alive with three languages, each of which looked and sounded different though all told the same story. The entry point to the story for individual children in the class could have been any of these languages and/or the visuals place-holding the story line. Mike videotaped

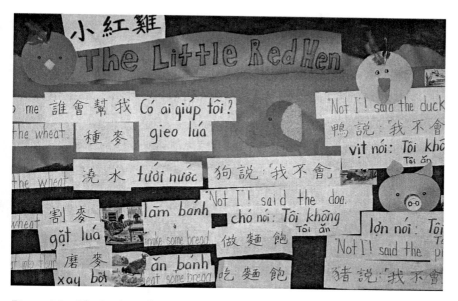

Figure 6.1 The Little Red Hen multilingual word wall.

the children learning and reciting the story in all language versions—which amounted to four or more languages for some of the children who spoke one or more languages other than the three used in the word wall. His videos attest to children's overwhelming enthusiasm and revelry in learning this story, so richly detailed on the multilingual word wall.

Through this project the children in Mike's kindergarten learned interest, pride and tolerance of multilingualism. They learned that different languages sound and look different when they tell the same story. They learned that English is one way of speaking, and the Roman alphabet is one way of writing, but that there are other languages, and these contribute rather than deduct from what children (and adults) know. They learned about the narrative unfolding of a story.

There were three other educational spin-offs of this project in three different directions. *The Little Red Hen* wants to communally bake bread, a staple food, and, as the story relates, she calls for help in order to do this. One follow-up to this story of procedural food preparation invited parents' participation in their children's learning by coming in to cook. This activity incorporated Mike's idea of extending anti-bullying and anti-racism to understanding and appreciating the ethnic foods that children bring to school in their lunch boxes.

A second effect of the project was that parents became less afraid to enter the school and the classroom. Some had been invited to demonstrate preparation of the foods they ate. Others waiting to pick up their children were curious about the languages on the felt board that were outside their expectations of textbook English performance, and welcomed difference, no matter whether the languages were familiar to them or not. Instead of lurking in the shadows, waiting for their children after school, they entered the classroom, curious and interested in the multilingual representation.

Thirdly, as Mike's knowledge about children's home languages built incrementally with increasing awareness following the EAs' multilingual contributions, he was spurred to think about his own ancestral language: Italian. He took the lesson of language pride home to his three young children, and asked his parents to use only Italian with their grandchildren.

The development of voice in Mike's kindergarten classroom, thus included the development of what might be thought of as the right to have an authorial or vocal presence in multiple languages, which incurs political representation in terms of script visibility, and a scaffolded learning of how to express oneself: grammatically in English, and representationally in languages that are not shared with others. It diminished silencing, and conferred the right to pride in language knowledge, which was a lesson in both language awareness and anti-racism for all. Children learned not only school-sanctioned ways with words, but ways of expression that welcomed the community into the classroom. Heteroglossia in this context reached into other language codes and contexts that were given legitimacy in the classroom. In this way, anticipation of textbook English unyieldingly trumping all as the legitimate language of the classroom, and of political participation, was tempered.

This is kindergarten where language was being celebrated and shared for linguistic awareness and anti-racist learning. How could this attitude and these practices toward language inclusion be incorporated in project-based learning in the higher grades where defined proficiencies in language and literacy learning are under a microscope, and successful performance in narrowly defined English language *skills* is essential to demonstrate curricular learning?

Rhea With Brian: *Ananse's Feast,* Grade 4/5 Special Education

Rhea's involvement in our multiliteracies group made me very aware of the complexity of children's learning issues in the classroom: Rhea is the special education teacher. As I had discovered in 2003, during my ethnographic study of what it meant to successfully acquire literacy in the JPS context, learning problems can be buried under convenient labels. Children labeled ESL are expected to have difficulties with textual English. However, their problems communicating in English can mask deeper and more complex learning problems. Most of the children in Rhea's pull-out special education class were at some stage of English language learning in addition to suffering multiple, and often compound, learning difficulties.

Rhea, a fearless and imaginative educator, wanted to involve her small Grade 4/5 special education group in the multiliteracies venture. She wanted to tackle the issue of multilingualism from an unorthodox perspective: the acknowledgment and use of nonstandard creolized languages in the classroom. This is a salient issue in the TDSB which welcomes into the school system at all levels significant numbers of children from Caribbean countries whose Englishes span a range of contested creolized vernaculars. Labeling what speakers consider a local variety of English a Creole is a delicate proposition: parents assume they speak *bad English*, not understanding that it is, in fact, *good Creole*. Typically, they understand school as a place for chastisement about the language they speak in informal contexts. As Cooper (2010) explains:

> Most Jamaicans can't easily read and write in our mother tongue. Call it broken English, dialect, patois, patwa, Creole, Jamaican Creole or just plain Jamaican. It doesn't make a difference. As the poet Mutabaruka puts it so wittily, "the language we talk, we can't write; and the language we write, we can't talk." (para.1)

Learning English as a textbook language, hardly the stuff of voice at the level of emancipated language expression, is crucial to children who speak a nonstandard tongue that few recognize as valid in its own right. The Caribbean Creoles used by diasporic communities in Toronto are, by and large, vernaculars, though Jamaican Patwa has a growing literature by artists such as Louise Bennett (viz., Miss Lou), a much-loved poet who lived in Toronto for many years until her recent death.[5] Without access to English as a second dialect assistance in schools, Creole-speaking children have difficulties expressing themselves in *standard English*, particularly in writing. Consequently, they are pulled out, kept back and eventually pushed out of school when teachers fail to understand and augment their language facility. Creole speakers become all too easily marginalized in their educational efforts and fall into unhelpful stereotypes.

We had a powerful ally on our side: Rhea is an experienced specialist teacher who holds a Master's degree, and is herself a speaker of a Caribbean creolized vernacular. It is important to recognize that there is no pan-Caribbean Creole; the island countries of the Caribbean are home to a number of syncretic, creolized languages with European language superstrates (e.g., English, French, Dutch), the historical legacy of colonial slave-trading. Rhea's home language is from Trinidad. Patwa, also known as Jamaican Creole, which is commonly spoken in the Toronto area, though manifesting similarities, is a different language (or more accurately, set of language varieties along a creole continuum) than Trinidadian Creole, Guyanese Creole, Lesser Antillean Creoles and so forth.

Children who speak creolized Englishes are often ashamed of their home languages, which is a racist legacy of colonial education. Whereas children in a classroom who speak major languages, such as Russian, Spanish, Hindi or Arabic, can lay claim to traditions of distinguished literary, philosophical and scientific thought, Creole speakers speak language varieties that may not have recognition beyond the local marketplace, as is evident in schools, where Creole speakers are misunderstood and marginalized. These children are failed by the system; they receive inadequate assistance in acquiring a version of English deemed legitimate for participation in education. In this way, they are silenced, stripped of their voice.

Rhea's story selection and project planning spoke eloquently to this situation. She chose a story from a folk tradition originating in West Africa that is popular in the Caribbean: an *Ananse* (variously known as *Anancy*, *Anansi*) folktale, featuring the loveable Ghanaian trickster, Ananse the spider. She based the class multimodal retelling on the written version, *Ananse's Feast: An Ashanti Tale* (Mollel, 1997). The story was retold in two varieties of English: textbook English by the children, and Trinidadian (Creole) by the teacher.

Ananse is known for his cunning, which tips into self-serving greed that is exposed to become his undoing. The Ananse fables teach through a moral, though the tradition is not heavy-handed, and Ananse retains his likeability. In Rhea's teaching of *Ananse's Feast*, the children stay faithful to the tropical foods eaten at Ananse's and Crab's tables, though the meals are described differently in English and in Trinidadian. The story has Ananse inviting Crab to dinner on the beach, but as Crab must crawl through the sand to reach Ananse's table, he is perennially sent back to the sea to wash his claws, a polite and healthful act before eating. The endless loop of washing and then dirtying his claws to get to the table results in Ananse eating all the food himself. However, Crab gets his come-uppance given the opportunity to reciprocate, and he extends a similarly disingenuous invitation to come for dinner at his place under the sea. To sink down to the table, Ananse needs to put rocks in his pockets. Crab promptly invites Ananse to take off his jacket before dining, which results in a quick trip back to the surface for Ananse, who bobs up and down help-lessly fighting his natural buoyancy until Crab has eaten the whole meal himself. The story is light-hearted but morally clear: greedy self-serving gets you neither friends nor food. Be genuine, honorable and considerate in your invitations.

The multimodal retelling of *Ananse's Feast* was an academic task that began with the grueling job of helping children with language difficulties to write in English. The children learned the story, which was a long and arduous procedure given their struggles with language, and they rewrote it, not in adapted form, but using textbook English. They performed the story using clay figures they had made themselves (see Figure 6.2), and captured the performed retelling as a claymation. They added a reggae soundtrack, and narrated the story, taking turns so each student read a portion of the script.

Rhea describes the writing process as labored: learners with special needs are not independent in their writing and they need a great deal of scaffolding. She wrestled with the dual-edged benefits and challenges of story repetition, which bordered on becoming boring through repeated exposure. Yet children with special learning needs require repetition to gain access to a text. Rereading, rewriting and practicing their dramatic script was important.

The technological dimension provided another steep learning curve. Brian, an educational assistant at JPS who is a technical whiz (and who also has an ancestral Caribbean background as an Indo-Guyanese Cana-dian), facilitated in Rhea's project helping children to engage other design factors available to them in multimodal learning, such as visual depiction of character and scenery, and musical soundtrack. As Rhea explains, chil-dren may have expressive strengths in art, drama and even programming that are lost in the unwavering focus on alphabetic expression in English, in which they universally do poorly. With a multimodal project, they had other avenues for expression in which they could be successful, and which could be individually contributed to the group project.

In a wonderful twist on our aim of inviting community languages into the classroom, Rhea told the children's rewritten story in Trinidadian (Cre-ole), while the children narrated the story in the language they struggled so hard to learn: *standard English*. The finished iDVD provided two versions of the retold story in comparative Englishes.

Figure 6.2   Preparation for the bilingual claymation of *Ananse's Feast*.

Rhea had also planned to include a Jamaican Patwa retelling of the *Ananse* story by a community member. However, this proved to be a delicate undertaking that met with resistance from Jamaican community members. In hindsight, this is unsurprising. Schools and officialdom function in English in Jamaica, though most Jamaicans are native speakers of Patwa who learn English in school (Devonish & Harry, 2004). Schools in Jamaica offer little in the way of systemic language support to bridge the low varieties of Jamaican Patwa native to Jamaicans, and the high variety of Jamaican English required for literate participation in Jamaican society. But we were no further ahead in Toronto; bringing language variation into discussions about multilingualism in such a way that it does not diminish community language knowledge remains an important avenue for research and development.

Using Trinidadian in the project had political and personal implications for the teacher as well as the children. The experience of hearing a creolized language used by a teacher in the school system validated the status of a Caribbean vernacular as a bona fide language. But Rhea, like Mike, also had an intense personal reaction. Having tried out her story version with her family at home to get their opinions, she met with rave reviews. But her youngest child made a trenchant observation, asking why she reserved her use of Trinidadian at home for punishment? Why didn't she use it for other kinds of talk with them, too?

In a follow-up workshop, Rhea related this moment, which caused her to reflect deeply on her own language use in the home. She explained that the project had opened her eyes to the importance of using her ancestral language with her own children. As she put it: "Knowing the importance of the first language and actually living it were different experiences and really helped me understand the importance of my other language."

Voice in this project was an interesting mélange of finding and learning the standard, sanitized language of textbooks and tests, which was a significant challenge for children with multiple learning difficulties compounded with limited knowledge of English, and pairing it with a vernacular language that had contextual authenticity. The layering of languages, including a Creole that verges on the subversive in school spaces, gave children two versions of the same story: one sanctioned, the other, more intimate and nonthreatening.

Special education means just that: each child has particular needs. The multimodal character of the project provided expressive media for children who are marginalized by a logocentric system. Nonlinguistic semiotic resources are not acknowledged in the alphabetic focus of modern literacy education, which means that children with diagnosed learning challenges that complicate encoding and decoding language are doomed to repetitive remedial education to attain a reading level that comes much more easily to others. But a multimodal project allows alternative routes for expression, which broadens the dimensions of voice beyond linguistic limits.

Using and combining different expressive media provided a small group of children with varied problems and talents with opportunities for distributing learning. As Gee (2004a) explains, "A team can behave smarter than any individual in it by pooling and distributing knowledge (p. 284). Distributing learning among group members, who were individually marked as slow learners, facilitated a collective success that validated their work. After seeing the finished bilingual movie, one child exclaimed, "Now I really like my story!"

MOVING FORWARD

This chapter took up the issues of creating dialogic spaces for learning and investigating concepts of voice. Our project-based orientation to language and literacy education attempted to cut across the vertical boundaries of disciplinary timetabling, where English, mathematics, social studies and so forth are approached as separate studies, to experiment with language inclusion in retold multimodal narratives. In the elementary scenario, where the classroom teacher is a generalist, teachers creatively merged time periods for longer stretches of project work. However, the participating specialist teachers (e.g., music, French as a second language), who are itinerant, were less able to contribute to project-based learning because of timetabling constraints. This was a problem.

We found that teachers needed more freedom in timetabling to collaborate and conduct interdisciplinary projects. In Ontario, we do not have blocks of time designated for project building. However, such an infrastructure has been piloted and implemented in two European countries: Portugal and Greece. In Portugal, the *Area-Escola* (A-E) is "an emerging school arena for the exercise of the different school attributions and functions—cooperative teaching, curriculum development, design of assessment instruments to monitor and improve student performance, and development of school/community relationships" (Amaro, 2000, p. 3). The A-E aims to develop connections between school, community and students' social and personal development by promoting interdisciplinarity in project work. Following the Portuguese example, Greece implemented a similar infrastructure reform:

> The Flexible Zone is a two hours [*sic*] curricular innovation introduced with the Cross-Curriculum approach where students and teachers can design, develop and implement projects using cooperative, problem-solving and synergistic methodologies with themes, issues and problems of everyday life that interest them. (Spinthourakis, Karatzia-Stavlioti, Lempesi & Papadimitriou, 2007, p. 2)

The teachers found it important to customize the timetable to maximize opportunities for students to plan, prepare and perform their projects; in effect, they created their own versions of a *flexible zone* in the teaching day. Their pedagogical revisions tore the fabric of the spatially and temporally packaged curriculum, fulfilling Sawyer's (2006) dictum that "teaching for the innovation economy must be improvisational, because if the classroom is scripted and overly directed by the teacher, students cannot co-construct their own knowledge" (p. 44).

Contemporary knowledge-building approaches to education in the digital age focus on problem-solving using diverse resources, including, prominently, digital mediation, distributed learning models and dialogic learning creatively orchestrated by the teacher (Bereiter & Scardamalia, 2000; Sawyer, 2006, 2008). Teachers' innovations in developing project-oriented multimodal literacy education demonstrated the depth of their professional knowledge and breadth of their creativity and organizational experience, which is undervalued and underutilized in transmission approaches to education.

Creating the conditions for dialogic learning in the linguistically het-erogeneous classroom provoked questions about the construction of voice in a multilingual, multimodal classroom. I envisioned voice in our project as polyphonous and multimedial, multilingual and multimodal, individual and collaborative: valued in variation. But children have to arrive at that complex point. So do teachers, parents, test makers, curriculum writers and policy makers. We are still a long way off from this enlightened point.

Conceptions of *voice* in the literature on language education reveal a wide range of interpretations, spanning expressive footprint, viewed in terms of authorial presence, though interpretable in the current communicative cli-mate into a variety of modes; political representation, which, though tend-ing to overgeneralization, speaks to gaps and negation in being heard; being able to communicate, which demands at some level social responsibility in education and in valuing participation; and lastly, speaking consciousness that understands speech as building on and contributing to the social con-struction of ideologically laden language in heteroglossic space.

Heteroglossic interfaces in speaking consciousness are learning spaces: this is what dialogic learning illuminates. But students need to have con-trol of a recognizable voice to access this learning. How do we get there? And how do we make this a conversation that does not restrict itself to English?

English is the voice needed for succeeding in school. Most students at JPS are learners of English, which is chronically sanitized in school, built to meet the bland middle ground of test standards, aspiring to competence in the use of *legitimate language* (Bourdieu, 1991), which is all but devoid of individual interpretation, as evidenced in test-marking schemes, such as the OSSLT essay rubric. Though developing voice requires gaining access to the language that codes political access and social mobility, it does not require abandoning the rich multitongued social existence of life. But how do we get educators and policy makers to see this? Indeed how do we get parents to understand this?

Mike and Rhea planned multimodal projects that invited the languages of the school and community into their classrooms in imaginative ways, introducing to kindergarten children a folktale taught in three languages, and producing in a junior special education class a multimodal folktale in two varieties of English. They brought together the languages of the home and the school, the page and the screen, and multiple modes of expression. In so doing, they created spaces in which students could participate col-laboratively in learning: spaces that facilitated distributed learning—not all children can count to ten in Vietnamese, but some can; not all children can write fluent English prose, but they are assisted in their narrative writ-ing by those who can. Group learning in this dialogic scenario is distrib-uted among the participants as a patchwork unlike assessed school learning that taps each individual's mastery of each skill. Individual participation in group creation of knowledge is scaffolded by the teacher, and in this case, the educational assistants, to create mini zones of proximal development (Vygotsky, 1934/1986). The knowledge created is not necessarily homogenized; it fits together as puzzle pieces to make a whole.

Our voyage through multilingual projects had brought us to an interesting juncture: we could see how to customize learning, and create projects addressing curricular learning needs that generated interest and personal investment. Our learning community had settled into a recognized aspect of the school infrastructure, and the classroom was extending into the community, and to other schools via digital connection. The ease with which teachers and children were playing with multiple modalities was progressing rapidly, and multimodal interpretations of paper narratives were introducing wonderful embodied approaches to language and literacy learning.

But there were also sticky issues. Children were producing beautiful multilingual stories, but these were still largely created as translations of English. This stimulated numerous questions:

1. How can we support multilingualism in a distributed learning model?
2. How much and how many language/s can be introduced in a given project?
3. What is the potential for language infusion in project building: introduction at the beginning, middle or end of a project? Can we start with a story in another language?

There were also engaging questions emerging about the development of voice in the linguistically diverse, digitally connected classroom:

1. Can student voice be nurtured in multiple languages in the classroom?
2. Can voice be developed in other modes?
3. Can languages be exploited in complementary modalities to nurture polyvocality individually and collectively?

These questions provided plenty of food for thought.

7   Multimodality, Language Inclusion and Third Space

THE LINGUISTICALLY DIVERSE CLASSROOM

Michelle tells me she has 16 different languages in her class of 23 kindergarten children. She confides that few of these languages are familiar (Indo-European) languages, such as French, Italian and German; they include Pashto, Yoruba, Oromo and Laotian as well as more recognizable local languages, such as Jamaican Patwa, Cantonese and Vietnamese. Some of these languages are new to her; this is a testament to the challenges facing teachers in the linguistically heterogeneous classroom. How can one teacher support 16 different languages?

Given the proliferation of languages on earth, language contact, which gives rise to bilingualism and multilingualism, is natural and inevitable. Crystal (1997) states that although less than a quarter of the world's countries officially recognize two or more languages, virtually all nations have some degree of cultural pluralism and, consequently, are multilingual. The urban cosmopolis today is a microcosm of international languages interlaced in political, economic, social and cultural life. Relocated to new urban geographies, transplanted speech communities find new linguistic neighbors, and new patterns of mixing and matching languages across personal connections and community interchanges in digital as well as physical space. As Cope and Kalantzis (2009b) state,

> Diversity is pivotal in today's life-worlds—much more profoundly and pervasively so than the straightforward demographic groupings that underwrote an earlier identity politics of gender, ethnicity, race and disability, which were the forms of politics that first unsettled the hoped-for homogeneity of mass society and the nation-state. (p. 173)

Encountering 16 languages in a single classroom is not a situation unique to this school, this city or this country. A generation ago, Heath (1983) made evident how schooling was geared to children with mainstream, middle-class socialization. Examination of curricular documents illustrates that this assumption has not changed appreciably. The place of multiple languages in the urban classroom complicates the social expectations on which the curriculum, and curricular assessment proceed. In Cookson's published letter towards the improvement of formal education in the United States—one of 15 letters written to President-elect Barack Obama (in Cookson & Welner, 2008), he stresses that American educational values, likewise, remain oblivious to this fundamental diversity:

> At the heart of the American educational dilemma is our unwillingness to embrace diversity and complexity. Our children live at the center of a complex set of social concentric circles: home, neighborhood, school, city or town, state, country, and world. These different environments are not separate but interlinked, permeable, and continuously shifting. Every American family is affected by global change, yet, most of our schools continue to operate in not so splendid isolation. (p. 13)

Language Policy and the Realities of the Multilingual Classroom

> Michael is a nice name. You could call him Michael. (School secretary's suggestion to a Chinese-speaking parent)

In Michelle's polyglot kindergarten, children's lack of familiarity with English is extended even to their own identity. Michelle recounts that children (with Chinese names, in particular) are often given an ad hoc *English* name on school registration. If parents do not have a name in mind, one is suggested by school personnel. This sometimes results in a child not knowing his or her new *English* name. Michelle describes trying to corral her kindergarten children after free play on the playground, repeatedly calling out the name on her register matching a child tearing around the schoolyard, only to discover that he did not recognize it as *his* name.

Patterns of possibility for socially sharing and maintaining minority languages are shaped by policy, both in terms of official statements and as realized in social practices that regulate the environmental welcome to multilingualism (Lo Bianco, 2003). Based on Ruiz's (1984) three political perspectives on linguistic pluralism—language as a *problem*, a *right* or a *resource*—Canada, as the birthplace of French immersion education, appears to take a positive stance, treating language as a fundamental right. Indeed, Canadian research has been foundational in establishing French immersion pedagogies that have become the model for bilingual programs worldwide (see Genesee, 1987; R. K. Johnson & Swain, 1997; Swain & Lapkin, 1981). However, the (monolingual English) classrooms for which French immersion was designed in Montréal, Québec, in the 1960s do not exist in the urban areas that are the context of this research. On closer examination, Canada's treatment of language as a right is extended to two languages only: English and French. Other languages, though welcomed in principle, are treated as a complication in the classroom.

The Canadian official languages policy funnels minority language speakers into an officially bilingual society, though the colonial seal of English and French never adequately recognized the language wealth of a nation founded on lands usurped from Native Peoples speaking a panorama of indigenous languages, and built on the backs of immigrants from source countries as distant as Ukraine and China. The provincial school system in Ontario does offer limited opportunities for assisting in the maintenance of the polyglot culture created by the multiculturalism act, but *international language education* is optional, unevenly available, normally held outside regular school hours, and oriented to those with an ancestral heritage. This system effectively segregates children's home language learning, and limits others' informed exposure to these languages, rather than welcoming them into the classroom where all children can learn about them.

The preschool linguistic socialization that school entrants bring to class is treated as a problem to be eradicated rather than as a resource to be developed. Since nearly half of the children attending school in the TDSB are nonnative speakers of either English or French (TDSB, n.d.), all classrooms are functionally English language learning environments. Cummins (2001b) observed teachers in California covertly coding minority students' identities as subordinate, and endemically pushing acquisition of English over a socially welcoming approach to children's all-around language development. A similar situation occurs in Ontario where curricular resources are focused on teaching only the official languages: English and French (via English), so teachers are effectively engaged in enforced language shift to teach an English medium curriculum to linguistically heterogeneous students. These patterns of language suppression are fixed into place by testing procedures that reinforce social reproduction and calculable, prescriptive expression in English writing.

Language is taught in the Ontario curriculum as oral communication, reading, writing and media literacy (Ministry of Education, 2006), but externally assessed as reading and writing performance (Education Quality and Accountability Office, 2010c), which taps a limited band of written proficiency in English on paper. Though access to the dominant discourse must be assured in school where social and academic competencies will require a strong command of textbook English, this is, at best, a partial competence in an increasingly digitally and culturally connected world. Ignoring cultural and linguistic diversity in the classroom and the digital lives children lead resonates with Marsh's (2006) delineation of how the complex media spaces of preschool children, which connect the global and the local, are virtually ignored at school in the United Kingdom, where the focus remains on "phonics, print-based literacy texts and canonical narratives" (p. 35). This is a classroom treating *diversity as deficit* (Rampton, 2006), with language approached prescriptively, following standards and norms. Moreover, results from consequential literacy tests in Ontario—focused on prescriptive English usage and conservative reading and writing *skills*—are worryingly interpreted as performance indicators that reverberate in political priorities, school funding and teacher allocation to reinforce a traditional understanding of literacy as written English.

The ideological basis of language education in Canada is that we are working with two national languages: English and French. Language and literacy curricula and gate-keeping tests assume that students come to school familiar with dominant *Canadian culture/s*. Not only is this hegemonic stance untrue, unfair and unrealistic in urban classrooms across the country; it is culturally undermining. A conservative approach to language and literacy education as reproduction of sociohistoric dominance, reading diversity as deficit, has no place in the classrooms of the country that first proposed and implemented multiculturalism as political policy. Yet, this is one of the upshots of the external assessment vehicle that determines school literacy success.

Marsh (2005) references how children's abilities to "appropriate, contest or recontextualise curriculum tasks" (p. 23) depend, in large part, on whether the teacher recognizes the unique cultural capital of each child as a positive contribution to literacy learning. Consider this against the school secretary's seemingly helpful suggestion to a Chinese parent on registering her child to spontaneously rename him Michael, devaluing and masking the child's Chinese heritage in a single administrative stroke.

Valuing Multilingualism in the Classroom

It is clear that we should never have abandoned the languages English language learners (ELL) bring into the classroom. Additive bilingualism (Lambert, 1974) and additive multilingualism (Cenoz & Genesee, 1998)—referring to enriching an individual's language repertoire, rather than replacing languages within it—have been shown to provide specific cognitive benefits (Bialystok, 2001; Bialystok, Craik, Kelin & Viswanthan, 2004; Cummins, 1981a, 1991, 2000; W. P. Thomas & Collier, 2001). Beyond cognitive advantages of being bilingual and multilingual vis-à-vis language processing, bilinguals have been found to have a variety of social, cultural, political and even economic advantages, though these are selective rather than blanket benefits (e.g., see Kharkhurin [2010] on bilinguals' nonverbal creativity; Vaillancourt [1996] on economic benefits to bilingual francophones in Canada). Wong Fillmore (1991, 2000) delineates painful social problems in family unity created in scenarios of language shift where additive bilingualism was not pursued. Tse (2001) recounts the speed with which a child can flip from the language of the home to the language of society, leaving parents and intergenerational communication in the wake.

Cummins, Bismilla, Chow et al. (2005) state, "Many teachers understand intuitively that human relationships are at the heart of schooling" (p. 41). Cummins' work on respecting and incorporating linguistic diversity in the classroom calls on teachers—and the political systems regulating their schools—to value children's culturally and linguistically diverse identities for school engagement that is positive, and constructive. Our learning community is committed to this view, and at JPS, teachers are experienced in welcoming children of varied linguistic, social and cultural backgrounds into the social space of the classroom. But teachers report encountering resistance to their efforts to reinforce community languages from parents who fear their children will be left behind because they are English language learners.

Valuing children's language knowledge in the classroom counteracts the sort of destructive advice that still somehow finds its way to immigrant families to switch from the home language to English in order help their children integrate socially and succeed educationally. Baetens Beardsmore (2003) delineates a number of fears about language learning and cultural allegiance that immigrant parents report, and suggests they may transfer these fears onto their children's language learning, and blame bilingualism for complicating their children's language development. In our context in Toronto, not only do parents fear whether their children will learn English fast enough to keep up at school, they trust that proficient use of English (and French) will signal their political belonging.

Hornberger (2001) points out that the nationalistic linking of language and nation is a relatively recent chapter in human history, dating back to the 18th and 19th century establishment of nation-states in Europe and the Americas. Since the 20th century, forces of globalization have dissipated this marginalizing ideology, merging economic and political structures into supranational constellations, and pulling the corners of the globe together in culturally remixed spaces. The urban classroom is now a global village, and teachers are faced with the difficult educational contradiction of responding to the possibilities of their culturally complex classes while answering to limited language and literacy curricula and assessment grounded in dated norms. Many immigrant newcomers are unaware that maintaining the language of the home when it is not a dominant social language is a benefit they provide for their children, not a hindrance. However, despite teachers' best advice to parents to use their home language, parents find covert confirmation of their fears in publically discussed standardized assessment procedures of English language and literacy competencies.

Meisel (2004) makes the case that "the human language faculty has an endowment for multilingualism" (p. 112), arguing, "monolingualism can be regarded as resulting from an impoverished environment where an opportunity to exhaust the potential of the language faculty is not fully developed" (p. 92). Homegrown efforts at language shift fortified by subtractive language learning in the classroom support the child's abandoning a sense of self constructed in and around the home language to take on a new language. The reductive construction of an either-or cultural and linguistic reality is at odds with contemporary hybridity. Decrying the value of home language use devalues multilingualism, which is a demonstrated asset to cognitive development, a support to cultural connections and social breadth, and a boost to economic horizons in the emerging global economy.

It is multilingualism rather than monolingualism that characterizes our world (Crystal, 1997). Languages open doors; limited linguistic proficiencies close them. Focusing on one or two national languages is an inadequate educational response to a multilingual world. But where are spaces for language inclusion to be carved in the linguistically diverse classroom where teachers are struggling with children's variable language and social knowledge under the pressures of a packed curriculum that will be externally assessed against conservative standards? How and where can welcoming spaces be created that will supersede the nationally conceived framework of language and literacy competence as English and French with the rest of them fitting in somehow?

Shifting Frontiers

Globalization is multidirectional, opening spaces for individual, social, cultural, economic and political connections with the larger world while merging grounded cultures in urban spaces. This is the glocal (R. Robertson, 1992, 1995)—the local and the global in synergetic interaction. As Jenkins (2004) demonstrates, children in urban contexts are socialized into glocal communities of increasing cultural and communicational connectivity, complexity and convergence. Eaton (2010) describes the language classroom of the children of today as:

> vastly different from that of the mid- to late twentieth century. The focus is no longer on grammar, memorization and learning from rote, but rather using language and cultural knowledge as a means to connect to others around the globe. Geographical and physical boundaries are being transcended by technology as students learn to reach out to the world around them, using their language and cultural skills to facilitate the connections they are eager to make. (p. 16)

The communicative technologies of today have superseded the industrial technologies of fixed print moving us into ever more democratic access to information and away from standardization, centralization and deficit learning models. Social memory is increasingly being constructed in globally networked patterns, not in confining national molds. But the question of how a single teacher can manage cultural and linguistic inclusion in classrooms of 16 mutually unintelligible languages remains.

Indeed, supporting 16 different languages in a single classroom would appear to be a patently ridiculous proposal. The inevitable political response to supporting minority languages in school classrooms is to boil all the languages down to English for administrative ease. Complexity is expensive. English is essential. French is required.

This is no solution. In an ever-shrinking world, it is important to interpret language capital on a global scale. Children in school today have aspirations and aims, not to mention current communications networks that go far beyond national borders. We should be preparing children for global language and literacy competencies that do not exclude the languages children know or need to know. But how?

Third Space, Literacy and Liminality

"It is the trope of our times to locate the question of culture in the realm of the *beyond*," states Bhabha (1994, p. 1), who probes "the *in-between* spaces through which the meanings of cultural and political authority are negotiated" (1990b, p. 4). Bhabha (1990b) describes how the global scattering of people becomes a regrouping in new places, the migratory flow rupturing fixed notions of national culture, and creating "a process of hybridity, incorporating new 'people' in relation to the body politic, generating other sites of meaning" (p. 4). He stresses that cultural identification is complex, its symbolic and affective constitution defeating linear historical conjunctions of nation and culture, and proposes a space of agency that does not turn "Territory into Tradition" (1990a, p. 300): a *third space* that opens up "a new area of negotiation of meaning and representation" (Rutherford, 1990, p. 211). This third space is carved out of words that dialogically and intertextually invite the exploration of subjectivity (Allen, 2000).

Culture, in this view, is dynamic; hybridity, a fundamental. Pieterse (2001) describes hybridity as "deeply rooted in history and quite ordinary" (p. 221), imprecisely covering "a wide register of multiple identity, crossover, pick-'n'-mix, boundary-crossing experiences and styles, matching a world of growing migration and diaspora lives, intensive intercultural communication, everyday multiculturalism and erosion of boundaries" (p. 221). He cautions against dated, 19th century negative equations of hybridity with loss of purity or authenticity, towards newer notions of hybridity as polygenetic and anti-essentializing (Pieterse, 1994).

Pieterse (2001) describes cultural histories as layered hybridizations. Language, too, is hybridized by nature though it is seldom acknowledged as such. In formal education, language is railroaded into historically set patterns and prescriptions that determine *correctness*. Far from the sociolinguistic ideal of language as socially appropriate, this mentality has been at fault in educationally proscribing natural language variation. For instance, the form *ain't*, whose roots are variously described as a form of *hain't* (a contraction of "have not" or "has not" according to the Oxford English Dictionary online) and a variant negative contraction form of *am (I) not* (Hudson, 2000) has been educationally dissuaded in classrooms out of fear of social reprisal for sounding coarsely uneducated resulting in a stilted *I am, aren't I* construction, and dialect affiliation in use.[1] Nelson (1954) describes this notion of grammar as "linguistic etiquette" (p. 299).

Language functions as a cultural badge; it is a concomitant of culture that is learned and sustained through cultural practices. Clyne (2003) argues that community also forms around language in culturally plural contexts. He points out that pluricentric languages find multiple interacting centers in contexts of cultural diversity. This, in fact, is realism for the "migration mélange" (Pieterse, 1994, p. 172) student body that constitutes the urban classroom. Their complex hybridized identities develop in the interstices of multiple centers bridging minority and majority communities and expectations.

Gutiérrez (2008) argues for an interactional concept of third space: "a particular kind of zone of proximal development" (p. 148), in which culturally totalizing notions of literacy are disassembled and reconstructed as welcoming, hybridized practices. In her treatment, *third space* is a place of physical engagement, not literary interpretation, as in Bhabha's theories. She envisions a collective reframing of literacy practices that welcome peripheral and liminal subjectivities in educational experience.

Kramsch (2009) discusses *third culture* in the context of language education, where third space folds the performance of the nonnative speaker into the negotiation of the conventional and the idiosyncratic. She draws broadly on concepts of *thirdness* from semiotics, philosophy, literary criticism, cultural studies, second and foreign language education and literacy pedagogy, presenting *thirdness* as a stance: "a way of seeing the relation of language, thought and culture" (p. 248) that breaks through typical dichotomies, such as native speaker and nonnative speaker, L1 and L2, language and literature. For Kramsch (2009), culture is a mode of belonging, of heterogeneity and fluidity, not a static state.

Sadly, educational policy makers, test engines and curriculum writers in the context we are working in see nothing unfixed or liminal about literacy, textuality and the performance of language and culture. Their notion of learning entails meeting fixed, discrete targets. In this educational climate, the experimentation we propose invites the creation of customizable texts in the classroom that fundamentally engage third space negotiation of children's language and literacy learning and cultural performance as an expression of self, not a model emulating past standards.

To do this, we engage the affordances of multimodal texts to create in-between spaces towards cultural inclusion and negotiation, and multilingual expression.

CUSTOMIZING MULTIMODAL TEXTS FOR MULTILINGUAL INCLUSION

The P R E F A C E.

I. *To entice witty Children to it,* that they may noe conceit a torment to be in the School, but dain-ty-fare. For it is apparent, that Children' even from their Infancy almoſt)are delighted with Pi-ctures, and willingly pleaſe their eyes with theſe ſights: And it will be very well worth the pains to have once brought it to paſs, that ſcarcrows may be taken away out of wiſdoms Gardens.

(Comenius, 1689, p. 9)

Multimodality refers to "the fact that all texts combine and integrate diverse semiotic resources" (Baldry, 2000, p. 21). Multimodal expression is old hat in teaching resources; in the above quote Comenius (1689) lauds the utility of pictures as an attention-grabbing device in his 17th century Latin primer. New in multimodalism is the ever-expanding digital capability to juxtapose, merge and hybridize multiple modes of expression. This flexibility invites multidimensional texts that are dynamic and mobile and offer multiple spaces for helpful communicative redundancy to house the languages children know alongside the languages they do not know. These texts offer each child what Carlos (see Chapter 1) found in his creative teacher's Grade 4 homeroom: simultaneous translation towards a message or a story that can be read comfortably by all, but across different language pathways. Multimodal texts offer moving images, and soundtracks as well as print options to channel these languages. They offer multiple channels for the development of voice.

Primary classrooms have always used multiple modes of expression. The written word is typically integrated with dramatic puppetry, visual arts and crafts, songs, movement and games towards a multisensory experience. These modes of expression predate the digitally programmable, networked resources of today that enable combining, connecting and remixing modes in novel and dynamic texts. Typically the multimodal practices of kindergarten dissipate as children's facility with print grows and school learning is more and more downloaded to the printed page. As Robinson (2006) comically puts it: "Truthfully what happens is as children grow up we start to educate them progressively from the waist up. And then we focus on their heads, and slightly to one side" (9:18–9:26).

Contemporary multimodality is permeating school boundaries; Bezemer and Kress (2008) find that "modes of representation other than image and writing—moving image and speech for instance—have found their way into learning resources, with significant effect" (p. 167). Traditional texts, too, have changed; Kress (2010) illustrates how the typical school textbook has become increasingly image-centered and modular, moving away from linear information flow.

Kress (2009b) describes the *mode* as "a socially shaped and culturally given resource for making meaning" (p. 54). He provides a contemporary road map, suggesting, *"image, writing, layout, music, gesture, speech, moving image, soundtrack* are examples of modes used in representation and communication" (p. 54). Modes, he maintains, are not fixed but culturally negotiated meaning-making devices. They span the senses, and though continuing to rely prominently on the visual and auditory, increasingly utilize haptic and other sense pathways (e.g., video gaming). Modes of meaning making can be linked, juxtaposed and mixed in dynamic combinations. Accessing and producing a contemporary multimodal text is, thus, a more synesthetic experience than engaging in alphabetic literacy.

Based on teachers' protean multiliteracies explorations, I theorized three axes for decision making in the creation of multimodal texts in the language and literacy classroom, intended to guide decision making (see Chapter 5):

- a paradigmatic axis for selection of appropriate meaning-making resource for the content and communicative intent: *aptness*, following Kress (2010).

- a diachronic axis, to map out sequential modal transformations: *transmodality*.

- a syntagmatic axis to consider modal complementarity and complexity: *multimodality*.

These are translated into teacher decisions in Figure 7.1.

Our early multiliteracies explorations indicated that the semiotic redundancy available in multimodal texts—texts that combine multiple modes of representation syntagmatically—avails the author of spaces for multiple language inclusion. The teachers set out to play with this idea: where and how could children's home languages be included in the process and product of multimodal story retelling? What third spaces could be made?

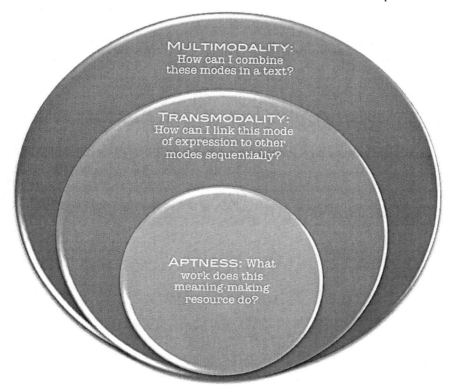

Figure 7.1 Three axes of decision making in creating multimodal texts.

My-Linh: *Stone Soup*, Kindergarten

My-Linh participated in our research from a public school in the Toronto District School Board located in a northeastern neighborhood abutting an area of high cultural diversity. Her JK–Grade 5 school had a demographic of similar linguistic and cultural heterogeneity to that of JPS, but with a slightly lower density of English language learners: 50% of the school population, according to TDSB figures.

My-Linh chose to base her kindergarten narrative retelling on *Stone Soup*, a traditional story about communal cooking, sparked somewhat unconventionally, to avert hunger. Her idea was to focus on breads of the world, a staple food common to all people though varied by shape and grain. The class worked towards a variation we called, tongue-in-cheek, *Stone Sandwiches*.

My-Linh orchestrated a multimodal journey that involved a connected train of learning experiences on the theme of basic foods spanning sight, sound, taste, touch and smell. The activities she led children into included traditional preparatory literacy activities, such as shared reading of picture book versions of *Stone Soup*; discussing favorite foods, and kinds of breads; drawing and painting; printing and spelling; assisted sentence writing; and programming bimodal picture stories of their favorite foods. She concurrently engaged children in a rich panorama of multisensory learning experiences.

There were two field trips during the year: one to a farm, where children learned about foods and how they were grown, and the second, a visit to a supermarket via public transit, where, with the guidance of grocery store workers, children shopped for sandwich ingredients and learned about the foods they saw. These were followed by participatory community functions: the first, to make a large pot of communal soup, which they all ate; and the second to customize personal sandwiches. Embedded within trip follow-ups were multiple opportunities for children's haptic experimentation with vegetables: art activities, where vegetables were both objects of and tools in painting, and spaces to help adults prepare and cook vegetables as food. These were jumping off points to traditional learning activities, such as description, naming, spelling and sentence writing. There were gustatory rewards, too, in eating their culinary creations, though one might well question the likely popularity of a blueberry and salami sandwich. To a child of 4–5, this apparently made for a promising combination!

Community languages were brought into the project in two ways. A preparatory questionnaire was sent home with children to discuss with family members the politesse around meals in the language/s of the home (see Figure 7.2). Children who spoke English at home were invited to fill in English phrases so all could be included in this exercise. The results revealed the language wealth of the classroom.

Another juncture for linking languages and cultures was in the nature of the project itself. Which breads did children recognize, know, eat, prefer? Which ones had they tried? The ensuing word wall listed *panini, challah, injera* and *roti* alongside buns, bagels, baguettes and sliced white bread. These words connected people with a staple food eaten, in different forms, around the globe, and in so doing, they presented foods in the languages of their cultural origins without ever having to state this.

The *Stone Sandwiches* project was conducted over the course of the kindergarten year. The process was captured in stills taken by the class teacher and my research assistant[2] with a digital camera. Following the sandwich preparation and eating celebration in class, My-Linh and I selected photographs to document the learning journey in a graphic format, using the program Comic Life. After working carefully on the draft to ensure the organization and representation of the multifaceted project, My-Linh took it to the children to fill in the speech bubbles we had programmed into picture frames, so children could use their own words to describe their actions.

The comic was a negotiated text, co-created (sequentially, and cumulatively) by teacher, research assistant, researcher and students. The final document was a teaching plan, a record of action research and a souvenir story for parents and their graduating student-authors, who were moving from Kindergarten into Grade 1. Figure 7.3 depicts a selection of the varied

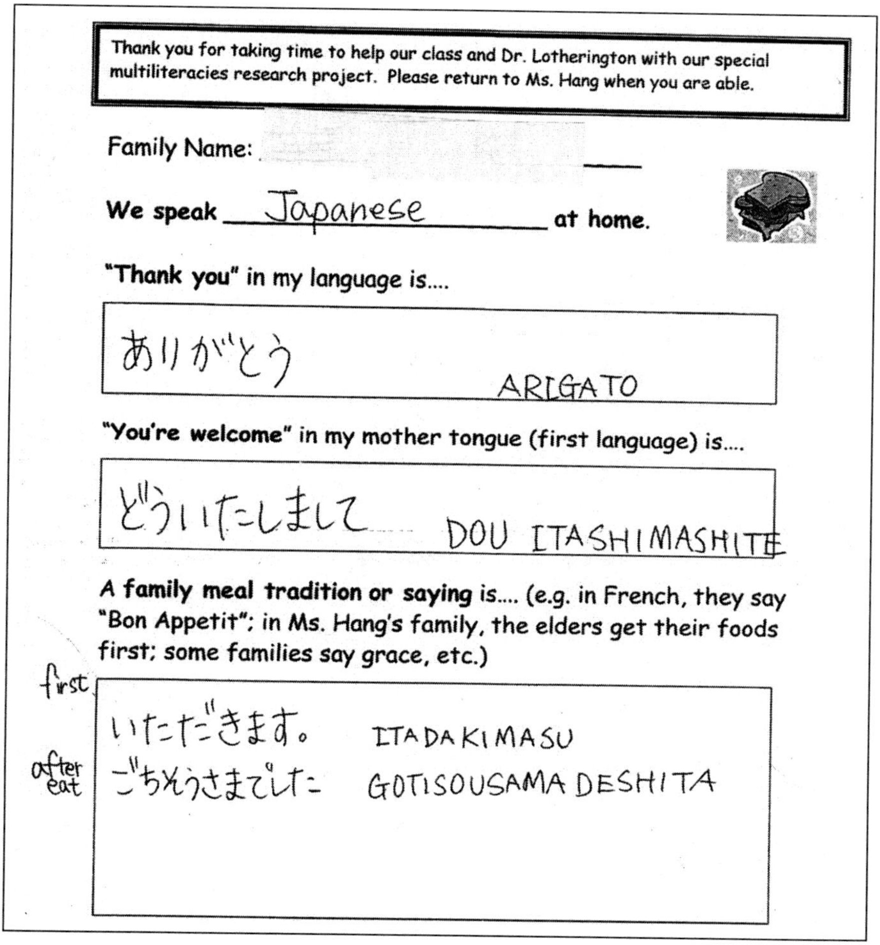

Thank you for taking time to help our class and Dr. Lotherington with our special multiliteracies research project. Please return to Ms. Hang when you are able.

Family Name: _____

We speak ___Japanese___ **at home.**

"Thank you" in my language is....

あリがとう   ARIGATO

"You're welcome" in my mother tongue (first language) is....

どういたしまして   DOU ITASHIMASHITE

A family meal tradition or saying is.... (e.g. in French, they say "Bon Appetit"; in Ms. Hang's family, the elders get their foods first; some families say grace, etc.)

first

after eat

いただきます。   ITADAKIMASU
ごちそうさまでした GOTISOUSAMA DESHITA

Figure 7.2   Survey questions to parents on home language use at mealtimes.

learning experiences that were linked in the final multimodal text (based on page 6 of the comic[3]).

The traditional narrative *Stone Soup* was the springboard for the *Stone Sandwiches* project, which combined semiotic resources, both transmodally and multimodally, in a multisensory journey into literacy learning. The inclusion of digital mediation was subtle, and simple: still photographs to document the learning progress that the teacher and researcher combined reflectively in comic form, and a draw program on school computers that children experimented with to describe their ideal sandwich. My-Linh brought families and family languages into the classroom and into thinking and discussion in two ways: by sending a questionnaire to

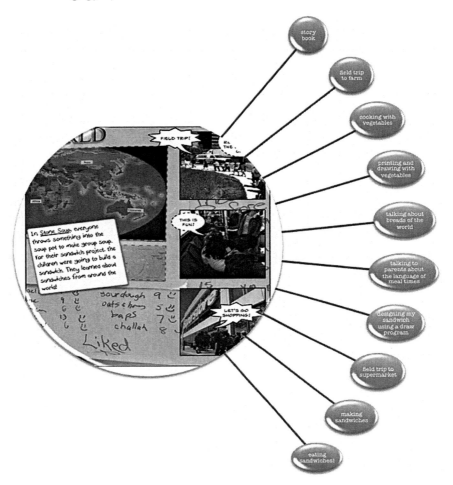

Figure 7.3 Anatomy of a multimodal text: *Stone Sandwiches.*

determine family practices around mealtimes, and by making a word wall of international breads.

My-Linh's classroom offered a seamless welcome to school children and to the community they lived in, inviting multicultural community members to take part in classroom learning activities, and taking the class into the community to learn from local merchants, and farmers on the outskirts of the city. As we saw in Mike's kindergarten class at JPS (see Chapter 6), multimodal play and multilingual inclusion are seen as natural and normal classroom learning in early childhood education. This welcoming learning space is rapidly dissipated as schooling comes to depend more and more exclusively on learning through reading, writing and listening (in the dominant language). As Robinson (2006) colorfully points out, the involvement of the body in learning is abandoned in formal education as teachers increasingly narrow their focus to one side of children's brains in the classroom. This describes how education peels away children's (and teachers') multisensory access to learning, honing in on visual, symbolic input and output (i.e., letters or numbers) in the dominant discourse: traditional literacy.

Could we implement a similarly strategic and welcoming third space for community involvement in the junior classroom, where the focus has shifted to learning through reading and writing print resources? How could a multimodal, linguistically inclusive approach to learning, such as that which teachers had quite naturally implemented in kindergarten, be implemented in the junior classroom?

Rhea, Farah and Liza: *Iqbal,* Grade 4/5 Special Education

At the junior level, Rhea and Farah decided to teach a juvenile novel that told the moving story of Iqbal Masih to the children in their Grade 4/5 classes: *Iqbal* by Francesco D'Adamo (2003). Iqbal was a young Pakistani boy sold into slavery to weave carpets. The novel documents his life as a child laborer, his daring escape, involvement with the anti-slavery lobby and ensuing public repudiation of child labor, and his horrific assassination at age 12. Rhea wanted to develop the children's social awareness beyond the borders of self-absorption typical of preteens in Toronto so they could empathize with the difficulties faced by children of a similar age living in another part of the world. Whereas many of the children at Joyce Public School live in families that struggle to make ends meet, all have access to free public schooling, and none face the loss of freedom, and nonstop manual labor that was Iqbal's lot in life.

The Grade 4/5 classes of Farah Rahemtula and Rhea Pereirra-Foyle combined forces to do this project. The teachers were joined by Liza Zawadzka, a specialist integrated arts teacher seconded to York University, who was interested in our multiliteracies project, and volunteered her expertise. Liza joined Rhea and Farah in planning and in classroom teaching, implementing arts-based activities complementary to and interpretive of the story line.

The children began their voyage to understanding Iqbal's life by weaving mini-carpets using scraps of wool on small pieces of cardboard to experience what it meant to be a *carpet-weaver* (see Figure 7.4). This learning task invited the intergenerational assistance of extended family members because handicrafts, such as weaving, are no longer commonly learned by young people. The children complained that it was hard to do, and hurt their fingers. This lesson helped them to understand the back-breaking labor faced all day, every day by child slaves, whose lives are constituted by weaving elegantly patterned carpets for buyers whose money will not reach them. In so doing, the children could empathize with Iqbal, whose life story they were reading.

After the children had become familiar with Iqbal's life by reading the novel, they plotted it as a series of scenes and interpreted these in movement.

Figure 7.4   Carpet-weaving at Joyce Public School.

This constituted a retelling of Iqbal's life story in another genre—an excellent test of reading comprehension. The class developed a narrative script, and choreographed dance and dramatic moves to enact it. Though at first the boys balked at the idea of dancing a narrative, they became motivated where creative movement could take on a martial arts veneer in scenes that involved fighting and assassination (see Figure 7.5). The story in movement was staged as a narrated shadow play, which involved scientific thinking to calculate the lighting for shadows against a screen. The performed shadow play was videotaped and programmed as a movie with narrated voice-over.

The last scene in the shadow play incorporated a research task the children undertook as part of their project: to look up the United Nations Convention on the Rights of the Child,[4] which told them about international protections that had been denied to Iqbal in his short life. These they took to their family members for help in translation. The conclusion of their video[5] showcases five children, each reciting one of the international rights of the child in a different language: four in the language of his or her home, and the fifth, in English (as a second language). Figure 7.6 presents a screenshot of their recitation, surtitled in English.

Figure 7.5 Learning to interpret Iqbal's life story in creative movement.

Their finished narrative project is moving, and inspiring, reaching far beyond the language and literacy demands of Grade 4/5 to absorbing, embodying and translating a juvenile novel into a contemporary, research-based multimodal assignment on injustice in the world. This is embodied literacy; the children literally inhabited a life they met in a book. It is *glocal* (R. Robertson, 1992, 1995) learning: students called on the local community to help them interpret and share information about internationally applicable children's rights in response to a story that happened at another time in another place. What is most amazing about this project is that whereas most of the children in this combined Grade 4/5 class were English language learners, many of the children had diagnosed learning challenges. Rhea teaches special education.

The multimodal literacies project arising from learning *Iqbal* moved dimensionally beyond textual comprehension and analysis to invoke multiple senses and modes of expression through the teachers' careful amalgamation of subject areas and creative combining of scheduled periods. In this way, teachers built a *flexible zone* project workspace (Spinthourakis et al., 2007). What Rhea, Farah and Liza created was an emancipatory, multimodal discovery zone for developing and sharing literacies that included intergenerational multilingual input. This is different in orientation and purpose from Gutiérrez's (2008) interactional conceptualization of third space as a *zone*

Figure 7.6   Screenshot of the multilingual conclusion of the children's video production of *Iqbal*.

of proximal development (ZPD) wherein participants disassemble and disrupt marginalizing literacy practices and welcome hybridized literacies in that it was not analytically focused on *literacy as political exclusion*. *Iqbal* was a dynamic multimodal text that drew on multiple modes of discovery and interpretative coding; it required learning to be embodied, historically and politically invested, inclusive of encyclopedic research and community language knowledge alike. This promoted "performance before competence" (Cazden, 1997, p. 303), both textual and interactive: an enabling space, facilitating and supporting multimodal participation that included, as one facet, the languages of the community—*third culture* (Kramsch, 2009). In this environment, literacy learning invited multilingual expression, and polyphonous development in creative, multimodal play.

ENABLING SPACES FOR LANGUAGE
INCLUSION IN MULTIMODAL TEXTS

Bhabha's conception of *third space* is a textual negotiation of meaning and representation that gives voice to cultural hybridity and challenges staid political determinations of culture and nationality (Rutherford, 1990). The children's texts described here develop *in-between spaces* for hybrid expression. These are not the elegantly discursive spaces Bhabha (1990a) interprets; they are enabling spaces in the process and product of literacy acquisition that exploit the complementarity and redundancy of multiple modalities for multilingual inclusion. These are spaces for customizing literacy learning in the classroom.

Multimodal texts are dimensionally complex; they provide multiple spaces for meaning-making that enable helpful redundancy by incorporating convergent modes of semiotic representation. Digital mediation provides opportunities to link these modes in novel ways to create customizable texts. The classroom multiliteracies projects, *Stone Sandwiches* and *Iqbal*, strategically include children's multilingualism to bridge classroom literacies and home language use. Though the spaces of home language engagement are fledgling at present, they successfully connect families and home language knowledge to children's academic language and literacy development. These connections are critically important for developing avenues for language support that no single teacher can supply in the linguistically heterogeneous classroom.

Gateways for Language Inclusion in Multimodal Text Creation

Our initial plans to support multilingualism in a distributed learning model in the linguistically heterogeneous classroom were predicated on post hoc translations or interpretations of children's story writing in English. Our first idea had been machine translation: we would run everything children wrote through a software program or online site to produce individualized translations, thus creating multiple individualized versions of stories that included all of the languages spoken by the children in the class.

The first red flag was the set of languages available in such programs, which were heavily weighted to major Western European and Asian languages. What would we do with children who spoke Kurdish, Macedonian, Twi and (Guyanese) Creolese? Things got worse when we trialed a machine translation of a *Once upon a time* opening story line using languages familiar to teachers and researchers. It was a dismal failure, risible even, producing mangled, and in some languages, quasi-translated prose. In discussions with distributers, we discovered that *postmachine human translation* was an expected and essential follow-up to machine translation. And that was the end of that.

Relying on software translation had been a bad idea; but using a digital connection for human translation, on the other hand, was a good idea. We ran a kindergarten child's story through Russian translation from two directions: the teacher appealed to the child's mother for help in translating her son's writing; and I emailed the same story to a graduate student who took not much more time than the software program to translate it into her—and the child's—native language, and email it back to me. We discovered online connection to human translators to be fast and efficient, given the numerous scripts available on Microsoft Word. Hypothetically, this meant we could forge digital connections between JPS and other elementary schools anywhere on the planet to develop text co-authorship in multiple languages. With this idea in mind, we had extended our research community to include teachers from two other schools: one in Toronto, and the other in Taipei.

Our mainstay, however, was connecting the classroom and the community. In Shiva's Grade 1 *Three Little Pigs* stories, a triple soundtrack was programmed into iMovie narratives, enabling English on one channel with a musical soundtrack playing on another, and an optional third channel for story translation into the home language. A number of parents participated in providing taped verbal translations of their children's stories, with the test case being in English and Yoruba. The end result required co-programming to get the home language in sync with the pictures, and the final product was not perfect, but it showed the possibilities for creating multiple channels for language inclusion. This created multimodal texts that had a choice factor: a switch from one language into another, paralleling the language selection feature on DVDs and video games. This is a dynamic multimodal text featuring choice via a transmodal switch.

In Michelle's kindergarten, modal redundancy in children's retold fables was implemented in the form of text boxes that provided an English narrative plus translation (see English-Tagalog dual captioning of *The Dinosaur and the Snake* in Figure 7.7). Michelle worked with both parents and EAs to co-program bilingual versions of the adapted stories her kindergarten children created in pictures and oral retelling based on Aesop's fable, *The Lion and the Mouse*. These translations required the agency of a parent or teaching assistant working as closely with the teacher as possible. The end result was an individualized multimodal text: a bilingual book customized for each author.

These experiments revealed that languages could be juxtaposed on a page, as in the dual language storybooks, and superimposed via a switch, as in the triple track iMovie. In other words, treating each language as a semiotic resource—a mode of communication—enables linguistically customizing multimodal texts. The redundancy built into multimodal texts can be used to fortify meaning and linguistic expression, and to share knowledge of languages.

What is needed is ready access to translation, which can be done with human resources, whether members of the school or the local community, or digitally connected educational partners. This distributes language support, learning and textual creation.

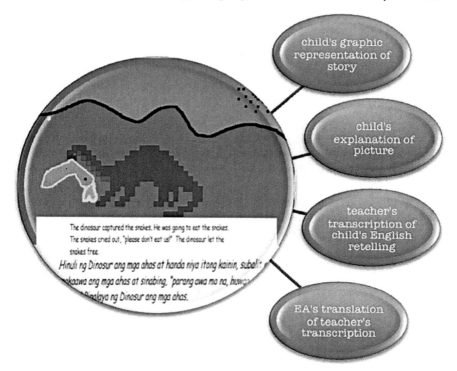

The dinosaur captured the snakes. He was going to eat the snakes.
The snakes cried out, "please don't eat us!" The dinosaur let the
snakes free.
Hinuli ng Dinosur ang mga ahas at handa niya itong kainin, subalit
nakaawa ang mga ahas at sinabing, "parang awa mo na, huwa...
Pinalaya ng Dinosur ang mga ahas.

child's graphic
representation of
story

child's
explanation of
picture

teacher's
transcription of
child's English
retelling

EA's translation
of teacher's
transcription

Figure 7.7 *The Dinosaur and the Snake* in English and Tagalog.

Multilingual Processing?

The dimensional complexity of multimodal texts opens up creative spaces
for expressive customization and play. Our learning community was at
play in designing multiliteracies pedagogies, and the children were playing with multimodal expression. Our design factor: to implement community languages in multimodal text creation, opened up a series of questions
about where in the teaching and learning process we could introduce home
languages.

The projects described in this section embedded multilingualism in text
creation via post hoc translation, which involved plenty of creative problem-solving to find linguistic resources. Could we bring diverse languages
into textual processing as well?

Translation occurred at the beginning of projects as well as at the end
of them. Sandra's Grade 2 digital animations of *Puppy and Horse Go to*
the Olympics were created as a class version of *Old Man Yu Moves the*
Mountain, a traditional story that was read in translation from Mandarin
Chinese. Using collegial assistance and an online connection, Sandra had

Puppy and Horse Go to the Olympics translated back into Mandarin Chinese, so the story underwent a spiral of translation from Chinese to English and back to Chinese.

The teachers guided children's creation of individually customized texts in different genres that resulted in multiple bilingual versions of adapted traditional stories:

- *The Three Little Pigs* retold in claymation in English and Yoruba, English and Cantonese, and English and Farsi in Shiva's Grade 1 class;
- *The Lion and the Mouse* retold in PowerPoint in English and Tagalog, and English and Russian in Michelle's kindergarten;
- *Ananse's Feast* re-created as a claymation and told in standard textbook English by Rhea's Grade 4 special education class and, sequentially in Trinidadian Creole English by the teacher; and
- a class retold version of *Old Man Yu Moves the Mountain* presented in English and Mandarin Chinese and individually programmed as web-based digital animations in Sandra's Grade 4 class.

Teachers also guided the creation of projects that were class multilingual productions:

- *The Little Red Hen* depicted on a felt board and co-taught in English, Cantonese and Vietnamese in Mike's kindergarten; and
- *Iqbal* interpreted in movement in a narrated shadow play, with a researched conclusion about the international rights of the child, voiced by five children in five different languages with English surtitles.

The inclusion of languages in class multiliteracies thus took many shapes in terms of genre, voice, authorship, languages incorporated and manner and place of linguistic incorporation. What they showed us was a world of possibility for utilizing the language wealth of the classroom. This extended everyone's knowledge from the children to the teachers to the parents, school volunteers, community members and digital partners to the principal and all involved researchers. What we found was increased curiosity about languages, pride in one's linguistic repertoire and motivation to create fun projects on the children's part. Though still a leap to full language inclusion, it was a brave and successful start to welcoming 16 different languages into the class.

8 Towards an Emergent Pedagogy of Multiliteracies

ONCE UPON A TIME . . .

Since my early days as a CUSO volunteer teaching English in Papua New Guinea, in the 1970s, when I was baffled by my Grade 9 students' easy dismissal of a village man's dynamic first person account of his encounters with Japanese and Allied soldiers during World War II, I have questioned the narrowness of what passes for literacy education in school. The wonder of hearing what it felt like to run an enemy line, dismissed by invading troops as a *native* who was de facto outside the battlefront, despite it being his homeland they so cavalierly usurped, and in his accomplishing what James Bond could only hope his script would work in, to become a true war hero, undecorated though he might be! The reason this history was not appreciated by children lucky enough to attend school? Joseph spoke in Tok Pisin, the local English-based auxiliary language, creolized into existence as a lingua franca but not into status as a carrier of historical information. He spoke with a historically authentic, and culturally contextualized voice, using the politically unsanitized language of the people, unauthenticated for school, where an idealized, sterilized version of the colonially imposed legitimate language (Bourdieu, 1991) was expected in a textbook. Wasn't that why children went to school?

My concerns about being a teacher of English as a second language increased as my teaching life took me into schools, colleges and universities in Singapore, England, Canada and Fiji, and then into the island states of the South Pacific. English, in every country I taught in, was an easy sell: students wanted either to learn English or to learn it better. In the process, I was conscious of the concomitant erosion of knowledge and learning opportunities encoded in languages that were preliterate, had small readerships or were out of favor with educational priorities. Valuable history, science, art and culture were carried in other languages and communicated outside of books. Joseph had been a goldmine of historical information, lost to the ears of his grandchildren's generation.

In the mid-1990s, I moved into sociolinguistics and language maintenance in Australia where there was widespread positive recognition of education in multiple languages in the state of Victoria. However, literacy—always a social concern—was firmly grounded in English and modern print resources. Consequential literacy testing seemed to completely miss popular social activities engaging the teenagers of Asian backgrounds participating in my research, which fused other communicative modalities (e.g., *karaoke*) into their bilingual and multilingual days (Lotherington, 2003b). At the same time, my preteen had begun to write strange emails to me that used oddball short forms. I asked for—and got—a tutorial in smileys. Where was recognition of these activities—conducted in different languages and different codes and mixing in other semiotic means of representation—in an understanding of literacy? Even more upsetting, not being a native speaker of English was designated a *risk factor* to literacy success (Australian Bureau of Statistics, 1997), suggesting that literacy was written English, and the ability to use other languages interfered. It was in this climate that the New London Group (1996) composed their manifesto on *multiliteracies.*

When I moved to York University in Toronto, a year before the dawning of the new century and millennium, I aimed to sort through this potpourri of observations about the changing worlds of literacy, and educationally mobilize sprouting theorizing on multiliteracies.

A BIG IDEA: MULTILITERACIES

Where would I begin to investigate multiliteracies—a theoretical notion in active development—in a communicative environment of persistent change? Even more challenging, how could I introduce a pedagogy of multiliteracies into formal education?

I entered the postmodern world of multiliteracies the way gamers do: by jumping into the middle and figuring it out as a participant. I wanted to ascertain, in the first instance, what constituted success in literacy acquisition for children in the linguistically heterogeneous, urban, elementary classroom. Were multiliterate practices taking hold in the classroom and the curriculum? My theoretical jumping off point was the New London Group's (1996) programmatic manifesto: *A Pedagogy of Multiliteracies: Designing Social Futures.*

The New London Group (1996) highlighted fissures between the limited project of school literacy education, the tools and mediating surfaces of literacy in a climate of rapid digitization, and the kaleidoscopic cultural splintering of urban geographies. With changing realties in *private, public* and *working lives* in mind, they looked to change literacy education towards critical access to "the evolving language of work, power, and community" (p. 60), enabling learners "to design their social futures and achieve success through fulfilling employment" (p. 60). They proposed that schools change the *what* and *how* of literacy pedagogy. The *what* of multiliteracies education concerned complex modal design considerations; the *how, overt instruction, critical framing, situated practice* and *transformed practice.*

Suitably motivated towards revolutionary change in literacy pedagogy, I entered a local elementary school with a highly culturally diverse student body that had been internationally recognized for its technologically innovative pedagogy—an ideal environment in which to work with contemporary multiliteracies. What I walked into was the beginnings of a continuing program of collaborative educational research.

Situating Multiliteracies Research in an Elementary School

I found in the public school an infrastructure of substantial complexity in which language and literacy teaching and testing were governed by political bodies at length from the children, teachers, school and even each other. The principal kept the body and soul of the school together; the teachers knit possibilities for children's learning out of curricular documents that catalogued skills and content, and tests that idealized students and cordoned literacy beyond recognition. Progressive changes in the curriculum were neutralized by conservative testing efforts. The system monitored the teaching of content, not the learning of children. How and where could I begin to explore the *what* of literacy education, when, like the proverbial blind man describing an elephant, it was perceived differently depending on the educational vantage point?

In the early years classrooms, children's multimodal activities showed me what the New London Group's (1996) idea of constructing and mixing linguistic, visual, audio, gestural and spatial modes of meaning might entail, whether digitally mediated or not. However, the multimodally expressive activities of kindergarten were funneled into print-based learning as children progressed into grade school. Though they had access to computers, children were not taught to touch type. I found children learning to print letters meticulously following a chart that would not have been out of place in my Grade 1 class half a century ago. The curriculum prioritized handwriting, despite the fact that literate communication in society depends heavily on navigating screens and keyboarding.

There were deep ideological fissures that surfaced along with the limitations on expressive media taught and tested as literacy. The cultural image of Canada and Canadians imbuing passages in literacy tests was shocking, resting on knowledge of Anglo-centric Canadiana beneath a thin veneer of smiling multiculturalism invested in ethnic names and brown faces. Children were assumed to have in common, by dint of living at a northern latitude, *the great white north* of romantic imagination. The inner-city children I observed in classrooms had in common their cultural and linguistic diversity, and their affiliation to pop culture, most of which was accessed digitally. Most had never even seen the great lake separating Canada and the United States that forms the southern border of the city of Toronto (viz.,

Lake Ontario). As Grade 4/5 teacher, Farah Rahemtula, explains: "The world is their condo, and it is concrete, unfortunately."

Idealizing the real in educational pursuits is not new. Drawing on Fillmore's (1981) delineation of the *ideal reader* of American standardized tests against the *real reader* in the classroom, Kay (1983) explains:

> The ideal reader is defined in terms of a particular text and a particular interpretation of that text. Given the text and the interpretation, the ideal reader is a device that is possessed of just the knowledge and skills required to extract that interpretation from the text. The ideal reader knows what the text presupposes and is able to learn what the text is designed to convey. (p. 1)

The literacy agenda of the classroom required real children to bridge substantial gaps in their knowledge. The work of elementary school teachers was fraught with practical issues. We recognized a need for change in literacy education—but where could we start? What could we change, and how could we change it durably and meaningfully within the complex hierarchical infrastructure of formal schooling?

Radford (2006) reminds us that formal education is a complex social organism, not a single, seamless administrative unit. Examining schools through the lens of complexity theory, he cautions against reductionist assumptions about cause and effect in educational policy and planning, explaining that the multiple components of institutional education are not atomistic variables but interconnected systems in nonlinear and dynamic relationship. In his view,

> research describes and explains and in doing so supports the network of communication between institutions and outside agencies. In this context research can promote the inherent self-organisational capacities of schools as adaptive and flexible institutions working within a complex society that makes multiple demands amidst continuously changing priorities. (Radford, 2006, p. 178)

I proposed a narrative rewriting intervention to the principal, based on a curious trend I noted in the kindergarten. Together with a couple of primary teachers, we began a small focused research project situated in the school.

Whence Goldilocks?

Children in the northwest quadrant of Toronto that is the catchment area of Joyce Public School live in a complex amalgam of multilingual existences. A preliminary year of ethnographic observations at JPS highlighted numerous gaps children and teachers had to bridge to catch up to the starting point anticipated in the language curriculum, including knowledge of

English; elementary familiarity with the symbolic sets used for encoding and decoding in school, including the Roman alphabet, and Arabic numerals; basic story schemas; and technological access. There was a 0.5 ESL teacher designated for a school serving a community comprising in excess of 90% immigrants, most of them recent. Every teacher in this scenario—then as now—is a de facto ESL teacher.

Our interventionist project got off to a well-meaning, if organizationally scattered start with the rewriting of *Goldilocks and the Three Bears*, a story that had attracted an uncanny following with kindergarteners who didn't know much English, how to read or stories in the traditional Western children's literature canon. I was curious about what they saw in Goldilocks and how they might reinterpret her as a character in 21st century inner-city Toronto, in an urban stretch where scavenger animals, such as raccoons, squirrels and pigeons might be seen amongst the high-rise apartment buildings, a long way from the *Once upon a time* cottage in the woods inhabited by a family of talking bears that Goldilocks finds and invades.

It was high time the little blond girl who walked brightly out of Victorian England into early 20th century American storybooks got updated for our multicultural reality in 21st century Toronto, Canada. How would children culturally reinterpret the story? What would their narrative retelling reveal? Could we enable children who begin school already on the outside of imagined school intake populations to enter stories as participants in literacy acquisition rather than as subjects of narration, in terms of both Freire's (1970/1998) *banking education*, and Bhabha's (1990b) critique of national identity wherein "nations, like narratives, lose their origins in the myths of time and only fully realize their horizons in the mind's eye" (p. 1). School configured a Canada of English and French identity, singularly devoid of the founding native peoples of this vast land, and providing nothing more than token names for the multicultural generations who created the modern nation on the outskirts of colonial narcissism. How could teachers at this inner-city school pry open this exclusivity to make texts more welcoming to real children?

A lot more than *Goldilocks and the Three Bears* needed a makeover.

MULTILITERACIES IN ACTION

The digital world on which the concept of *multiliteracies* had been predicated had changed dramatically from the mid-1990s to the early 2000s. Web 2.0, also known as the semantic web, brought in collaborative possibilities that have indelibly altered the shape and creation processes of a text; the ways in which information is accessed, constructed, assessed, referenced, linked and appropriated; and the kinds of conversations, forums and activities linking learners and teachers. Epistemologies of literacy and literacy education have continued to change, accordingly.

As Gardner (2008) states: "I can attest that belief in the power of education—for good or for ill—is ubiquitous. We have little difficulty in seeing education as an enterprise—indeed, the enterprise—for shaping the mind of the future" (p. 17). Our research agenda was dedicated to bettering education for real children at JPS—which meant imagining the future these children would inherit.

A serious critique of school literacy motivating the pedagogically interventionist research we had begun with the rewriting of *Goldilocks and the Three Bears* was the assumed primacy of print. Literacy, understood as the dominant language written down, focused on old technologies and models from past centuries. Our work had to imagine future literacies as a fundamental responsibility to students.

The research was fundamentally collaborative, merging theory and practice; and situated at the coal face of education: the classroom. Our context was glocal; the families whose children attend JPS have traversed the world to settle in our city. Outside of select communities and official image-making, Canada is and has always been a complexly and enduringly multilingual nation, not a bilingual society. In the emerging global society, we should be positioned as leaders in nurturing of the language wealth in our classrooms. Our focus had to tackle politically sensitive entrenched norms and ideals.

After considerable experimentation, our collaborative research developed a three-pronged pursuit towards developing multiliteracies pedagogies in the classroom, as shown in Figure 8.1

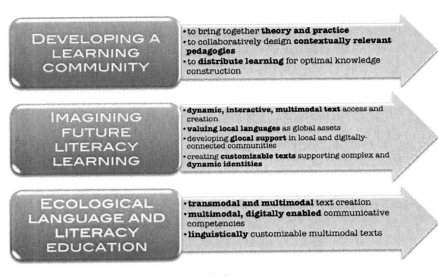

Figure 8.1   Our multiliteracies research directions.

The Theory-Practice Loop: Establishing a Learning Community

My agenda to understand rapid and dynamic social and linguistic changes in how we communicate, and to move these observations into 21st century language and literacy education depended on teachers' collaborative good will, intelligence, knowledge, creativity, organizational skills and willingness to try new ways of teaching. I entered their institutional context, and, in so doing, had to learn to work within it, which was a socialization all on its own.

Ayers (2010) argues: "In the always-contested space of education at all levels, we are, each and all of us, works-in-progress, participating, intentionally or unwittingly, in history-in-the-making (p. 7). Our early multiliteracies investigations were beset by bumps in the road: finding our feet in a collegial learning community where the expectations and patterns of knowledge sharing of university researchers and elementary school teachers were very different; dealing with the complexities of formal education, which in 2005 meant working according to work-to-rule legislation that cut off our workshops; dealing with digital crises, including official edicts from the TDSB and Ministry of Education. One year, our OSX Macs were downgraded to OSIX (which, though outdated, was the officially supported operating system) despite having been upgraded through public research funds, and the school wireless Internet was disconnected in an official *equalization* exercise, cutting away many of JPS's innovations. These decisions, taken above the level of school administration, defied logic to the point of cranial collapse, and they seriously undercut our research progress.

At a recent conference in England,[1] Viv Edwards pointed out that the largest constraint in the classroom is the imagination. The principal and the teachers saved the day time and time again. The school principal believed in her teachers:

> The staff as a whole usually gives 150%. If I ask for 100 I always get 150%. They always *wow* me. But their passion, their passion and my passion is to provide these children with the absolute best education possible. (C. Paige, personal communication, February 8, 2010)

The teachers believed in their students and in best teaching practice. We worked altruistically to improve children's learning, and to improve our understanding of how we might do this in the century we actually live in.

To be certified in Ontario, teachers must minimally earn two degrees: a Bachelor's degree—whether in Arts, Sciences, Fine Arts—and a Bachelor of Education degree. Many of the elementary school teachers I work with hold additional special qualifications, and a number of teachers have earned Master of Education degrees. They are well educated, and respectably remunerated. However, teachers are not always treated like professionals in political commentary where there is a tendency to understand their work as the clerical management of designated information in the classroom, or worse, as assembly-line supervisors, ensuring quality control in the processing of students as they pass along a conveyor belt. The political tendency to overlook or downplay teachers' creative abilities, organizational mastery, familiarity with the materials they teach, and their wizardry in turning dry lists of curricular objectives into meaningful learning experiences for children of all ages, levels of understanding and backgrounds, is wasteful.

Cope and Kalantzis (2009b) advise:

> A pedagogy of multiliteracies requires that the enormous role of agency in the meaning-making process be recognized, and in that recognition, it seeks to create a more productive, relevant, innovative, creative and even perhaps emancipatory, pedagogy. (p. 175)

The principal's vision of a *learning community*—a community of practice dedicated to focused, in-house educational research and professional development (PD)—gave shape to my interest in and experience with collaborative action research. With the best of intentions but minimal funding, we wobbled off to a start.

The dedication and patience of teachers, not to mention their much-needed organizational skills, helped to build a self-renewing motivational cycle. We matured into a supportive and dedicated body for research and focused professional development that has invisibly stitched itself into the running of the school. Our learning community, now in its 8th year, hosts teacher candidates and visitors as well as graduate students, teachers and fellow researchers. The principal puts in as much time as she can, given myriad, unceasing calls on her attention from morning till well after school is out for the day. We have successfully created a community dedicated to multidimensional learning—a fundamental building block of our action research to bring together theory and practice.

Recently, through a badly timed invitation, a well-meaning junior member of our learning community erroneously invited a Ministry official to our final show-and-tell exhibition in June when participants internally showcase their multiliteracies research and classroom products. This is a day of internal critique and celebration relying on trust, where we candidly discuss where to go from here, not a day to bring in those who feel it is their place to externally judge. The principal took me aside, and offered to ask the official to leave, but I decided she might as well stay, given the circumstances. The upshot was revealing.

At a suitable juncture, the official jumped into the conversation with a tedious demonstration of acceptable graphic novel construction, giving a step-by-step account of how to follow a (limited) pattern set in a recent Ministry publication. The teachers sat patiently, listening; the room, typically very noisy, went quiet. The protocol seemed unnecessarily boring and restrictive, and I wondered, rather rebelliously, upon her insistence that the background of the graphic presentation be black; what was wrong with purple? Fortunately, soon after the official finished her impromptu tutorial, she swanned importantly out of the colloquium. The university researchers sighed audibly. The teachers, accustomed to such hierarchical performances, did not take offense at the official's condescending lecturette. Curious about how they could politely listen to such limiting and limited ideas, we took up the difference between her top-down regimented do-it-this-way formal PD, and the informal, do-it-yourself multilateral collaboration we had developed. At the flip of an invisible switch, everything changed: the mood of the group (productively noisy), attitude to pedagogical exploration (not invited in a black background, square box graphic reproduction), motivation to try out new ideas (no one supervising the *correctness* of your background), envisioned engagement with the learners (why not pink!), interface with curricular content (let's do music as well by adding a soundtrack to the comic), transmodal links and multimodal collages (how about animation, too?). In a trice, the place of the teacher had shifted from robotic social reproducer to creative and skillful guide to knowledge construction.

At the end of the day, it is the moral imperative of the researcher to be accountable to those who sanction and fund the program of research, the public in whose interests the research is conducted, and, most of all, the research participants. Interventionist research is, itself, a Goldilocks venture: the researcher enters someone else's house. But unlike Goldilocks, the researcher tries to improve, repair or replace damaged or badly fitting systems, not use them to self-advantage.

The teacher is a crucial interpreter of the educational project, connecting life in and out of school, without whom "the nexus between instruction and education is dissolved, while the problem of teaching is conjured away by the cardboard schemata exalting educativity" (Gramsci, 1971, p. 36). Cheryl, as administrator of our host school, sees our collaboration as honoring teachers' knowledge and understanding of their students:

> These teachers feel so empowered; it's their ideas and they're [trying them out], and . . . they have the opportunity to work with absolutely outstanding educators. It's a gift for you, but it's also a gift for them. (C. Paige, personal communication, February 8, 2010)

What we have learned about teaching ourselves in our collaborative research community at JPS is a critically important achievement of this research venture.

WHAT DID WE LEARN?

Children, most of whom had migrated relatively recently to Canada, entered Joyce Public School to find a provincial educational agenda designed for idealized students learning to read and write according to 20th century norms in Canada's official languages: English (predominantly in this context), and French. The educational system was complex; the curriculum, standardized, and students were individually tested (externally) on paper against provincial ideals. Meanwhile, in social life, literate practices had evolved into collaborative and interactive screen-based activities programmed on dynamic multimodal canvasses.

It was clear that literacy education required a fundamental rewrite. Generally recommending that schools be dismantled and restructured is not a workable starting place though, so we pitched our focus on the *how* of literacy education within the existing infrastructure. The curriculum is politically awkward to change. Our collaborative research focused on revising pedagogies towards the creation of multimodal texts. The teachers were responsible for linking *how to* ideas to the curricular mandate. This facilitated teaching literacy creatively, inclusively and contemporaneously, allowing us to, as one teacher put it, "change the default thought."

Project-Based Learning: Collaborative and Distributed Learning

Tapscott (2010) provides a commercial gloss on contemporary knowledge construction:

> Of course, you still need a knowledge base, and you can't Google your way through every activity and conversation. But what counts more, is your capacity to learn lifelong, to think, research, find information, analyze, synthesize, contextualize, critically evaluate it; to apply research to solving problems; to collaborate and communicate.
>
> This is particularly important for students (and employers) who are increasingly competing in a global economy. Labour markets are now global and given networked business models, knowledge workers are being subjected to market forces in real-time. They must learn, adapt and perform like never before. (para. 36–37)

This description of learning for the contemporary workplace—as being able to source information, think creatively, collaborate with others and actively problem-solve—recalls progressive approaches to education across the 20th century that moved away from individual learning of externally standardized curricula: Vygotsky's (1934/1986) *zone of proximal development* constructing learning within social collaboration; J. Dewey's (1938/1998) experiential philosophy of education; Illich's (1970/1972) critique of formal schooling's failure to provide space for exploration and application of learning; Freire's (1970/1998) critical literacy revolution advocating *problem-posing* education. The just-in-time learning Tapscott (2010) describes reverberates in the research and development of contemporary researchers and practitioners working with

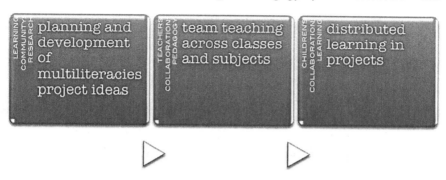

Figure 8.2 Levels of collaboration in multiliteracies action research.

problem-based models of education (Bereiter & Scardamalia, 2000; Katz & Chard, 2000), and with education for the information economy (Gee, 2004b; Sawyer, 2006, 2008).

The collaborative impetus founding our learning community and classroom multiliteracies projects, paired with our focus on narrative learning, created the conditions for project-based learning. This model evolved on a third level as well: as an organizational teaching strategy. Presently, classroom projects are mandatorily collaborative, engaging at least two teachers and, more often, a small team, so no teacher gets lost, stuck or stranded on his or her own in the classroom. Collaborative learning thus emerges on three levels, as shown in Figure 8.2.

Collaborative interfaces enable distributed learning in tune with just-in-time problem-based models. As Gee (2000) explains, "Networks and networking, within what I call 'distributed systems', are the master theme of our 'new times'" (p. 43). The networked classroom opens spaces for customized learning. Given the reach of digital connections, the classroom can easily be connected with other classrooms around the world (though different time zones complicate this). Our learning collective established links with an elementary public school in northeast Toronto, and a private school in Taipei, Taiwan (via Skype). Both successfully implemented their own interventionist multiliteracies projects.

Collaborative learning has transformed practice, from models of professional development to distributed learning patterns in the classroom that maximize children's abilities by having them voluntarily choose their roles in a team, rather than requiring each to do the same thing competitively, emphasizing what they cannot do—the modus operandi of standardized testing. The movement away from standardized education towards customized learning (see Sawyer, 2008) allows the teacher to welcome 16 languages into the classroom, and open the door to intergenerational participation, and, via digital links, to international peer collaboration.

Multimodal Literacies: Customizing Texts for Linguistic Inclusion

How could *Goldilocks and the Three Bears* be retold through a child's eyes? Indeed, why have we not been asking that all along? Textuality has changed dimensionally from the static, two-dimensional page; it has acquired dynamism in audio-visual design (e.g., animations), and haptic activation (e.g., gaming); it has gained the fourth dimension of time in social interactivity (e.g., texting), enabling novel collaborative text-building (e.g., wikis). Literacies have changed very dramatically. So must the classroom.

Teachers designed engaging narrative retelling projects that were tied to traditional stories and curricular aims of their choosing. As we progressed through the yearly project cycle, teachers linked modal communication and orchestrated multimodal ensembles that engaged children creatively and critically in distributed learning patterns towards customizable texts. They moved children into print and beyond into modes and media, utilizing artistic, musical, graphic, photographic and even whole body expression (e.g., dance). Teachers approached digital media as co-learners, sharing know-how in teams, and offering program choices to children who had to critically evaluate the software they wanted to use, even in kindergarten.

Technology-enhanced learning naturally accommodates collaboration and problem-solving—there are never enough machines around, no matter what hardware is in use, so children must share. They then have to learn to navigate the screen-based environment in question, which requires active problem-solving. Projects engaged teams of learners in different configurations that encouraged distributed learning patterns. In so doing, teachers supported the positive individual contribution of each student, based on his or her talents, rather than always insisting all students achieve the same standardized learning goals that leave some children in perpetual remediation.

Teachers motivated thinking in different modes and media. I routinely hear people defend essay writing as a genre that facilitates thinking. Quite apart from the fact that few of us in life require professional essay writing skills, essays tend to be uncritically viewed as a sort of vitamin supplement to the development of thinking in schools. Mandatory tests grade whether students have filled out the spatially and medium-limited pattern with acceptably organized content, rather than original thinking. The teachers circumvented this kind of formatted test of comprehension, inspiring and guiding children into bold multimedia productions that required strategic and creative thinking far beyond the reaches of the five-paragraph essay.

Teachers guided children to adapt stories from books into scripts, plays, slide presentations, web-based animations, claymations, movies, comic books, songs and even operettas, treating programming as fundamental to literacy acquisition. We discovered that children could program (via basic iconic navigation) before they could read and write alphabetic print, and that programming stories on the computer supported learning to read alphabetic print. We looked to creativity, to inclusion and to future literacies (see

Figure 8.3), finding educational substance in the words of fellow Toronto-nian, media scholar Marshall McLuhan:

> In a culture like ours, long accustomed to splitting and dividing all things as a means of control, it is sometimes a bit of a shock to be re-minded that, in operational and practical fact, the medium is the mes-sage. This is merely to say that the personal and social consequences of any medium—that is, of any extension of ourselves—result from the new scale that is introduced into our affairs by each extension of our-selves, or by any new technology. (McLuhan, 1964, p. 7).

Multimodal texts clustered semiotic resources that opened ideal spaces for language inclusion: (e.g., speech bubbles with sound files, dual track

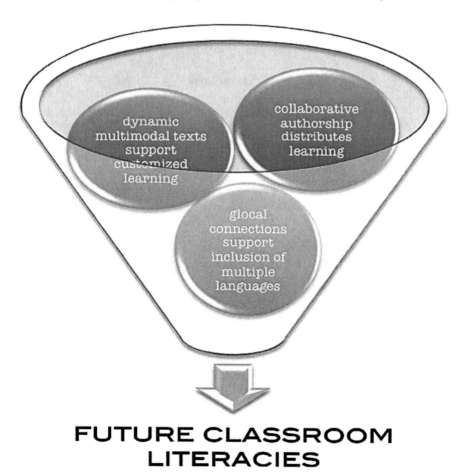

Figure 8.3   Aiming towards the future in classroom literacy learning.

movies, bilingual and multilingual books). Modes in complex arrangement created helpful message redundancy. A story could be subtitled in another language, or a bilingual narration programmed in postproduction voice-overs. Teachers initiated partnerships with educational assistants, children's parents, school volunteers, research assistants and other teachers.

Children need to learn whatever dominant language is required for agency in social learning and doing—English in our case. But this does not have to be at the expense of other languages they know or want to know or are able to share, which can and should be incorporated into imaginative and customizable pedagogies as indicated in this book. This is a mission for all of us in a rapidly globalizing era. Cultural belonging requires a broad palette of communicative proficiencies in a range of media in our digitally connected world. Freedman and Ball (2004) advise:

Figure 8.4   Ecological language and literacy learning.

We need to consider how the multiplicity of voices shapes the ideologies that the next generation will develop and that will guide us all in the coming century. These voices demand that we set a research agenda that includes the complexities of our world's societies, its schools, and its other settings where ideological becoming is nurtured. (p. 9)

We found new opportunities for the development of voice in multimodal productions, inviting children to give shape to their voice in the language of the home while developing a voice in school English, too. The promise of multimodal expression led us to think about whether voice could be developed in different modes.

By trial and error, we evolved ways and means of including children's languages in school projects, though questions of how to build this level of exposure into more supportive pathways remain. Figure 8.4 depicts our model of ecological language development.

The Old in the New

Jewitt (2002) explains:

"Old" technologies always occupy new technologies (as witnessed by the running boards on cars, the keyboards on computers). The question of whether or not these technologies are best suited to the spaces they occupy is something that can only be resolved over time. I suggest that that time is now. (p. 194)

Intellectual products take different shapes. Schools are out of date. Children still need to be able to access and critically grapple with connected print. They need to understand that books have encoded thought using scribal and print technologies over millennia. This immense body of knowledge will not all turn up in fun games. It is up to us as a society to highlight the worlds encoded in books against a high-octane commercial backdrop of flashy attention-grabbing games. This is not easy.

That being said, children need to game, too—as learners, participants, programmers, *prosumers* (Toffler, 1980) and *remixers* (Lessig, 2001). Formal education, complex though its infrastructure may be, is culpable in not moving in step with the times in accessing, connecting, celebrating, critiquing, modeling and inspiring thought and knowledge construction when even the best of our schools is modeled on industrial era technologies.

The fundamental shift in the semiotic materiality of literate communication enables modally complex texts that are dynamic, interactive and customizable. The new media engaged call on creative and critical processes appropriate to expressive possibilities. These welcome collaborative authorship structures, enabling children to work with partners in class

or via web-based connections in novel configurations. They require epistemological revision of *literacy*, and appropriate pedagogical responses.
Black as a background to presentations, for example, is a conscious design
choice, not a correctly followed prepared formula that is beyond critique.
Choosing the background color requires the author to understand the
potential of color as a meaning-making mode. This is a consequential decision in text creation.

Children still need to learn to write canonically, with culturally appropriate formal spelling, and they must be able to judge when to use what
codification system. Texting is texting; it runs on other standards. Handwriting continues to be a very useful portable technology though manual
encoding technologies are used less and less as we become enmeshed in
a cyberworld; human-machine interfaces, such as keyboarding and navigating screens, must become a fundamental part of curricular learning.
Without this, we teach a saber-tooth curriculum (Peddiwell, 1939/2004) to
children in the 21st century.

Formal education must press on from epistemological visions of literacy
as alphabetic conventions, text grammars and stock, sanitized, static textbook passages. Though being proficient in the print literacy of yesterday is
still necessary, it is insufficient to literacy education today. The refocusing
of literacy priorities requires an urgent critical overhaul of curricular foci
and, essentially, testing procedures.

MEETING THE CHALLENGES OF THE FUTURE

Goldilocks led our learning community into an educational infrastructure
that was in disorder. The porridge, chairs and beds of formal schooling
were too cold, too hot, too weak, too soft and too hard in terms of conceptions of literacy, recognition and utilization of linguistic heterogeneity,
and testing concerns. Goldilocks' makeover pinpointed the serious need for
educational housecleaning. We have created a way to change the existing
order, working in one school in one city and connecting to colleagues and
students in other schools with minimal hardware, software from the public
domain and the courage to make a difference.

My first foray into multiliteracies in Melbourne, Australia (Lotherington, 2003b), alerted me to the distance between imagined literacies and
children's multilingual, multimodal abilities. On checking national literacy
testing in Australia to see how things have changed over the past decade
and a half, I find the following candid description:

In 2008, the National Assessment Program—Literacy and Numeracy
(NAPLAN) commenced in Australian schools. Every year, all students
in Years 3, 5, 7 and 9 are assessed on the same days using national tests
in Reading, Writing, Language Conventions (Spelling, Grammar and

Punctuation) and Numeracy. (Australian Curriculum and Assessment Reporting Authority, 2010, para. 1)

The information on this standardized paper-and-pencil test is available online; general information about the test is provided in video form; and numerous reports on student achievement can be downloaded in pdf format (Australian Curriculum and Assessment Reporting Authority, 2010). It is precisely this oxymoronic situation that promulgated my experimental investigations of multiliteracies.

Our work has grown and changed in tune with evolving technoculture, multimodal practices and educational ideas. The number of researchers participating has grown, and the work of the learning community now invokes theories of play in multimodal project creation, having found support for *ludic* pedagogies (de Castell & Jenson, 2003) in teachers' increasingly more sophisticated multiliteracies projects. We are rethinking *communicative competence* (Canale, 1983; Canale & Swain, 1980)—fundamentally theorized in second language education by my PhD supervisor, Michael Canale—for the digital era we live in (also see Leung, 2005), and systematically tracking avenues for assessment appropriate to multimodal literacies. And we continue to think about supportive and sustainable language networks that extend the walls of the classroom.

On the local front, we need to communicate to teachers across the full trajectory of public schooling, to bridge the media-savvy children of elementary schools to appropriate follow-on care at middle and secondary school. This requires permeating the consciousness of policy makers to make political change. In most urgent need of change is the fortress of standardized testing that undercuts expressive new literacies in favor of easily judged past models.

The work of a small group of teachers and researchers has illuminated a pathway for teaching literacy more imaginatively, engagingly, inclusively and coherently with the social world children will inherit upon leaving school. We have developed spaces for language inclusion so that children do not need to drop their backgrounds at the school door, only to be picked up again when they go home. We have demonstrated why a new vision of inclusive, multimodal literacy is crucial to the relevance of education, and how it can be accomplished with minimal financial input.

Though we are far from living happily ever after, I take heart from the Grade 2 children who so imaginatively rewrote *Goldilocks and the Three Bears* years ago. Given a far-fetched assignment to update a traditional story, they showed us a world of possibility within. Surely we can continue to do the same.

Notes

NOTES TO THE PREFACE

1. http://www.vsocan.org

NOTES TO CHAPTER 1

1. See Mishra and Hodge (2005) for an engaging discussion on postcolonialism.
2. *Musical Instrument Digital Interface.*
3. Real names are used for the school and the teachers and staff, but not for the children, in accordance with our informed consent procedures which permit choice in nonanonymity disclosure for participating teachers. Our research collective worked hard to achieve university and school board ethics committee approval for this condition on the request of the school which wanted to be named in the research.
4. Statistics provided by the school.
5. http://schools.tdsb.on.ca/joyce/main/index.html
6. Now Sandra Chow.
7. http://www.eqao.com/
8. Statistics provided by the school.
9. http://schools.tdsb.on.ca/joyce/main/about/technology.html

NOTES TO CHAPTER 2

1. See http://laws.justice.gc.ca/eng/C-18.7/page-2.html#anchorbo-ga:s_3 for the Multiculturalism Act.
2. Figures from http://www40.statcan.ca/l01/cst01/demo12c-eng.htm
3. Facts and figures are available at http://www.tdsb.on.ca/
4. Figures from http://www40.statcan.ca/l01/cst01/demo12c-eng.htm
5. See http://www.tdsb.on.ca/programs/continuing_education/int_lang/default .asp and http://www.tcdsb.org/curriculum/internationallanguages.html# LANGUAGE%20LISTIN .
6. A good example is the *Kitāb Gharā'ib al-funūn wa-mulaḥ al-'uyūn* (*The Book of Curiosities of the Sciences and Marvels for the Eyes*) available for viewing online at the Bodleian Library, University of Oxford: http://cosmos. bodley.ox.ac.uk/content.php/boc?expand=732
7. http://www.bookofkells.ie/book-of-kells/
8. This fact is according to the British Library. *The Diamond Sutra* can be seen at: http://www.bl.uk/onlinegallery/sacredtexts/diamondsutra.html

9. Gutenberg's Bible can be viewed at: http://www.bl.uk/onlinegallery/sacred-texts/gutenberg.html
10. Photography in Figures 2.3 and 2.4 is courtesy of Maya Woloszyn.
11. The *Lisbon Hebrew Bible* manuscript can be viewed at: http://www.bl.uk/onlinegallery/onlineex/expfaith/judmanu/lisbbible/zoomify74023.html
12. See the mouse's tale/tail on page 28 of the original manuscript, *Alice's Adventures Under Ground*, at: http://www.bl.uk/onlinegallery/ttp/alice/accessible/pages28and29.html#content
13. Image from the public domain available under the Creative Commons Attribution/Share-Alike License retrieved from http://commons.wikimedia.org/wiki/File:Chaucer_knight.jpg
14. This information was personal communication from Dr. Bruce Barker-Benfield, Curator of Medieval Manuscripts at the Bodleian Library, University of Oxford, who personally guided our small Christ Church seminar group, headed by Dr. Julia Cresswell, through the parchment pages of the medieval bestiary, MS. Bodley 764, on July 29, 2010.

NOTES TO CHAPTER 3

1. I wish to acknowledge with gratitude the Social Sciences and Humanities Research Council of Canada for awarding me the SSHRC small research grant: *Rewriting Goldilocks: Emergent Transliteracies*.
2. http://www.torontopubliclibrary.ca/uni_spe_osb_collection.jsp
3. The Ontario Ministry of Education licenses software for educational download to school teachers under the Ontario Software Acquisition Program Advisory Committee (OSAPAC): http://www.osapac.org
4. These collages are shaped as posters, using ComicLife, to highlight selected original hypercards from children's stories.
5. http://www.ytv.com/

NOTES TO CHAPTER 4

1. My sincere gratitude to Research and Field Development, Faculty of Education, York University for supporting our work towards and presentation of a professional workshop on multiliteracies pedagogies for teachers across Toronto.
2. My grateful appreciation to the York University Educational Research Centre librarian for clarifying this process. Ontario-based teachers can search out software titles at: http://www.osapac.org
3. All children are given pseudonyms.

NOTES TO CHAPTER 5

1. I gratefully acknowledge the Social Sciences and Humanities Research Council of Canada for awarding standard research grant 410–2005–2080 in support of: *Emergent Multiliteracies in Theory and Practice: Multicultural Literacy Development at Elementary School*.
2. The men's team, though top contenders, did uncharacteristically poorly at the 2006 Torino Winter Olympics, not even making the medal rounds; the women's team, also top contenders, played very well, winning the gold medal.

3. Lego is the brand name for snap together toy building bricks: http://www.lego.com

NOTES TO CHAPTER 6

1. See: http://www.edu.gov.on.ca/eng/general/elemsec/speced/iep/iep.html#what
2. There are ongoing arguments over the authorship of this work attributed to V. N. Vološinov, alleging M. Bakhtin actually wrote overtly Marxist orientations to language and attributed them to friends. This argument is not taken up here.
3. See para. 11: http://www2.parl.gc.ca/content/lop/researchpublications/936-e.htm
4. Nia Vardalos, who grew up in Winnipeg, Canada, spotlighted this issue in her film: *My Big Fat Greek Wedding*, where the children's brown-bagged home-cooked *moussaka* is crudely mocked at school.
5. http://louisebennett.com/

NOTES TO CHAPTER 7

1. *Ain't* is particularly ascribed to African American Vernacular English (AAVE). See Labov (1972).
2. My sincere thanks to my graduate assistant, Robert Wood, for his excellent photographic documentation.
3. The full comic can be accessed at: http://www.multiliteracies4kidz.ca/stone_sandwiches.html
4. http://www.unicef.org/crc/
5. The video can be viewed at: http://www.multiliteracies4kidz.ca/iqbal.html

NOTES TO CHAPTER 8

1. NALDIC Annual Conference 17: *Integrated Language, Integrated Curriculum*. Reading, England, November, 14, 2009.

References

Abbott, J. (2006). *King Alfred of England*. Teddington, Middlesex, England: The Echo Library.

Abram, D. (1997). *The spell of the sensuous*. New York, NY: Vintage Books.

Agnello, M. F. (2001). *A postmodern literacy policy analysis*. New York, NY: Peter Lang.

Allen, G. (2000). *Intertextuality*. London, England: Routledge.

Amaro, G. (2000). *Curriculum innovation in Portugal: The "Area Escola"—an arena for cross-curricular activities and curriculum development* (Innodata Monographs 5). Switzerland: International Bureau of Education. Retrieved from Education Resources Information Center website: http://www.eric.ed.gov/ERIC WebPortal/search/detailmini.jsp?_nfpb=true&_&ERICExtSearch_Search Value_0=ED448073&ERICExtSearch_SearchType_0=no&accno=ED448073

Anonymous. (1856). *The three bears* (Second series of Aunt Mavor's Picture Books for Little Readers). London, England: Routledge.

Anonymous. (1888). *The three bears* (Young Folk series). New York, NY: McLoughlin.

Anonymous. (circa 1901). *The three bears*. Akron, OH: Saalfield.

Appadurai, A. J. (1996). *Modernity at large: Cultural dimensions of globalization*. Minneapolis, MN: University of Minnesota Press.

Ashliman, D. L. (2004). *Folk and fairy tales: A handbook*. Westport, CT: Greenwood Press.

Australian Bureau of Statistics. (1997). *Aspects of literacy: Assessed skill levels (Australia 1996)*. Canberra, Australia: Australian Government Publishing Service.

Australian Curriculum and Assessment Reporting Authority. (2010). *National assessment program literacy and numeracy: Welcome*. Retrieved from the ACARA website: http://www.naplan.edu.au/home_page.html

Ausubel, D. (1960). The use of advance organizers in the learning and retention of meaningful verbal material. *Journal of Educational Psychology, 51*(5), 267–272.

Ayers, W. (2010). Class warriors. *Academic Matters, May*, 3–7.

Baetens Beardsmore, H. (2003). Who is afraid of bilingualism? In J.-M. Dewaele, A. Housen & L. Wei (Eds.), *Bilingualism: Beyond basic principles* (pp. 10–27). Clevedon, England: Multilingual Matters.

Bakhtin, M. M. (1981). Discourse in the novel (C. Emerson & M. Holquist, Trans.). In M. Holquist (Ed.), *The dialogic imagination: Four essays by M. M. Bakhtin* (pp. 257–422). Austin, TX: University of Texas Press. (Original work published 1975)

Baldry, A. (2000). Introduction. In A. Baldry (Ed.), *Multimodality and multimediality in the distance learning age* (pp. 11–39). Campobasso, Italy: Palladino Editore.

Ball, A. F., & Freedman, S. W. (Eds.). (2004). *Bakhtinian perspectives on language, literacy and learning*. Cambridge, England: Cambridge University Press.

Barlow, J. P. (1996). *A declaration of the independence of cyberspace*. Retrieved from https://projects.eff.org/~barlow/Declaration-Final.html

Barton, D. (1994). *Literacy: An introduction to the ecology of written language*. Oxford, England: Blackwell.

Bäuml, F. H. (1980). Varieties and consequences of medieval literacy and illiteracy. *Speculum, 55*(2), 237–265.

Bazerman, C. (2004). Intertextualities: Vološinov, Bakhtin, literary theory, and literacy. In A. F. Ball & S. W. Freedman (Eds.), *Bakhtinian perspectives on language, literacy and learning* (pp. 53–65). Cambridge, England: Cambridge University Press.

Beavis, C. (1997). Computer games, culture and curriculum. In I. Snyder (Ed.), *Page to screen: Taking literacy into the electronic era* (pp. 234–255). St. Leonards, New South Wales, Australia: Allen & Unwin.

Benson, H. H. (2000). *Socratic wisdom: The model of knowledge in Plato's early dialogues*. Oxford, England: Oxford University Press.

Bereiter, C., & Scardamalia, M. (2000). Process and product in problem-based learning (PBL) research. In D. H. Evensen & C. E. Hmelo (Eds.), *Problem-based learning: A research perspective on learning interactions* (pp. 185–195). Mahwah, NJ: Erlbaum.

Bettelheim, B. (1977). *The uses of enchantment: The meaning and importance of fairy tales*. New York, NY: Knopf.

Bezemer, J., & Kress, G. (2008). Writing in multimodal texts: A social semiotic account of designs for learning. *Written Communication, 25*(2), 166–195.

Bhabha, H. K. (1990a). DissemiNation: Time, narrative, and the margins of the modern nation. In H. K. Bhabha (Ed.), *Nation and narration* (pp. 291–322). London, England: Routledge.

Bhabha, H. K. (1990b). Introduction: Narrating the nation. In H. K. Bhabha (Ed.), *Nation and narration* (pp. 1–7). London, England: Routledge.

Bhabha, H. K. (1994). *The location of culture*. London, England: Routledge.

Bialystok, E. (2001). Metalinguistic aspects of bilingual processing. *Annual Review of Applied Linguistics, 21*, 169–181.

Bialystok, E., Craik, F. I. M., Kelin, R., &Viswanthan, M. (2004). Bilingualism, aging, and cognitive control: Evidence from the Simon task. *Psychology and Aging, 19*(2), 290–303. doi: 10.1037/0882–7974.19.2.290

Blommaert, J. (2005). *Discourse: A critical introduction*. Cambridge, England: Cambridge University Press.

Bogdan, R. C., & Biklen, S. K. (2003). *Qualitative research for education: An introduction to theory and methods* (4th ed.). Boston, MA: Allyn & Bacon.

Bourdieu, P. (1977). The economics of linguistic exchanges. *Social Science Information, 16*(6), 645–668. doi: 10.1177/053901847701600601

Bourdieu, P. (1991). *Language and symbolic power*. Cambridge, MA: Harvard University Press.

Briggs, K. M. (1970). *Dictionary of British folk-tales in the English language: Part A: Folk narratives*. London, England: Routledge & Kegan Paul.

Brunelle, M. D. (2003). Why free software matters for literacy educators. In B. C. Bruce (Ed.), *Literacy in the information age: Inquiries into meaning making with new technologies* (pp. 107–113). Newark, DE: International Reading Association.

Bruner, J. (1986). *Actual minds, possible worlds*. Cambridge, MA: Harvard University Press.

Bruner, J. (1991). The narrative construction of reality. *Critical Inquiry, 18*(1), 1–21.

Burn, A. (2009). *Making new media: Creative production and digital literacies*. New York, NY: Peter Lang.

Canadian Heritage. (2010). Development of official-language communities program: Minority language component. Retrieved from http://canadianheritage. gc.ca/pgm/lo-ol/pgm/dclo-elm-eng.cfm

Canale, M. (1983). From communicative competence to communicative language pedagogy. In J. C. Richards & R. W. Schmitt (Eds.), *Language and communication* (pp. 2–27). London, England: Longman.

Canale, M., & Swain, M. (1980). Theoretical bases of communicative approaches to second language teaching and testing. *Applied Linguistics, 1,* 1–47.

Castells, M. (2010). *The rise of the network society* (2nd ed.). Chichester, West Sussex, England: Wiley-Blackwell.

Cazden, C. B. (1997). Performance before competence: Assistance to child discourse in the zone of proximal development. In M. Cole, Y. Engestrom & O. Vasquez (Eds.), *Mind, culture and activity: Seminal papers from the laboratory of comparative human cognition* (pp. 303–310). Cambridge, England: Cambridge University Press.

Cenoz, J., & Genesee, F. (1998). Psycholinguistic perspectives on multilingualism and multilingual education. In J. Cenoz & F. Genesee (Eds.), *Beyond bilingualism: Multilingualism and multilingual education* (pp. 16–32). Clevedon, England: Multilingual Matters.

Churchill, S. (1998). *Official languages in Canada: Changing the language landscape.* Ottawa, Ontario, Canada: Canadian Heritage.

Cilliers, P. (1998). *Complexity and postmodernism: Understanding complex systems.* London, England: Routledge.

Clanchy, M. (2002). Does writing construct the state? *Journal of Historical Sociology, 15*(1), 68–70.

Clandinin, J. D., & Connelly, E. M. (2000). *Narrative inquiry: Experience and story in qualitative research.* San Francisco, CA: Jossey-Bass.

Clyne, M. G. (2003). Towards a more language-centred approach to plurilingualism. In J.-M. Dewaele, A. Housen & L. Wei (Eds.), *Bilingualism: Beyond basic principles* (pp. 43–55). Clevedon, England: Multilingual Matters.

Comenius, J. A. (1689). *Joh. Amos Comnienii Orbis sensualium pictus: hoc est, Omnium fundamentalium in mundo rerum, & in vita actionum, pictura & nomenclatura* [Early English Books Online, British Library. Reel position: Wing / 2651:16]. Retrieved from http://www.library.yorku.ca/find/Record/1865464

Cookson, P. W., & Welner, K. G. (Eds.). (2008, December). *Fellows' Education Letters to the President.* Tempe, AZ: Education Policy Research Unit, & Boulder, CO: Education and the Public Interest Center. Retrieved from http://epicpolicy. org/publication/Letters-to-Obama

Cooper, C. (2010, August 8). Reading and writing. *The Gleaner.* Retrieved from http://www.jamaica-gleaner.com/gleaner/20100808/cleisure/cleisure3.html

Cope, B., & Kalantzis, M. (Eds.). (2000). *Multiliteracies: Literacy learning and the design of social futures.* London, England: Routledge.

Cope, B., & Kalantzis, M. (2009a). A grammar of multimodality. *The International Journal of Learning, 16*(2), 361–425.

Cope, B., & Kalantzis, M. (2009b). "Multiliteracies": New literacies, new learning. *Pedagogies, 4*(3), 164–195.

Crystal, D. (1997). *English as a global language.* Cambridge, England: Cambridge University Press.

Crystal, D. (2001). *Language and the Internet.* Cambridge, England: Cambridge University Press.

Crystal, D. (2008). Texting. *ELT Journal, 16*(1), 77–83.

Cummins, J. (1981a). *Bilingualism and minority language children.* Toronto, Ontario, Canada: Ontario Institute for Studies in Education of the University of Toronto.

Cummins, J. (1991). Interdependence of first- and second-language proficiency. In E. Bialystok (Ed.), *Language processing in bilingual children* (pp. 70–89). Cambridge, England: Cambridge University Press.

Cummins, J. (1992). Heritage language teaching in Canadian schools. *Journal of Curriculum Studies, 24*(3), 281–286.

Cummins, J. (1996). *Negotiating identities: Education for empowerment in a diverse society.* Los Angeles, CA: California Association for Bilingual Education.

Cummins, J. (2000). Language, power and pedagogy: *Bilingual children in the crossfire.* Clevedon, England: Multilingual Matters.

Cummins, J. (2001a). HER Classic: Empowering minority students: A framework for intervention. *Harvard Educational Review, 71*(4), 649–655.

Cummins, J. (2001b). *Negotiating identities: Education for empowerment in a diverse society* (2nd ed.). Los Angeles, CA: California Association for Bilingual Education.

Cummins, J. (2006). Identity texts: The imaginative construction of self through multiliteracies pedagogy. In O. Garcia, T. Skutnabb-Kangas & M. E. Torres-Guzmán (Eds.), *Imagining multilingual schools: Languages in education and glocalization* (pp. 51–68). Clevedon, England: Multilingual Matters.

Cummins, J., Bismilla, V., Chow, P., Cohen, S., Giampapa, F., Leoni, L., Sandhu, P., & Sastri, P. (2005). Affirming identity in multilingual classrooms. *Educational Leadership, 63*(1), 38–43.

Cummins, J., Bismilla, V., Cohen, S., Giampapa, F., & Leoni, L. (2005). Timelines and lifelines: Rethinking literacy instruction in multilingual classrooms. *Orbit, 36*(1), 22–26.

Cummins, J., & Danesi, M. (1990) *Heritage languages: The development and denial of Canada's linguistic resources.* Toronto, Ontario, Canada: Our Schools.

D'Adamo, F. (2003). *Iqbal: A novel* (A. Leonori, Trans.). New York, NY: Atheneum.

Davis, B., Sumara, D., & Luce-Kapler, R. (2008). *Engaging minds: Changing teaching in complex times* (2nd ed.). New York, NY: Routledge.

de Castell, S., & Jenson, J. (2003). Serious play: Curriculum for a post-talk era. *Journal of the Canadian Association for Curriculum Studies, 1*(1), 47–52.

de Castell, S., & Jenson, J. (2007). Introduction. In S. de Castell & J. Jenson (Eds.), *Worlds in play: International perspectives on digital games research* (pp. 1–8). New York, NY: Peter Lang.

Delpit, L. (1988). The silenced dialogue: Power and pedagogy in the education of other peoples' children. *Harvard Educational Review, 58*(3), 280–298.

Delpit, L. (1995). *Other people's children: Cultural conflicts in the classroom.* New York, NY: New Press.

Delwiche, A. (2010). Media literacy 2.0: Unique characteristics of video games. In K. Tyner (Ed.), *Media literacy: New agendas in communication* (pp. 175–191). New York, NY: Routledge.

Deschenes, S., Cuban, L., & Tyack, D. (2001). Mismatch: Historical perspectives on schools and students who don't fit them. *Teachers College Record, 103*(4), 525–547.

Devonish, H., & Harry, O. G. (2005). Jamaican Creole and Jamaican English: Phonology. In E. W. Schneider, K. Burridge, B. Kortmann, R. Mesthrie & C. Upton (Eds.), *A handbook of varieties of English* (Vol. 1, pp. 450–480). Berlin, Germany: Mouton de Gruyter.

Dewey, J. (1998). *Experience and education: The 60th anniversary edition.* Indianapolis, IN: Kappa Delta Pi. (Original work published 1938)

Dewey, M. (2009). English as a lingua franca: Heightened variability and theoretical implications. In A. Mauranen & E. Ranta (Eds.), *English as a Lingua Franca: Studies and findings* (pp. 60–83). Newcastle upon Tyne, England: Cambridge Scholars Press.

Dewing, M., & Leman, M. (2006). *Canadian multiculturalism* (Current Issues Review 93–6E). Library of Parliament. Retrieved from http://www2.parl.gc.ca/content/lop/researchpublications/936-e.htm

Duff, P. A., & Li, D. (2009). Indigenous, minority, and heritage language education in Canada: Policies, contexts, and issues. *Canadian Modern Language Review,* 66(1), 1–8. doi: 10.1353/cml.0.0100

Duffy, A. (2004). *Class struggles: Public education and the new Canadian* (Special report: The 2003 Atkinson Fellowship in Public Policy). Retrieved from the Atkinson Charitable Foundation website: http://www.atkinsonfoundation.ca/updates/Document_1106172663284/view

Dyson, A. H. (1993). *Social worlds of children learning to write in an urban primary school.* New York, NY: Teachers College Press.

Dyson, A. H. (2003). *The brothers and sisters learn to write: Popular literacies in childhood and school cultures.* New York, NY: Teachers College Press.

Eaton, S. E. (2010). *Global trends in language learning in the twenty-first century.* Calgary, Alberta, Canada: Onate Press. Retrieved from http://www.eatonintl.com

Education Quality and Accountability Office (EQAO). (2007). *Grade 3 Assessment of reading, writing and mathematics, primary division. Student Booklet, Language 1.* Retrieved from the Education Quality and Accountability Office website: http://www.eqao.com/Parents/Elementary/036/BookletsandGuides.aspx?Lang=E&gr=036&yr=07

Education Quality and Accountability Office (EQAO). (2008). *Grade 3 Assessment of reading, writing and mathematics, primary division. Student Booklet, Mathematics.* Retrieved from the Education Quality and Accountability Office website: http://www.eqao.com/Parents/Elementary/036/BookletsandGuides.aspx?Lang=E&gr=036&yr=08

Education Quality and Accountability Office (EQAO). (2010a). *Improvement planning.* Retrieved from the Education Quality and Accountability Office website: http://www.eqao.com/IP/ImprovementPlanning.aspx?status=logout&Lang=E

Education Quality and Accountability Office (EQAO). (2010b). *Student resources.* Retrieved from the Education Quality and Accountability Office website: http://www.eqao.com/Students/students.aspx?Lang=E

Education Quality and Accountability Office (EQAO). (2010c). *What parents need to know about province-wide testing.* Retrieved from the Education Quality and Accountability Office website: http://www.eqao.com/Parents/Elementary/036/036.aspx?Lang=E&gr=036

Education Quality and Accountability Office (EQAO). (2011). *Ontario Province-wide Tests. Ontario Secondary School Literacy Test, 2007–2008.* Retrieved from the Education Quality and Accountability Office website: http://www.eqao.com/Test/OSSLT/Question.aspx?Lang=E&itemID=10_B2_S6_Q1

Egan, K. (1993). Narrative and learning: A voyage of implications. *Linguistics and Education, 5*(2), 119–126.

Egan, K. (2000). Forward to the 19th century. *Teaching Education, 11*(1), 75–77.

Egan, K. (2001, August). The cognitive tools of children's imagination. Paper presented at the Annual European Conference on Quality in Early Childhood Education. Retrieved from the Imaginative Education Research Group website: http://www.ierg.net.

Eisenstein, E. L. (1979). *The printing press as an agent of change.* Cambridge, England: Cambridge University Press.

Elementary Teachers' Federation of Ontario (ETFO). (2010). *EQAO testing.* Retrieved from the Elementary Teachers' Federation of Ontario website: http://www.etfo.ca/issuesineducation/eqaotesting/pages/default.aspx

Elms, A. C. (1977). "The three bears": Four interpretations. *The Journal of American Folklore, 90*(357), 257–273.

Feuerverger, G. (1997). "On the edges of the map": A study of heritage language teachers in Ontario. *Teaching and Teacher Education, 13*(1), 39–53.

Fillmore, C. J. (1981). Real readers and ideal readers. *Proceedings of the 32nd Georgetown Roundtable on Languages and Linguistics*. Washington, DC: Georgetown University Press.

Finnegan, R. (1988). *Literacy and orality: Studies in the technology of communication*. Oxford, England: Basil Blackwell.

Finnegan, R. (2005). The how of literature. *Oral Tradition, 20*(2), 164–187.

Fitzmaurice, S. (2000). *The Spectator*, the politics of social networks, and language standardisation in eighteenth-century England. In L. Wright (Ed.), *The development of standard English 1300–1800: Theories, descriptions, conflicts* (pp. 195–218). Cambridge, England: Cambridge University Press.

Flutter, J. (2007). Teacher development and pupil voice. *Curriculum Journal, 18*(3), 343–354. doi: 10.1080/09585170701589983

Fox, J., & Cheng, L. (2007). Did we take the same test? Differing accounts of the Ontario Secondary School Literacy Test by first and second language test-takers. *Assessment in Education, 14*(1), 9–26. doi: 10.1080/09695940701272773

Freebody, P., & LoBianco, J. (1997). *Australian literacies*. Canberra, Australia: Language Australia.

Freedman, S. W., & Ball, A. F. (2004). Ideological becoming: Bakhtinian concepts to guide the study of language, literacy, and learning. In A. F. Ball & S. W. Freedman (Eds.), *Bakhtinian perspectives on language, literacy and learning* (pp. 3–33). Cambridge, England: Cambridge University Press.

Freire, P. (1998). *Pedagogy of the oppressed* (new rev. 20th anniversary ed., M. B. Ramos, Trans.). New York, NY: Continuum. (Original work published 1970)

Freire, P., & Macedo, D. P. (1987). *Literacy: Reading the word and the world*. South Hadley, MA: Bergen and Garvey.

Gal, I. (2002). Adults' statistical literacy: Meanings, components, responsibilities. *International Statistical Review, 70*(1), 1–51.

Gardner, H. (2003, April). Multiple intelligences after twenty years. Paper presented to the American Educational Research Association, Chicago, IL. Retrieved from http://www.howardgardner.com/Papers/papers.html

Gardner, H. (2008). The five minds for the future. *Schools: Studies in education, 5*(1–2), 17–24.

Garrison, D. R., & Anderson, T. (2003). *E-learning in the 21st century: A framework for research and practice*. London, England: Routledge Falmer.

Gayá Wicks, P., & Reason, P. (2009). Initiating action research: Challenges and paradoxes of opening communicative space. *Action Research, 7*(3), 243–262. doi: 10.1177/1476750309336715

Gee, J. P. (2000). New people in new worlds: Networks, the new capitalism and schools. In B. Cope & M. Kalantzis (Eds.), *Multiliteracies: Literacy learning and the design of social futures* (pp. 43–68). London, England: Routledge.

Gee, J. P. (2003). *What video games have to teach us about learning and literacy*. New York, NY: Palgrave Macmillan.

Gee, J. P. (2004a). New times and new literacies: Themes for a changing world. In A. F. Ball & S. W. Freedman (Eds.), *Bakhtinian perspectives on language, literacy and learning* (pp. 279–306). Cambridge, England: Cambridge University Press.

Gee, J. P. (2004b). *Situated language and learning: A critique of traditional schooling*. New York, NY: Routledge.

Gee, J. P. (2007). Are video games good for learning? In S. de Castell & J. Jenson (Eds.), *Worlds in play: International perspectives on digital games research* (pp. 323–335). New York, NY: Peter Lang.

Gee, J. P. (2008). Literacy, video games, and popular culture. In K. Drotner & S. Livingston (Eds.), *The international handbook of children, media, and culture* (pp. 196–212). Los Angeles, CA: Sage.

Geertz, C. (1973). *The interpretation of cultures: Selected essays*. New York, NY: Basic Books.

Genesee, F. (1987). *Learning through two languages: Studies of immersion and bilingual education*. Cambridge, MA: Newbury House.

Giroux, H. (2000). *Impure acts: The practical politics of cultural studies*. New York, NY: Routledge.

Graff, H. J. (1987). *The labyrinths of literacy: Reflections on literacy, past and present*. London, England: Falmer Press.

Graff, H. J. (2001). Literacy's myths and legacies: From lessons from the history of literacy, to the question of critical literacy. In P. Freebody, S. Muspratt & B. Dwyer (Eds.), *Difference, silence and textual practice: Studies in critical literacy* (pp. 1–30). Cresskill, NJ: Hampton Press.

Gramsci, A. (1971). *Selections from the prison notebooks of Antonio Gramsci* (Q. Hoare & G. N. Smith, Eds. & Trans.). London, England: Lawrence & Wishart.

Graves, D. H. (1983). *Writing: Teacher and children at work*. Portsmouth, NH: Heinemann Educational.

Graves, D. H., & Kittle, P. (2005). *Inside writing: How to teach the details of craft*. Portsmouth, NH: Heinemann.

Grubium, J. F., & Holstein, J. A. (2009). *Analyzing narrative reality*. Thousand Oaks, CA: Sage.

Guilherme, M. (2002). *Critical citizens for an intercultural world: Foreign language education as cultural politics*. Clevedon, England: Multilingual Matters.

Gutiérrez, K. D. (2008). Developing a sociocritical literacy in the third space. *Reading Research Quarterly, 43*(2), 148–164.

Hamer, N. (2009). The lion, the witch and the cereal box: Reading children's literature across multimedia franchises. In S. S. Peterson, D. Booth & C. Jupiter (Eds.), *Books, media and the Internet: Children's literature for today's classrooms* (pp. 121–135). Winnipeg, Manitoba, Canada: Portage & Main.

Harklau, L. (2003). *Generation 1.5 students and college writing* (CAL Digests: EDO-FL-03–05). Retrieved from the Center for Applied Linguistics website: http://www.cal.org/resources/digest/0305harklau.html

Harris, M. (1976). History and significance of the emic/etic distinction. *Annual Review of Anthropology, 5*, 329–350.

Hawisher, G. E., & Selfe, C. L. (Eds.). (2000). *Global literacies and the worldwide web*. London, England: Routledge.

Heath, S. B. (1983). *Ways with words: Language, life, and work in communities and classrooms*. Cambridge, England: Cambridge University Press.

Holquist, M. (Ed.). (1981). *The dialogic imagination: Four essays by M. M. Bakhtin*. Austin, TX: University of Texas Press.

Hornberger, N. (2001). Multilingual language policies and the continua of biliteracy: An ecological approach. *Language Policy, 1*(1), 27–51.

Hudson, R. (2000). *I amn't. Language, 76*(2), 297–323.

Hymes, D. (1996). *Ethnography, linguistics, narrative inequality*. London, England: Taylor and Francis.

Ibrahim, A. (2004). Operating under erasure: Hip-hop and the pedagogy of affect(ive). *Journal of Curriculum Theorizing, 20*(1), 113–133.

Ibrahim, A. (2008). Operating under erasure: Race/language/identity. *Canadian and International Education Journal, 37*(2), 56–76.

Illich, I. (1972). *Deschooling society*. New York, NY: Harrow Books. (Original work published 1970)

Innes, M. (1998). Memory, orality and literacy in an early medieval society. *Past and Present, 158*, 3–36.

International Committee of the Fourth International (ICFI). (1998). *World socialist web site: Canada*. Retrieved from http://www.wsws.org/articles/2005/mar2005/wkrs-m29.shtml

Jenkins, H. (2004). The cultural logic of media convergence. *International Journal of Cultural Studies, 7*, 33–43. doi: 10.1177/1367877904040603

Jenkins, H. (2006). *Convergence culture: Where old and new media collide*. New York, NY: New York University Press.

Jewitt, C. (2002). The move from page to screen: The multimodal reshaping of school English. *Visual Communication, 1*(2), 171–195.

Jewitt, C. (Ed.). (2009). Introduction: Handbook rationale, scope, and structure. In C. Jewitt (Ed.), *The Routledge handbook of multimodal analysis* (pp. 1–7). Abingdon, Oxon, England: Routledge.

Johnson, B. (2010, July 19). Illiteracy is bad for us—so why don't we do something about it? *The Daily Telegraph*, p. 16.

Johnson, D. (2009). *How do work stoppages and work-to-rule campaigns change elementary school assessment results?* Unpublished manuscript.

Johnson, R. K., & Swain, M. (Eds.). (1997). *Immersion education: International perspectives*. Cambridge, England: Cambridge University Press.

Johnson, S. (2005). *Everything bad is good for you: How today's popular culture is actually making us smarter*. New York, NY: Riverhead Books.

Katz, L. G., & Chard, S. C. (2000). *Engaging children's minds: The project approach* (2nd ed.) Stamford, CT: Ablex.

Kay, P. (1983, March). *Three properties of the ideal reader* (Berkeley Cognitive Science Report Series). Retrieved from http://www.terpconnect.umd.edu

Kellner, D. (2003). Toward a critical theory of education. *Democracy and Nature, 9*(1), 51–64.

Kellner, D. M. (2004). Technological transformation, multiple literacies and the re-visioning of education. *E-Learning and Digital Media, 1*(1), 9–37.

Kharkhurin, A. V. (2010). Bilingual verbal and nonverbal creative behavior. *International Journal of Bilingualism, 14*(2), 211–226.

Kramsch, C. (2009). Third culture and language education. In L. Wei & V. Cook (Eds.), *Contemporary applied linguistics: Vol. 1. Language teaching and learning* (pp. 233–254). London, England: Continuum.

Kress, G. (1997). *Before writing: Rethinking the paths to literacy*. New York, NY: Routledge.

Kress, G. (2000). Multimodality: Challenges to thinking about language. *TESOL Quarterly, 34*(2), 337–340.

Kress, G. (2003). *Literacy in the new media age*. London, England: Routledge.

Kress, G. (2009a, November). *The future of language*. Public lecture presented at Technology Enhanced Learning and Teaching, Languages of the Wider World, School of Oriental and African Studies, and University College London, Centre for Excellence in Teaching and Learning, London, England.

Kress, G. (2009b). What is a mode? In C. Jewitt (Ed.), *The Routledge handbook of multimodal analysis* (pp. 54–67). Abingdon, Oxon, England: Routledge.

Kress, G. (2010). *Multimodality: A social semiotic approach to contemporary communication*. Abingdon, Oxon, England: Routledge.

Kress, G., & van Leeuwen, T. (2006). *Reading images: The grammar of visual design* (2nd ed.). London, England: Routledge.

Kunz, J.L. (2008). *Multicultural Canada in the 21st century: Harnessing opportunities and managing pressures*. Government of Canada, Policy Research Initiative. Retrieved from http://www.policyresearch.gc.ca/page.asp?pagenm=rp_mult_bkg

Labov, W. (1972). Negative attraction and negative concord. *English grammar. Language, 48*(4), 773–818.

Labov, W. (1997). Some further steps in narrative analysis. *Journal of Narrative and Life History, 7,* 395–415. Retrieved from http://www.ling.upenn.edu/~wlabov/sfs.html

Labov, W. (2006). Narrative preconstruction. *Narrative Inquiry, 16*(1), 37–45.

Labov, W., & Waletzky, J. (2004). Narrative analysis: Oral versions of personal experience In C. B. Paulston & G. R. Tucker (Eds.), *Sociolinguistics: The essential readings* (pp. 74–104). Malden, MA: Blackwell.

Lai, A. (2007). Two translations of the Chinese Cinderella story. *Perspectives: Studies in Translatology, 15,* 49–56.

Lambert, W. (1974). Culture and language as factors in learning and education. In F. E. Abour & R. D. Meade (Eds.), *Cultural factors in learning and education* (pp. 91–122). Bellingham, WA: 5th Western Washington Symposium on Learning.

Landay, E. (2004). Performance as the foundation for a secondary school literacy program: A Bakhtinian perspective. In A. F. Ball & S. W. Freedman (Eds.), *Bakhtinian perspectives on language, literacy and learning* (pp. 107–128). Cambridge, England: Cambridge University Press.

Lankshear, C. (1997). *Changing literacies.* Buckingham, England: Open University Press.

Lankshear, C., & Knobel, M. (2003). *New literacies: Changing knowledge and classroom learning.* Buckingham, England: Open University Press.

Lankshear, C., & Knobel, M. (2006). *New literacies: Everyday practices and classroom learning* (2nd ed.). Maidenhead, Berkshire, England: Open University Press and McGraw-Hill Education.

Lessig, L. (2001). *The future of ideas: The fate of the commons in a connected world.* New York, NY: Random House. Retrieved from http://the-future-of-ideas.com

Leung, C. (2005). Convivial communication: Recontextualizing communicative competence. *International Journal of Applied Linguistics, 15*(2), 119–144.

Li, X. (2008). A tale of two provinces: Who makes stronger vertical equity efforts. *Canadian Journal of Educational Administration and Policy, 83,* 1–19.

Livo, N. J. (1994). *Who's afraid . . . ? Facing children's fears with folktales.* Englewood, CA: Teacher Ideas Press.

Lo Bianco, J. (2001). Language policies: State texts for silencing and giving voice. In P. Freebody, S. Muspratt & B. Dwyer (Eds.), *Difference, silence and textual practice: Studies in critical literacy* (pp. 31–71). Cresskill, NJ: Hampton Press.

Lo Bianco, J. (2003). Making language education policies: A needed response to globalization. *Modern Language Journal, 87*(2), 286–288.

Lotherington, H. (1998). Education in post-colonial Fiji: Language choices and social reality. *Journal of Intercultural Studies, 19*(1), 57–67.

Lotherington, H. (2003a). Emergent metaliteracies: What the Xbox has to offer the EQAO. *Linguistics and Education, 14*(3–4), 305–319.

Lotherington, H. (2003b). Multiliteracies in Springvale: Negotiating language, culture and identity in suburban Melbourne. In R. Bayley & S. Schechter (Eds.), *Language socialization in bilingual and multilingual societies* (pp. 200–217). Clevedon, England: Multilingual Matters.

Lotherington, H. (2005). Writing postmodern fairy tales at Main Street School: Digital narratives and evolving transliteracies. *McGill Journal of Education, 40*(1), 109–119.

Lotherington, H., & Chow, S. (2006). Rewriting *Goldilocks* in the urban, multicultural elementary school. *The Reading Teacher, 60*(3), 244–252.

Lotherington, H., Neville-Verardi, D., & Sinitskaya Ronda, N. (2009). English in cyberspace: Negotiating hypertext literacies. In L. B. Abraham & L. Williams

(Eds.), *Electronic discourses in language learning and language teaching* (pp. 11–42). Amsterdam, The Netherlands: John Benjamins.

Lotherington, H., Sotoudeh, S., Holland, M., & Zentena, M. (2008). Project-based community language learning: Three narratives of multilingual storytelling in early childhood education. *Canadian Modern Language Review*, 65(1), 125–145.

'Lotherington, H., & Xu, Y. (2004). How to chat in English and Chinese: Emerging digital language conventions. *ReCALL*, 16(2), 308–329.

Lotherington-Woloszyn, H. (1995). Television's emergence as an English as a second language and literacy socializer in Fiji. *Pacific-Asian Education*, 7(1 & 2), 60–66.

Louie, A. (1999). *Yeh-shen: A Cinderella story from China*. New York, NY: Puffin.

Luke, A. (1993). *The social construction of literacy in the primary school*. Melbourne, Victoria, Australia: Macmillan Education Australia.

Luke, A. (2000). Critical literacy in Australia: A matter of context and standpoint. *Journal of Adolescent & Adult Literacy*, 43(5), 448–461.

Luke, A. (2008). On the situated and ambiguous effects of literacy. *International Journal of Bilingual Education and Bilingualism*, 11(2), 246–249.

Luke, A., & Freebody, P. (1997). Critical literacy and the question of normativity: An introduction. In S. Muspratt, A. Luke & P. Freebody (Eds.), *Constructing critical literacies: Teaching and learning textual practice* (pp. 1–18). St. Leonards, New South Wales, Australia: Allen & Unwin.

Luke, C. (1995). Media literacy and cultural studies. In S. Muspratt, A. Luke & P. Freebody (Eds.), *Constructing critical literacies: Teaching and learning textual practice* (p. 19–49). St. Leonard's, New South Wales, Australia: Allen & Unwin.

Luke, C. (2000). What next? Toddler netizens, playstation thumb, techno-literacies. *Contemporary Issues in Early Childhood*, 1(1), 95–100.

Lye, T. (1677). *A spelling book: or, Reading and spelling made easie: Wherein all the words of our English Bible are set down in an alphabetical order, and divided into their distinct syllabls. Together with the grounds of the English tongue laid in verse, wherein are couch'd many moral precepts. By the help whereof, with Gods blessing, little children and others of ordinary capacities, may in few months be enabled exactly to read and spell the whole Bible* (2nd ed.). London, England: printed for Tho. Parkhurst, at the Bible and Three Crowns in Cheapside near Mercers-Chappel, and at the Bible on London-Bridge. [Electronic reproduction. Ann Arbor, MI: UMI 1999- (Early English books online) Digital version of: Early English books, 1641–1700; 2034:6. s1999 miun s] Retrieved from http://theta.library.yorku.ca/uhtbin/cgisirsi/x/0/0/5?searchdata1=a1841023{CKEY}

Lyotard, J. F. (1984). *The postmodern condition: A report on knowledge* (G. Bennington & B. Massumi, Trans.). Minneapolis, MN: University of Minnesota Press.

Marsh, J. (2004). The techno-literacy practices of young children. *Journal of Early Childhood Research*, 2(1), 51–66.

Marsh, J. (2005). Ritual, performance and identity construction: Young children's engagement with popular cultural and media texts. In J. Marsh (Ed.), *Popular culture, new media and digital literacy in early childhood* (pp. 21–38). London, England: Routledge Falmer.

Marsh, J. (2006). Global, local/public, private: Young children's engagement in digital literacy practices in the home. In K. Pahl & J. Rowsell (Eds.), *Travel notes from the new literacy studies: Instances of practice* (pp. 19–38). Clevedon, England: Multilingual Matters.

Marsh, J., & Millard, E. (2000). *Literacy and popular culture: Using children's culture in the classroom*. London, England: Paul Chapman.

Marshall, C., & Rossman, G. B. (2006). *Designing qualitative research* (4th ed.). Thousand Oaks, CA: Sage.

Mateas, M., & Stern, A. (2007). Build it to understand it: Ludology meets narrative in game design space. In S. de Castell, & J. Jenson (Eds.), *Worlds in play: International perspectives on digital games research* (pp. 268–281). New York, NY: Peter Lang.

Maybin, J. (2009, November). Conceptions of voice. Presentation at the Centre for Language, Discourse and Communication, King's College, London, England.

Maynes, M. J. (1985). *Schooling in Western Europe: A social history.* Albany, NY: State University of New York Press.

McLuhan, M. (1962). *The Gutenberg galaxy: The making of typographic man.* Toronto, Ontario, Canada: University of Toronto Press.

McLuhan, M. (1964). *Understanding media: The extensions of man.* New York, NY: McGraw-Hill.

Meisel, J. M. (2004). The bilingual child. In T. K. Bhatia & W. C. Ritchie (Eds.), *The handbook of bilingualism* (pp. 91–113). Malden, MA: Blackwell.

Ministry of Education. (1994). *For the love of learning.* Queen's Printer for Ontario. Retrieved from http://www.edu.gov.on.ca/eng/general/abcs/rcom/full/volume2/chapter7.html

Ministry of Education. (2000a). *The Ontario curriculum Grades 11 and 12: Classical studies and international languages.* Queen's Printer for Ontario. Retrieved from http://www.edu.gov.on.ca

Ministry of Education (2000b). *The Ontario curriculum Grades 11 and 12: Native languages.* Queen's Printer for Ontario. Retrieved from http://www.edu.gov.on.ca

Ministry of Education. (2006). *The Ontario curriculum Grades 1–8: Language* (revised). Queen's Printer for Ontario. Retrieved from http://www.edu.gov.on.ca/eng/curriculum/elementary/language.html

Ministry of Education. (2007). *English language learners: ESL and ELD programs and services. Policies and procedures for Ontario Elementary and Secondary Schools, kindergarten to Grade 12.* Queen's Printer for Ontario. Retrieved from http://www.edu.gov.on.ca/eng/document/esleldprograms/index.html

Mishra, V. (2001). Multiculturalism. *The Year's Work in Critical and Cultural Theory, 8*(1), 227–246. doi:10.1093/ywcct/8.1.227

Mishra, V., & Hodge, B. (2005). What was postcolonialism? *New Literary History, 36*(3), 375–402.

Mitchell, C., & Reid-Walsh, J. (2002). *Researching children's popular culture: The cultural spaces of childhood.* London, England: Routledge.

Mollel, T. M. (1997). *Ananse's feast: An Ashanti tale.* New York, NY: Clarion Books.

Mure, E. (1967). *The story of the three bears.* Toronto, Ontario, Canada: Oxford University Press. (Original work written 1831)

Muspratt, S., Luke, A., & Freebody, P. (Eds.). (1997). *Constructing critical literacies.* Creskill, NJ: Hampton Press.

Negroponte, N. (1995). *Being digital.* New York, NY: Knopf.

Nelson, F. W. (1954). Revolution in grammar. *Quarterly Journal of Speech, 40*(3), 299–312.

New London Group. (1996). A pedagogy of multiliteracies: Designing social factors. *Harvard Educational Review, 66*(1), 60–92.

Nishimura, M. M. (2009). *The medieval imagination: Images in the margins.* Los Angeles, CA: J. Paul Getty Museum.

Norton, B. (1997). Language, identity, and the ownership of English. *TESOL Quarterly, 31*(3), 409–429.

Olson, D. (1994). *The world on paper: The conceptual and cognitive implications of writing and reading.* Cambridge, England: Cambridge University Press.

Ong, W. J. (1980). Literacy and orality in our times. *Journal of Communication, 30*(1), 197–204.

Ong, W. J. (1982). *Orality and literacy: The technologizing of the word*. London, England: Routledge.

Opie, I., & Opie, P. (1974). *The classic fairy tales*. London, England: Oxford University Press.

Palfrey, J., & Gasser, U. (2008). *Born digital: Understanding the first generation of digital natives*. New York, NY: Basic Books.

Peddiwell, J. A. (2004). *The sabre-tooth curriculum* (classic ed.). New York, NY: McGraw-Hill. (Original work published 1939)

People for Education. (2009). *Wanted: A renewed vision for public education* (Annual Report on Ontario's Schools 2009). Retrieved from People for Education website: http://www.peopleforeducation.com/research-info

Petrie, G. M. (2003). ESL teachers' views on visual language: A grounded theory. *The Reading Matrix, 3*(3), 137–168.

Petrie, G. M. (2005). Visuality and CALL research. In J. Egbert & G. M. Petrie (Eds.), *CALL research perspectives* (pp. 97–107). Mahwah, NJ: Erlbaum.

Phillips, E. D. (1954). The three bears. *Man, 54*, 123.

Pieterse, J. N. (1994). Globalisation as hybridisation. *International Sociology, 9*(2), 161–184.

Pieterse, J. N. (2001). Hybridity, so what? The anti-hybridity backlash and the riddles of recognition. *Theory, Culture & Society, 18*(2–3), 219–245.

Prensky, M. (2001). Digital natives, digital immigrants. *On the Horizon, 9*(5), 1–6.

Prensky, M. (2006). *Don't bother me Mom, I'm learning*. St. Paul, MN: Paragon House.

Prensky, M. (2008). Programming is the new literacy. *Edutopia*, February. Retrieved from http://www.edutopia.org/magazine/feb08

Propp, V. (1968). *Morphology of the folktale* (2nd ed., L. Scott, Trans.). Austin, TX: University of Texas Press.

Radford, M. (2006). Researching classrooms: Complexity and chaos. *British Educational Research Journal, 32*(2), 177–190.

Rampton, B. (2006). *Language in late modernity: Interaction in an urban school*. Cambridge, England: Cambridge University Press.

Reason, P., & Bradbury, H. (2008). Introduction. In P. Reason & H. Bradbury (Eds.), *Handbook of action research: Participative inquiry and practice* (2nd ed., pp. 1–10). London, England: Sage.

Robbins, M. (2002). Preface. In M. Pearson, *University-community design partnerships: Innovations in practice* (pp. 1–4). Washington, DC: National Endowment for the Arts.

Robertson, H.-J. (2005). Lost in translation. *Phi Delta Kappan, 86*(5), 410.

Robertson, R. (1992). *Globalization: Social theory and global culture*. London, England: Sage.

Robertson, R. (1995). Glocalization: Time-space and homogeneity-heterogeneity. In M. Featherstone, S. Lash & R. Robertson (Eds.), *Global modernities* (pp. 25–44). London, England: Sage.

Robinson, K. (2006, February). Ken Robinson says schools kill creativity [Video podcast]. Retrieved from TED (Technology, Entertainment, Design) website: http://www.ted.com/talks/lang/eng/ken_robinson_says_schools_kill_creativity.html

Rodari, G. (1996). *The grammar of fantasy: An introduction to the art of inventing stories* (J. Zipes, Trans.). New York, NY: Teachers & Writers Collaborative. (Original work published 1973)

Rumbaut, R. G., & Ima, K. (1988). *The adaptation of Southeast Asian refugee youth: A comparative study. Final report to the Office of Resettlement*. San

Diego, CA: San Diego State University. (ERIC Document Reproduction Service No. ED 299 372). Retrieved from Education Resources Information Center website: http://www.eric.ed.gov

Ruiz, R. (1984). Orientations in language planning. *NABE: The Journal for the National Association for Bilingual Education, 8*(2), 15–34.

Rutherford, J. (1990). The third space: Interview with Homi Bhabha. In J. Rutherford (Ed.), *Identity, community, culture, difference* (pp. 207–221). London, England: Lawrence & Wishart.

Ryan, M.-L. (2004a). Introduction. In M-L. Ryan (Ed.), *Narrative across media: The languages of storytelling* (pp. 1–40). Lincoln, NE: University of Nebraska Press.

Ryan, M.-L. (2004b). Will new media produce new narratives? In M.-L. Ryan (Ed.), *Narrative across media: The languages of storytelling* (pp. 337–359). Lincoln, NE: University of Nebraska Press.

Santa Ana, O. (2004). Introduction: The unspoken issue that silences Americans. In O. Santa Ana (Ed.), *Tongue-tied: The lives of multilingual children in public education* (pp. 1–8). Lanham, MD: Rowman & Littlefield.

Saussure, F. de (1974). *Cours de linguistique générale.* Paris: Payot. (Original work published 1916)

Savage-Rumbaugh, S., Shanker, S. G., & Taylor, T. J. (1998). *Apes, language, and the human mind.* New York, NY: Oxford University Press.

Sawyer, R. K. (2006). Educating for innovation. *Thinking Skills and Creativity, 1,* 41–48.

Sawyer, R.K. (2008). *Optimising learning: Implications of learning sciences research* (OECD document EDU/CERI/CD(2008)12). Retrieved from the Organisation for Economic Co-operation and Development (OECD) website: http://www.oecd.org/dataoecd/39/52/40554221.pdf

Semali, L. M., & Watts Pailliotet, A. (1999). Introduction: What is intermediality and why study it in US classrooms? In L. M. Semali & A. Watts Pailliotet (Eds.), *Intermediality: The teachers' handbook of critical media literacy* (pp. 1–29). Boulder, CO: Westview.

Shaffer, D. W., Squire, K., Halverson, R., & Gee, J. P. (2005). Video games and the future of learning. *Phi Delta Kappan, 87*(2), 104–111.

Shameem, N. (2002). Multilingual proficiency in Fiji primary schools. *Journal of Multilingual and Multicultural Development, 23*(5), 388–407.

Shohamy, E. (2007). Language tests as language policy tools. *Assessment in Education, 14*(1), 117–130. doi: 10.1080/09695940701272948

Sinclair, G. (2010, May). *Exploring Canada's digital future.* Featured "Big Thinking" lecture at the Congress of the Humanities and Social Sciences, Concordia University, Montréal, Québec.

Singh, P. (2009). Trawling through language policy: Practices and possibilities post-1994. *Language Learning Journal, 37*(3), 281–291.

Snyder, I. (Ed.). (1997). *Page to screen: Taking literacy into the electronic era.* St. Leonards, New South Wales, Australia: Allen & Unwin.

Snyder, I. (Ed.). (2002). *Silicon literacies: Communication, innovation and education in the electronic age.* London, England: Routledge.

Southey, R. (n.d.). *The three bears.* Oxford, England: Oxford University Press. (Original work published 1837)

Spinthourakis, J.-A., Karatzia-Stavlioti, E., Lempesi, G.-E., & Papadimitriou, I. (2007, October). *Flexible Zone Project: A curricular approach to social integration* (Greece case study report 2). Retrieved from Educational Policies that Address Social Inequality (EPASI) website: http://www.epasi.eu/CaseStudyGR2.pdf

Spivak, G. C. (1988). *In other worlds: Essays in cultural politics.* New York, NY: Routledge.

Squire, K. D. (2008). Video-game literacy: A literacy of expertise. In J. Coiro, C. Lankshear, M. Knobel & D. Leu (Eds.), *Handbook of research on new literacies* (pp. 635–670). New York, NY: Erlbaum.

Stoller, F. (2006). Establishing a theoretical foundation for project-based learning in second and foreign language contexts. In G. H. Beckett & P. C. Miller (Eds.), *Project-based second and foreign language education: Past, present, and future* (pp. 19–40). Greenwich, CT: Information Age.

Street, B. (1984). *Literacy in theory and practice*. Cambridge, England: Cambridge University Press.

Street, B. (1995). *Social literacies: Critical approaches to literacy in development, ethnography and education*. London, England: Longman.

Street, B. (2000). Literacy events and literacy practices: Theory and practice in the New Literacy Studies. In M. Martin-Jones & K. Jones (Eds.), *Multilingual literacies* (pp. 17–29). Amsterdam, The Netherlands: John Benjamins.

Swain, M., & Lapkin, S. (1981). *Bilingual education in Ontario: A decade of research*. Toronto, Ontario, Canada: Ministry of Education.

Tagliamonte, S., & Denis, D. (2008). LOL for real! Instant messaging and teen language. *American Speech, 83*, 3–34.

Tapscott, D. (2010, August 12). *The future of education: Reboot required*. Retrieved from the Canadian Broadcasting Corporation (CBC) News website: http://www.cbc.ca/consumer/story/2010/08/11/f-school-tapscott.html

Tatar, M. (2002). *The annotated classic fairy tales*. New York, NY: Norton.

Thomas, S., Joseph, C., Laccetti, J., Mason, B., Mills, S., Perril, S., & Pullinger, K. (2007). Transliteracy: Crossing divides. *First Monday, 12*(12). Retrieved from http://firstmonday.org/htbin/cgiwrap/bin/ojs/index.php/fm/article/view/2060/1908

Thomas, W. P., & Collier, V. P. (2001). *A national study of school effectiveness for language minority students' long-term academic achievement*. Berkeley, CA: Center for Research on Education, Diversity & Excellence.

Thurlow, C., & Brown, A. (2003). Generation Txt? The sociolinguistics of young people's text-messaging. *Discourse Analysis Online, 1*(1). Retrieved from http://extra.shu.ac.uk/daol/articles/v1/n1/a3/thurlow2002003-paper.html

Toffler, A. (1980). *The third wave*. New York, NY: Morrow.

Toronto District School Board. (n.d.) *Fact sheet*. Retrieved from the Toronto District School Board website: http://www.tdsb.on.ca/_site/ViewItem.asp?siteid=308&menuid=4721&pageid=4131

Tse, L. (2001). *"Why don't they learn English?" Separating fact from fallacy in the U.S. language debate*. New York, NY: Teachers College Press.

Tunsbridge, N. (1995, September). The cyberspace cowboy. *Australian Personal Computer, 12*, 64–70.

Upitis, R. (2004). School architecture and complexity. *Complicity: An International Journal of Complexity and Education, 1*(1), 19–38.

Vaillancourt, F. (1996). Language and socioeconomic status in Quebec: Measurements, findings, determinants and policy costs. *International Journal of the Sociology of Language, 121*, 69–92.

Valdés, G. (2004). The teaching of academic language to minority second language learners. In A. F. Ball & S. W. Freedman (Eds.), *Bakhtinian perspectives on language, literacy and learning* (pp. 66–98). Cambridge, England: Cambridge University Press.

van Lier, L. (2006). Foreword. In G. H. Beckett & P. C. Miller (Eds.), *Project-based second and foreign language education: Past, present, and future* (pp. xi–xvi). Greenwich, CT: Information Age.

Venezky, R. L., & Davis, C. (2002). *Quo vademus? The transformation of schooling in a networked world* (OECD/CERI Report, version 8C). Retrieved from the

Organisation for Economic Co-operation and Development (OECD) website: http://www.oecd.org

Vincent, D. (2000). *The rise of mass literacy: Reading and writing in modern Europe.* Cambridge, England: Polity.

Vološinov, V.N. (1973). *Marxism and the philosophy of language* (L. Matejka & I. R. Titunik, Trans.). New York, NY: Seminar Press. (Original work published 1929)

Vygotsky, L. S. (1978). *Mind in society: The development of higher psychological processes* (M. Cole, V. John-Steiner, S. Scribner & E. Souberman, Eds.). Cambridge, MA: Harvard University Press.

Vygotsky, L. (1986). *Thought and language* (A. Kozulin, Ed. & Trans.). Cambridge, MA: MIT Press. (Original work published 1934)

Warner, M. (1994). *From the beast to the blonde: On fairy tales and their tellers.* London, England: Chatto & Windus.

Watson, J., & Callingham, R. (2003). Statistical literacy: A complex hierarchical subject. *Statistics Education Research Journal,* 2(2), 3–46.

Wenger, E. (1998). Communities of practice: Learning as a social system. *The Systems Thinker,* 9(5). Retrieved from http://www.open.ac.uk

Wenger, E., McDermott, R. A., & Snyder, W. M. (2002). *Cultivating communities of practice: A guide to managing knowledge.* Boston, MA: Harvard Business Press.

Willinsky, J. (1987). The seldom-spoken roots of the curriculum: Romanticism and the new literacy. *Curriculum Inquiry,* 17(3), 267–291.

Wong Fillmore, L. (1991). When learning a second language means losing the first. *Early Childhood Research Quarterly,* 6(3), 323–347.

Wong Fillmore, L. (2000). Loss of family languages: Should educators be concerned? *Theory Into Practice* 39(4), 203–221.

Zipes, J. D. (2004). *Speaking out: Storytelling and creative drama for children.* New York, NY: Routledge.

Zipes, J. D. (2007). *When dreams came true: Classical fairy tales and their tradition* (2nd ed.). New York, NY: Routledge.

Index